W9-AOV-937

Exploring Health Careers

Exploring Health Careers

Maureen McCutcheon

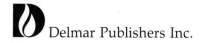
Delmar Publishers Inc.

NOTICE TO THE READER

Cover photos from *Nursing Assistant: A Nursing Process Approach*, 6E by Hegner and Caldwell. Used with permission.

Delmar Staff:
  Executive Editor: David Gordon
  Administrative Editor: Marion Waldman
  Editorial Assistant: Catherine Eads
  Project Editor: Carol Micheli
  Production Coordinator: Barbara A. Bullock
  Art/Design Supervisor: Judi Orozco
  Electronic Publishing Supervisor: Lisa Santy

For information, address Delmar Publishers Inc.
3 Columbia Circle, Box 15-015
Albany, New York 12212

Printed in the United States of America
published simultaneously in Canada
by Nelson Canada,
a division of The Thomson Corporation

1 2 3 4 5 6 7 8 9 10 XXX 99 98 97 96 95 94 93

Library of Congress Cataloging-in-Publication Data

McCutcheon, Maureen.
  Exploring health careers / Maureen McCutcheon.
    p.   cm.
  Includes index.
  ISBN 0-8273-4897-5
  1. Medicine—Vocational guidance.   2. Allied health personnel
  —Vocational guidance.   I. Title.
    [DNLM: 1. Allied Health Personnel.   2. Health Occupations.
  W21.5 M477e]
  R690.M354   1992
  610.69—dc20
  DNLM/DLC
  for Library of Congress   92-14924
                                                            CIP

▶ DEDICATION

Exploring Health Careers is dedicated to future health care professionals, the students who want to learn about health care occupations, and to their teachers and mentors who nurture that interest and help to make it a reality.

▶ TABLE OF CONTENTS

ALPHABETICAL LISTING OF DEPARTMENTS:

▶ PREFACE

Exploring Health Careers was written primarily to assist students to determine the health care career most suited to their individual goals by learning the specifics of each role and the factors that impact upon professional performance. It may be used effectively in any health occupations or general career exploration course, or in a related health career training program.

The text has been written from the perspective of health care specialties or departments within acute care, clinic, or office settings. With that focus, each chapter presents all facets of a specialty, including terms, career descriptions, professional skills, and procedures performed that would be encountered by students interacting with professionals in that work site. Each chapter of the textbook prepares students to experience that specialty of health care.

The text presents two types of information: general job skills and health care careers. Chapter 1 relates to job skills that contribute toward the successful performance of health care workers. Other chapters are presented in alphabetical order and relate to health care specialties. Organizational charts, educational requirements, desired personal characteristics, job satisfaction, career advancement, employment opportunities, and work hours are also covered. Frequently used medical terms and abbreviations and an introduction to structure and function of some body systems have been included to increase understanding of department activity and communication among staff.

Workbook chapters correspond with textbook chapters. My experience with using this material has shown that active participation in the learning process increases knowledge acquisition. The workbook provides a bond with staff mentors who appreciate the students' interest generated and guided by this tool. The workbook provides an instructive guide to mentors as well, a structure around which discussions can be centered. Mentors have been more receptive to students who have some understanding of department goals, activities, terms, and careers and who actively seek information.

Students who go to a department with some comprehension of activities and careers gain maximum benefit from the association with professional mentors there and are more likely to be welcomed into the department. The effort invested by the students' preparation is rewarded with extra effort by mentors. In addition, students have felt more confident when talking with mentors because they are aware of the department's goals, activities, terms, and hierarchy.

Program expectations and student responsibilities are clearly stated in the chapter objectives. Select body system reviews, average salaries, a glossary, and references for health care careers are provided in the Appendix.

An *Instructor's Guide* is available for the convenience of the teacher. Information on establishing a staff-mentored program, problem-solving situations, student selection process, and possible pitfalls and solutions in clinical areas are included. Examples of class schedules, quizzes, texts, and answers to workbook puzzles are also included.

The author, Maureen McCutcheon, received a Bachelor of Science in Nursing from Saint John College in Cleveland, Ohio and a Master of Education from Kent State University. She has worked at The Cleveland Clinic Foundation, Cook County Hospital, The New York Hospital, Memorial Hospital for Cancer and Allied Diseases, and Lakewood Hospital. She has worked as a staff nurse, an instructor in staff development, LPN and RN schools of nursing, for the Red Cross, and as a nursing supervisor. She currently teaches a health occupations course for the Lakewood School System that is based at Lakewood Hospital. She is a member of the American Vocational Association, the Ohio Vocational Association, and the National Education Association. She has previously published a medical/surgical textbook for LPNs.

▶ ACKNOWLEDGMENTS

I wish to thank the administration of the Lakewood School System for observing the need for a medical careers program and allowing me the autonomy to create and develop the course. In particular: Dr. Daniel M. Kalish—Superintendent of Schools; Alan Penn—Director, Vocational Education; Judith Sellers—Former Director, Vocational Education; Sarah Sweeney—Personnel Administrator; William McNamera—Assistant Principal; and to special colleagues Eileen Ptacek, Carol Litzler, and Joseph Ertler.

I wish to thank the administration of Lakewood Hospital for hosting the medical careers program, encouraging staff mentors, supporting the educational goals of the program, and nurturing community youth: Jules W. Bouthillet—Chief Executive Officer; Gail Bromley, M.S.N., R.N.—Vice President, Clinical Services; Fred De-Grandis—Vice President, Legal Services; Pamela L. Gorski, M.B.A.—Director, Auxiliary Services; James L. Stewart Jr., M.D.—Vice President, Medical Affairs; John Bolan—Director of Human Services; Joy Kovar—Employee Relations Manager, Human Services; Barry Dore—Compensation/Benefits Manager.

In addition to the mentors and medical photographer, I wish to thank the following staff who reviewed the manuscript associated with their specialty and allowed photographs in their departments. They made substantial contributions to the development and accuracy of information.

Biometrics Department: Ilse Hazners, B.S.; Judy Kinder, R.C.T.; Sharon Suter, R.EEG.T.

Communication Disorders Department: Theresa S. Dawson, M.A., CCC-SLP—Supervisor of Speech Pathology

Dental Office: Marie A. Albano, D.D.S.

Dietary Department: Bonny Ayers, R.D., L.D.—Assistant Dietary Director/Clinical and Patient Services

Emergency Department: Sue Jachnick, B.A., R.N.—Clinical Nursing Coordinator, Emergency Room; Matt Burke, EMT-P—Supervisor, EMS

Medical Laboratory: Rosemary Kirchner, M.T. (ASCP)—Chief Medical Technologist

Medical Library: Jo Ann Hudson—Director

Medical Photography: Steven Robertson

Medical Records Department: Janet Griffin, A.R.T.—Assistant Director

Mental Health Department: Grace Herwig, M.S.N., M.B.A., R.N.—Clinical Nurse Specialist, Mental Health; Mary Ellen Reichard, B.A., R.N.—Clinical Nurse Manager, Department of Psychiatry; Cynthia D. Sansom, A.C.S.W.—Director of Social Service Department

Nursing Department: Rosalie DeBlase, R.N., M.S.N.—Clinical Nurse Specialist, Critical Care; Barbara Soltis, R.N., M.S.N., C.R.R.N.—Certified Rehabilitation Nurse, Certified Nurse Consultant

Occupational Therapy Department: Sandy Dadante O.T.R./L—Manager of Occupational Therapy

Pharmacy Department: Scott Jamieson, R.Ph.—Director of Pharmacy

Physical Therapy Department: Carol Bieri, P.T.—Director of Rehabilitation Services; Judith Bryan, P.T.

Radiology Department: Joan Ellsworth, R.T.—MRI Technologist; Judy Wilms, R.T.—MRI Coordinator; Dennis Schisler, R.T.—MRI Technologist

Respiratory Therapy Department: Mary Ann Marsal, B.A., R.R.T.—Chief Respiratory Therapist

Support Departments:
- Admitting: James Yaeger, A.A.M.—Admitting and ER Registration Manager
- Business: Julie Abouserhal—Office Coordinator of Patient Accounting
- Central Service/Storeroom: Tim Kirwelnz—Material Handler
- Material Service: Paul F. Aalders—Director, Material Services

Surgery Department: Mary Jane Wolf, R.N.—Director of Surgery

Special thanks go to the professionals at Delmar Publishers Inc. for their foresight, encouragement, and able assistance in the development, preparation, and publication of this project: Marion Waldman—Administrative Editor, Health Services; Cathy Eads—Editorial Assistant; Carol Micheli—Project Editor; Judi Orozco—Art Supervisor; Russell Berg—Art Coordinator; Joseph Reynolds—President.

I also wish to acknowledge my indebtedness to the reviewers for their thoughtful comments and creative recommendations that added immeasurably to the writing and usefulness of the manuscript.

Faye Munoz
Tri-Cities Regional Occupation Program
Whittier, CA

Judith Mabrey
Health Occupations
Putnam County Vocational School
Cookeville, IN

Virginia Rullman
Diversified Cooperative Health Occupations
Instructor/Coordinator
D. Russel Lee Career Center
Hamilton, OH

Linda Stutzman
Health Occupations Coordinator
EHOVE Career Center
Milar, OH

Luetisha Newby
Health Occupations Education Consultant
Michigan Dept. of Education
Vocational-Technical Education Svce
Lansing, MI

Peggy A. Grubbs
Health Occupations Instructor
Hillsborough County School Board
Tampa, FL

And finally I thank those special people in my life who offered continuing encouragement throughout the project: Margaret Saunders McCarthy, M.A.; Ruthanne Dillhoefer, M.A., M.Ed.; Jean Marie Gallagher, B.S.N., R.N.; Rosemary Metro; Barbara Stepanek; my children—Kelly, Casey, and Kate.

► INTRODUCTION

Hospital Organizational Chart

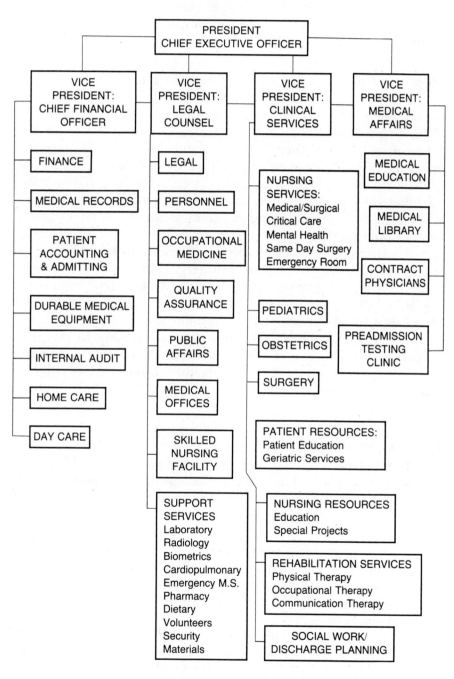

Welcome to the world of health care! At the beginning of a career quest, several topics need to be considered. First, an area of interest. If you decide upon health care, the next search is for a specific career. The following questions and answers may help you to decide a career course.

How can I decide what career I want to select?

One of the most effective methods of determining a career is to spend time working or volunteering in the area of general interest. Talking with professionals about their jobs, observing the duties they perform each day in their work site, and discussing the personal characteristics and academic courses that would help to attain success in that field are ways to learn about a career. A survey program about health careers located in a hospital offered by a high school, technical school, college, or retraining program is ideal for an extended on-the-spot experience.

Another way to discover career interests is to read about a job setting such as emergency room or surgery. Think about all the career professionals that interact in that setting, learn about the skills performed there, and how much education it takes to become each one of those professionals. Then determine if you like the work and how much time, money, and effort you are willing to invest to prepare yourself for a career. This textbook and accompanying workbook were written to help you evaluate careers in a health care setting. All the careers in a particular field of health care are presented in a chapter.

Why choose a health care career?

There are several good reasons why a career in health care is advantageous: worthwhile work, job satisfaction, position availability, and the opportunity to work with people of all ages in every area of the country. Other reasons include the variety of specialties, interaction with professional people, feelings of involvement with work, pride in a role, feeling of team spirit, membership on a professional team, opportunity to specialize, and ability to utilize the qualities of ingenuity, leadership, and entrepreneurship. Health care careers often serve as a springboard to other professions and management positions.

Health care is dynamic and exciting work. New procedures and instruments are continuously under development so careers do not become stagnant. New illnesses and treatments are constantly being recognized. Research in science, biotechnology, and human behavior continues to result in discoveries that impact on health, health care, and communication.

How safe are care givers?

Universal standards to protect caregivers from illness and infection have been developed by the Centers for Disease Control in Atlanta, Georgia. Infection control measures continue to be developed from research on bacteria and viruses, their habitats, and modes of transmission. Standards include recommended tests and vaccinations for tuberculosis and hepatitis B. Caregiving practices include when to wear protective clothing, such as gloves, masks, gowns, goggles, hats, and shoe covers, and proper hand-washing techniques.

Generally, measures are recommended to protect caregivers from contact with the body fluids of blood, sputum, emesis, urine, and stool. Protective measures are addressed in the safety section of the workbook chapters where necessary.

What is included in each chapter?

Chapter objectives, commonly used *medical terms*, and *goals* are meant to be reviewed before associating with department professionals to better understand their work and discussions. Compare the credentials of your mentors with those listed in the *Education and Credentials* section, the organizational chart with the *Career Hierarchy*, and the approximate range of annual income with the *Salary Chart*. (Incomes vary widely between geographical areas of the country, and between suburban and inner city facilities. Wages are usually higher on the East Coat, West Coast, and inner cities, lower in the southern states and suburban facilities.)

Career descriptions delineate tasks that sum up a role or profession. Compare them with job descriptions in the work site. Some health care workers have greater responsibility than others, depending on state laws and facility policies.

Skills sections describe tests, procedures, and processes. These will change as technology develops and communication techniques improve.

To become a health care worker, what education programs are offered?

There are many educational programs, offered in a variety of settings, that lead to certificates, diplomas, and degrees. From lowest to highest, there are certificates, diplomas, associate degrees, bachelor degrees, master's degrees, medical, osteopathic and nursing doctor degrees, and doctor of philosophy degrees.

Where are health career programs offered?

Health career programs are offered as on-the-job training, in high schools, vocation or technical schools, junior or community colleges, four-year colleges, universities, graduate schools (at universities), and medical, osteopathic, and dental schools.

When I graduate from a program, will my education be complete?

After graduation from an accredited program, many careers require passing a state or organizational board exam to be permitted to practice. This license or certificate may need to be renewed. This may require continuing education, a process designed to ensure up-to-date knowledge of the career practitioners. Some programs require an internship to ensure supervised practice before independent practice is granted.

What are the legal implications of health care?

Patients have a right to expect that they will be cared for safely by qualified persons who are pleasant, caring, and knowledgeable. Certain tasks are not to be done by workers until an accredited educational program has been completed and required exams passed. Persons in a training program must be extremely careful to carry out only those tasks they were taught, only when properly supervised, and only when given permission to do so by the instructor and professional staff.

Will I be expected to remain in the same career all my life?

Health care is unique in offering a variety of specialties within a career as well as encouraging members to use one career as a stepping stone to another career. Some programs may recommend or require experience in another health care career before accepting an applicant.

How will I remember all the information about health care careers?

The *Exploring Health Careers Workbook* provides information that corresponds with the textbook and provides insight into the careers being explored. In addition to *Guidelines for Keeping a Journal* of activities, a *Career Summary* provides a place to record an evaluation of compatibility with personal career goals.

1
Job Skills

After completing this chapter, you will be able to:
- Identify work habits that are important to employers
- Apply specific job skills to health care workers
- Perform job skills at entry-level proficiency
- Describe the steps of the problem-solving process

Employability skills:
Attitude
Communication
Critical thinking
Pride
Teamwork
Work habits

▶ INTRODUCTION

Valued staff members bring certain characteristics to the work site that enhance their usefulness on the job. Most health care workers have those characteristics, Figure 1-1.

Staff members with a positive attitude and good job skills are fine representatives of the health care agency. Employers depend on their employees' good work habits, their employability skills. Characteristics of good work habits include a positive attitude, regular attendance, punctuality, responsibility, dependability, communication techniques, and ability to set goals and follow directions. Other desirable work habits include taking pride in one's work (Figure 1-2), problem-solving skills, and team spirit.

▶ PRINCIPLES AND PRACTICE

Professional persons in health care usually have good job skills. They have learned them and put them into practice every day. Listed below are 1) explanations of job skills as they relate to health care workers and 2) methods to improve each skill.

Positive attitude: This is the most important job skill! An employer values workers who **look on the bright side** of things, who

FIGURE 1-1. Dependable employees come to work every day.

FIGURE 1-2. Good employees take pride in their work.

want to work, and who are **willing to learn**. **Enthusiastic** workers are a real asset on the job and a positive influence in the workplace, Figure 1-3. Workers who look at the negative side of every situation have a depressing influence on the rest of the employees. Working with complainers can make everyone feel unhappy. When workers feel unhappy or argue with each other, less work gets done and mistakes may be made.

Practice: Be thankful that you are in the health careers program. **Compliment** yourself on what you have learned and how well you have worked on the job. **Praise** a classmate for a job well done, an answer well spoken, or a problem well solved. **Feel good** about being on your job site. **Want to learn. Try** to do good work every day. Understand that every task is helpful in the health care system and ultimately to patient care. **Every task is important**—even those that do not involve direct patient care.

Attendance: Workers must **come to work** to qualify as good workers. Come to work **every day**. It is also good to come into work to relieve a team member who is ill (even on the workers' time off) or to help team members if the unit becomes very busy and scheduled staff is not sufficient. If workers do not come to work when scheduled, other workers may become angry because they will be overworked and patient care will suffer. Also, workers with good attendance may

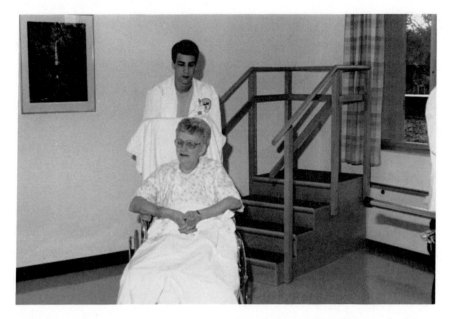

FIGURE 1-3. A positive attitude creates a workplace where people look forward to being.

have to do the absent workers' jobs plus their own. Soon, workers with regular attendance feel burdened and may seek employment elsewhere.

Practice: Come every day to the work site. Even if you feel tired or irritable when you get up in the morning, get dressed and report "on duty." Decide that you **want to have a good attendance record** and **care about being a team member**, Figure 1-4. Of course, if you feel sick or have a fever or an upset stomach, you will not want to expose patients to your illness.

Punctuality: Workers need to come to work **on time every day**. In a health care facility, patient care continues twenty-four hours a day, seven days a week. When an eight-hour or twelve-hour shift is over, workers are ready to go home. It is important that relief workers arrive **before their tour of duty** is scheduled to begin, so they will be **ready to work** when their tour begins. Thus, there will be a smooth transition between shifts and patient care will continue without interruption. When workers arrive late, irritation and angry feelings may result. To avoid jeopardizing patient safety and ensure efficient care, on-duty workers must wait until relief workers arrive and get organized for their work shift.

Practice: Come on time every day. Organize your life so that you **arrive early for work** every day. **Do not depend on others,** family

FIGURE 1-4. *Teamwork is a part of every career in health care.*

members or classmates, to wake you up and drive you to work/ school. Also, arrange your work in the work site so that you can **leave on time** and arrive promptly for class.

Responsibility: Valued workers can be depended upon to **fulfill the duties** of the job every day. These workers are reliable. The employer knows that reliable workers **make good decisions**. Though there is a certain freedom of choice on a job site, good workers do not take advantage of them. Running errands to many departments, the possibility of using the hospital telephone, and parking in restricted lots present freedoms and decision-making opportunities. Good workers feel responsible to the employer and do not take advantage of those freedoms. They accept the responsibility that freedom brings. They go directly to departments on errand runs, and do not stop to visit with friends. They understand that telephone lines are for business and do not use the hospital phone for personal calls. They respect the facility requests related to parking.

Practice: Call the teacher if unable to report to work or if you will be late. **Follow directions,** Figure 1-5. **Ask** questions when in doubt. **Conduct** yourself with maturity in the work site. That is, do not shout at classmates, push and shove one another, and chase friends through the hospital. **Dress** in uniform every day. **Speak respectfully** to coworkers and classmates.

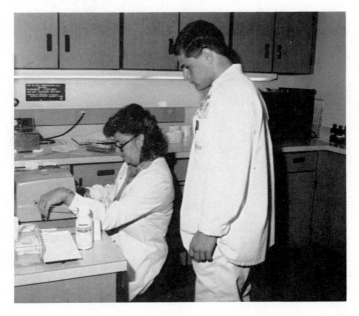

FIGURE 1-5.   *Ability to follow directions is important for patient safety.*

Dependability: Valued workers are **worthy of trust**. The employer knows that dependable workers will be **on the job** performing properly each day. Dependable workers **do a good job every day** without needing to be supervised. They are motivated to do their best.

Practice: Report directly to the work site after classroom activities. **Remain** in the workstation until time to leave. Do not leave your workstation to visit friends. **Work** when on the job; do not waste time or do other projects. Always try to do a good job. **Respect the privacy** of patients and coworkers. Complete homework, notebook, and class tasks on time but not on the job.

Communication skills: An employer expects a worker to be **honest** and **polite**. **Listen** to directions and **ask** necessary questions. It is good to question if you do not understand. It is not good to make sarcastic remarks about rules, methods, or tasks. Remember that you are a "guest" of the health care agency. You have **limited "rights."** Your experience in health care is different from those with whom you are working. Be **sensitive** to the feelings of others. If you do not like the work, feel good that you have learned something about yourself. But be careful how you share that information with your mentors to avoid hurt feelings.

Practice: Ask questions when you do not know what to do,

FIGURE 1-6. Ask questions if you do not know what to do.

Figure 1-6. **Admit** mistakes. **Speak respectfully** to professionals in the workstation. **Think before** you speak. Say what you really want to say. **Look** at the person when you speak. Tell the **truth. Talk loud enough** to be heard. **Listen** carefully.

Follows directions: Workers need to **follow the rules** of the job and the guidelines of the program. Rules are directions to ensure a safe environment and an effective, efficient workplace. Follow rules precisely. Carry out tasks exactly as taught, Figure 1-7. If you feel rules should be changed, follow the process to accomplish that. Do not just do what you want to do.

Practice: Report on and off duty. **Park where instructed** to park. If you ride the bus, **wait where instructed to wait** until the bus arrives. **Speak softly** in the halls. **Eat** only where allowed. **Wear your uniform** every day. **Do not smoke** in the facility. **Do not chew gum** in the facility.

Pride in work: An employer seeks workers who are proud of their jobs. Workers who feel good about a **job well done** will strive to continue this quality performance. Workers like to work in a job that they can be proud of and perform well. If workers do not like the work or do not perform well, they need to seek other employment.

Practice: Enjoy completing assigned tasks accurately. Tell yourself that you are doing a **good job**. Record the aspects of your job that

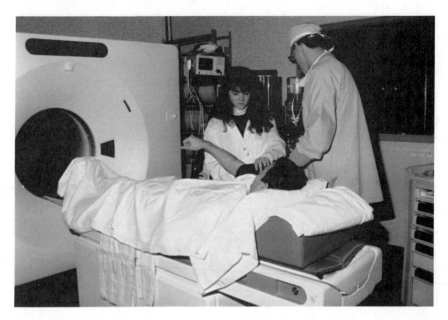

FIGURE 1-7. Carry out tasks exactly as taught.

you especially **like** and that you **perform well**. Write down **compliments** that you receive.

Pride in the health careers program: Professional people in the work site are aware that **this educational program is special**. They know that students are carefully selected. Many wish that a health careers program had been available when they were in school. Students need to realize that the **actions and words of each student** in the work setting **reflect on the entire class**. This means that the attitudes of the professional workers toward the entire program will be based on the individual student's **job performance** and work skills.

Practice: Dress like your professional mentors, Figure 1-8. **Speak** politely, using correct grammar. **Pay attention** when a patient or professional talks to you. Look at the person who speaks to you. **Show respect** for the patients, the program, the job site, the employer, and the staff. **Walk**, do not run in the halls. **Stand tall** and straight; keep your hands out of your pockets and your feet on the floor. **Wear** a clean lab coat/uniform, minimal makeup, small pieces of jewelry, and no perfume. Remember that in a health care facility, there is to be **no smoking, no rowdiness, no loud voices, and no gum chewing.**

Teamwork: Ideal workers **care about others** and are **sensitive** to their hopes, feelings, and needs. They reach out and **help one**

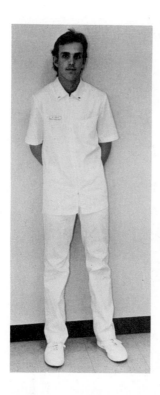

FIGURE 1-8. A clean, neat appearance is appreciated by patients, staff, and by the well-groomed worker.

another. They are not argumentative. They do not say nasty things about their fellow workers.

Teammates **work together** to get the job done, Figure 1-9. When their tasks are finished, they ask their teammates how they can help with their work. They exchange days off to help another team member. They come to work on their day off if a team member is ill. They think about the **needs of others** and **goals of the job** site. They are **willing to work**.

Practice: Think about how your comments influence others. **Say only positive comments** to classmates and professionals. Do not say anything negative or hurtful about another's clothes, relationships, or habits. **Become aware** of how patients, staff, and classmates are feeling. Then avoid doing and saying things that will cause them to feel sad or angry. When your assigned tasks are completed, **ask for more work**. Ask how you can **help** other workers.

Self-discipline: Workers who **manage themselves** are assets to the workplace. These workers are **in control** of their lives and **can concentrate** on their jobs, Figure 1-10. They can **do what needs to be done** to accomplish their goals. They do not wait for others to manage their lives. They get up on time, get themselves to their job, and

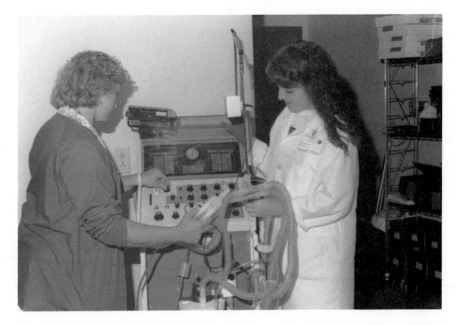

FIGURE 1-9. Teammates work together to get the job done.

accomplish the tasks to be done. They do their homework on time and study every night. Life's tasks do not overwhelm them and take them by surprise. They have a plan and they go about accomplishing it.

Practice: Set your alarm; **get yourself up** in the morning. Use a **battery** clock so that when the electricity goes off, you will not be late for work or school. **Study** every night. **Come** to work or school ten minutes early each day. **Launder** your uniform yourself; do not depend on someone else. **Stand** with good posture in the clinical site, unless you must sit to accomplish assigned tasks. **Get enough rest.**

Works well with others: Valued employees **respect other** people and allow others to be themselves. These workers are **pleasant** to everyone at work. They do not participate in arguments or "take sides." They act as **peacemakers** on the job. They do not talk about boyfriends or girlfriends on the job, brag about expensive gifts they have received, or talk about home or school problems.

Practice: Be pleasant and courteous to classmates and those in the job site. Offer your class notes to a student who was absent. Take the time to help another student with a skill or terms that you know. Encourage others to be **kind.** Do not criticize or complain about others.

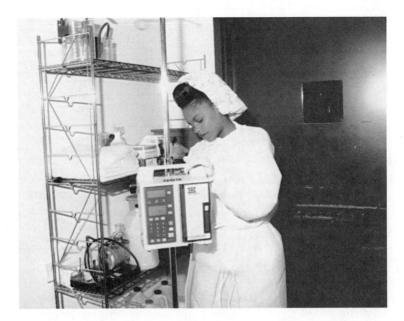

FIGURE 1-10. *Concentrating on the task at hand is important in health careers.*

▶ PROBLEM-SOLVING PROCESS

Problem solving is the procedure used to make decisions. Every activity involves a decision by the doer. For example, getting out of bed, eating breakfast, and going to school are three actions requiring decisions. Some actions become so automatic that they no longer seem like choices. But they are choices, whether the doer takes a long time to decide or acts "without thinking about it." The process of making decisions also becomes automatic.

The **steps of problem solving** may be labeled with different terms, but the process remains the same. While learning the process, write out each step. The seven steps of problem solving are represented by **GILMAEC**, an acronym for the following:

G   —**gather** data
I   —**identify** the problem
L   —**list** actions
M   —**make** a plan
A   —**act**
E   —**evaluate**
C   —**change** the plan

1. **Gather data; assess the situation.** Problem solving is what good detectives do. Just like Sherlock Holmes or Hercule Peirot, each person can learn to solve problems. The more information the problem solver learns about a situation, the better chance there is that a good decision can be made. There are many "sides to a story" and many facts in every situation. So review all aspects. Write a list of the "facts of the case." There should be at least six facts on your list for every situation to be solved.

2. **Identify the problem.** This is the hardest step. It takes the most time. The **real issue** is difficult to figure out. It is hard to separate the real problem from the facts of the case and the actions of the characters in the situation. **A problem is rarely an action.** The action is usually a symptom or a sign of a problem. For example, a student may be rude to a nurse at the hospital. Although that behavior is not acceptable on the job, the problem is not rudeness. The rudeness is a symptom of the problem. The problem is immaturity. This immaturity resulted in a job performance that lacks the job skills of responsibility and appropriate communication.

   The problem-solving process is constantly being used in health care. For example, a doctor uses a symptom as a guidepost to the real diagnosis, the real problem, the real cause of the symptoms. A fever may be a sign of infection, the real problem. Numbness may be a sign of poor circulation, the real problem. Headaches may indicate high blood pressure, the real problem.

3. **List all possible actions,** even if some may not seem like good choices. When the list is complete, evaluate each action. List at least six action choices.

4. **Make a plan.** That is, select an action. Think about the consequences of each action before making your choice. Then choose the action that will result in the most desirable outcome.

5. **Act.** Do it. Carry out the plan.

6. **Evaluate the action.** Was it effective? Did it achieve the goal? Is there a better way?

7. **Change the plan** if there is an action that would be more effective. Continue steps 5 through 7 until the problem is resolved or the situation improved.

Problem-solving steps must be followed **in order**. Eventually, small decisions can be made quickly and without the doer being completely aware of each step. For example, deciding to take the 7:30 A.M. or 7:45 A.M. bus. Big decisions require conscious problem solving, i.e., carefully going through each step of the problem-solving process in order. For example, what college should I attend? Am I ready to have a baby?

Health care workers make many important decisions about patient care every day. Sometimes those decisions must be made quickly, such as when a patient experiences a cardiac arrest. Sometimes decisions take longer because extensive fact gathering is necessary. The public has a right to expect that health care workers follow the problem-solving, decision-making process. The public expects health care providers to make the right choices for their well-being.

Sample Problem Solving, Using GILMAEC

Situation: You are a student in the health careers program driving to your hospital job site and thinking about where to park.

G—Gather Data. You need to park the car and go to the hospital classroom, dressed in your uniform in time for class. There are two garages at the hospital, north and south. Students have been directed to park in the north (one block away) not the south garage (connected to the hospital and reserved for out-patients and visitors, many of whom are elderly). Students receive free parking in the north garage. The teacher stamps the garage ticket to indicate free parking. Other parking options are metered parking spaces on the street in front of the hospital and a surface lot outside the emergency department labeled for ER patients only. Class begins at 8:00 A.M. It is now 7:53. It takes seven minutes to walk from the north garage to the hospital, three minutes from the south garage. It takes four minutes to get your uniform out of your locker. It is raining.

I—Identify the Problem. Where to park the car in order to get to class on time and follow program regulation.

L—List Actions. Park in the north garage as students have been instructed to do, receive free parking, and be late to class. Park in the close, convenient, but "off limits" south garage and pay for parking. Park in south "off limits" garage and trick a hospital employee to stamp garage ticket to receive free parking. Park at a metered place on the street and leave the work site to add coins twice during the morning. Park in the emergency department lot marked "for patients only."

M—Make a Plan. Park in the south garage attached to the hospital, avoid the rain, and be on time to class. Request an employee to stamp your parking ticket to avoid parking charge.

A—Act. Parked in the south garage. Pressured an employee in the emergency room to stamp the parking ticket to avoid charge and hoped the teacher did not find out.

E—Evaluate. You evaluated as positive arriving to class on time and getting free parking after "pressing" an emergency room employee. You realized a negative when the teacher assigned an after-school detention when she discovered that your car was parked in the south garage and that an emergency room employee was lead to believe that you qualified for free parking.

C—Change the Plan. In the future, park in north garage, even if arriving late and in rainy weather.

2
Biometrics
Department

OBJECTIVES

After completing this chapter, you will be able to:
- Explain the goal of the biometrics department
- Identify selected anatomical structures
- Describe each career in this department
- Identify required education and credentials for each career
- Describe the skills performed in this department

TERMS

Blood pressure:
Systolic
Diastolic

Diagnostic tests:
Electrocardiograph
Stress test
Ultrasound
Echocardiograph
Electroencephalograph

Problems:
Aneurysm
Arteriosclerosis
Thrombosis
Seizures

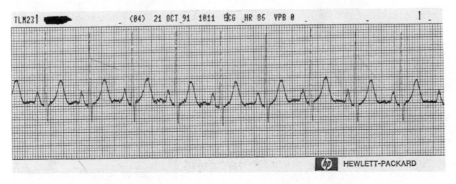

FIGURE 2-1. *An EKG strip showing normal sinus rhythm.*

▶ INTRODUCTION

In the biometrics department, life-sustaining organs are visualized and their functions assessed. The physical condition and degree of performance of the heart, blood vessels, brain, and nerves are recorded, Figure 2-1. Most tests are done by technicians and technologists and interpreted by physicians. Some are performed by physicians, assisted by technicians.

Division of duties and types of careers within departments may differ according to facility policy. When the department deals with all heart and lung functions, it is called the **cardiopulmonary** department. Biometrics and respiratory therapy may be divisions within that department. The **biometrics** department conducts tests to measure heart, blood vessels, and brain function. **Respiratory Therapy** (or the **pulmonary** department) conducts lung function tests and performs treatments related to breathing.

▶ GOAL

The goal of the biometrics department is to record accurate assessments of the heart, blood vessels, brain, and nerves by performing certain tests that will allow physicians to identify the physical condition and degree of function of cardiovascular and neurological structures.

▶ CAREER HIERARCHY

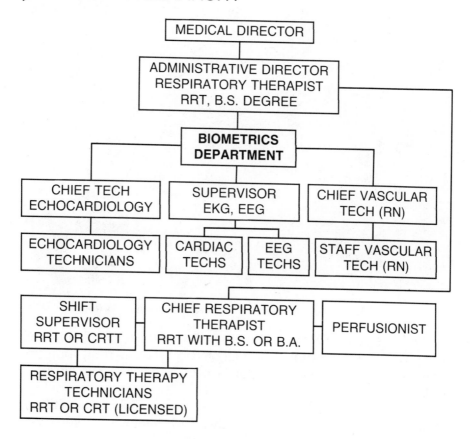

▶ CAREER DESCRIPTIONS

There are several careers in the biometric field. A tech's title will vary according to the type of educational program completed, field of specialty, the employer's policy, and geographic location. Technicians may enter the field after a short on-the-job training program or attendance at a seminar. Technologists enter the field after a longer formal program, often in a college setting.

The biometrics staff works with patients of all ages, conditions, and levels of consciousness, Figure 2-2. They work with newborns and elderly, conscious and unconscious patients. They screen for circulatory problems and organ disfunction in well people. They also help to identify the effects of CPR on heart function in critically ill patients during resuscitation efforts after cardiac arrest.

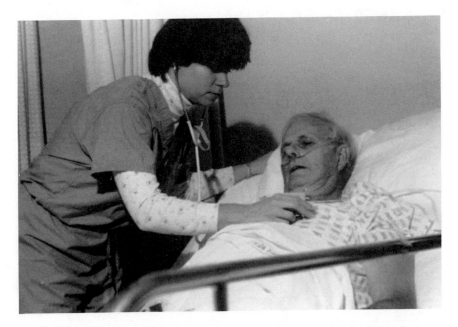

FIGURE 2-2.   *The biometrics staff works with many types of patients.*

Biometrics staff are important members of the health team. They help physicians determine abnormal physical status so that appropriate medications and treatments can be prescribed to sustain or regain health.

Technicians in biometrics are electrocardiographic (EKG), echocardiographic (ECG), and cardiac. Technologists in biometrics are cardiovascular, electroencephalographic (EEG), and vascular.

Employment opportunities vary. Biometrics staff work in hospitals, clinics, and physician offices. They work with ambulatory patients and in critical care areas of acute care institutions. EEG technologists can work in a neurologist's office, psychiatric facility, or in the research department of a university, pharmaceutical company, or the military. The **job market** is good, though jobs for EEG technologists are not as numerous as in other health careers.

Work hours for cardiac (EKG) techs are day and evening every day of the year; respiratory therapists often perform EKGs during the night in acute care facilities. Vascular and EEG technologists work Monday through Friday on the day shift. In clinics and physician offices, work hours are day shift Monday through Friday, with some evening and Saturday hours.

Career advancements include chief tech and department director positions. Lateral moves include changing from office to hospital or clinic positions. Technicians can return to school to become technologists. Continuing education courses help to increase technical skills, increase responsibility, and enhance job security because of the ability to do more and different kinds of tests. On a personal level, when techs perform a variety of tests, the job is more interesting. With a bachelor's or master's degree, teaching may be an option.

Desired personal characteristics include good verbal communication skills, accurate work habits, ability to work in a stressful environment, and an aptitude to work with technical equipment. Other attributes include sensitivity to the needs of patients and professional staff, being responsible, self-directive, and able to follow instructions.

Job satisfaction comes from performing an essential service, doing a job well, working closely with professional people, and continuously increasing knowledge as technology expands and equipment is updated.

Cardiologists specialize in the diagnosis and treatment of cardiovascular diseases. A cardiologist serves as the medical advisor to biometrics and works with staff to perform certain diagnostic tests. This specialist reviews the graphs and printouts from diagnostic tests performed in this department and interprets those results. A summary of every test is written and sent to each patient's physician.

Electrocardiographic technicians are responsible for performing electrocardiographs (EKGs), the most common test performed on the heart. The EKG traces electrical impulses from the heart onto special graph paper, showing the effectiveness of heart muscle contractions and the presence and extent of heart muscle damage. It is a health screening test, a tool to diagnose heart disease.

Technicians attach electrodes, and manage the electrocardiograph machine to record a graphic tracing for interpretation by a physician, usually a cardiologist. Technicians review tracings for quality, screen the machine's computerized data, report serious or life-threatening heart rhythms, post the tracing paper, and file the printout. In the hospital, technicians are responsible for transporting the machine to patients' bedsides, attaching electrodes, and running EKGs even during cardiac resuscitation. In addition, technicians are responsible for the care and cleaning of the EKG machines and for maintaining supplies.

The trend in health care is to hire a person who has several job skills. So, many community colleges have expanded the EKG technician program to the cardiac technician program.

Cardiac technicians record electrocardiographs (EKGs) and attach leads for Holter monitor tests (portable EKGs). After the Holter monitor has been worn by a patient for twenty-four hours and the EKG recorded on tape cassettes, technicians run those tapes through a scanner to detect irregular heartbeats and record simultaneous patient activities that may have precipitated those arrhythmias. These records are then submitted to a physician for interpretation of heart function.

Cardiac technicians also work with physicians in stress tests and thallium scans. During stress tests, technicians run the computer and assist the physician with the nuclear scanner after injection of thallium. They also check cardiac pacemaker function by running an EKG-type test to determine if a pacemaker is controlling the heart rate properly.

Cardiovascular technologists perform diagnostic tests to obtain information about the structure and function of the heart and blood vessels. This information helps physicians diagnose congenital and acquired heart disease, coronary artery disease, causes of hypertension, and peripheral vascular disease. These tests include echocardiography, cardiac Doppler flow studies, stress tests, arrhythmia scanning, pacemaker function tests, and EKG procedures. Cardiovascular technologists teach patients about health maintenance and prevention of illness.

Echocardiographic technicians, Figure 2-3, perform echocardiographs (ECGs) using sounds that are not audible by the human ear. The echoes of these ultrasound waves graphically picture structures of the heart. No radioactive materials are used.

Vascular technologists are trained to perform tests on veins and arteries. These tests include duplex scans and Doppler ultrasound. To qualify for acceptance into a vascular technologist program, it may be necessary to work for one year in a health care facility, have a Bachelor of Science degree, or be a member of another health care career, such as a cardiac technician or nurse.

Electroencephalographic technologists are responsible for performing electroencephalographs (EEGs) and nerve conduction and evoked potential studies. Technologists work with sleep studies, recording brain activity and nerve conduction. Responsibilities include positioning patients, applying electrodes to the head, and setting controls on the instrument that traces brain activity on special graphic paper. Technologists are responsible for the quality of the tracing. They need to recognize when changes occur in patients and react appropriately.

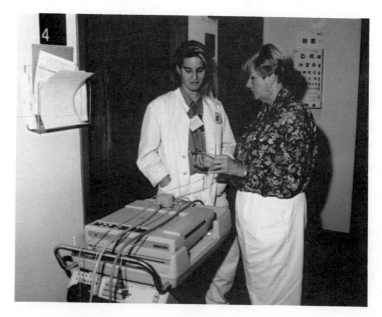

FIGURE 2-3. *This machine pictures the structures of the heart.*

Neurologists are physicians who specialize in studying about the structure and function of the brain, spinal cord, nerves, and diseases associated with the nervous system. These physicians are responsible for interpreting EEGs, nerve conduction velocity, and evoked potential tests.

▶ EDUCATION AND CREDENTIALS

CAREER NAME	YEARS OF EDUCATION AFTER HIGH SCHOOL	DEGREE OR DIPLOMA	TESTED BY: REGISTERED BY:
Cardiologist (M.D . or D.O.)	11 years: 4 yrs. college 4 yrs. medical school 3 yrs. postgraduate training	M.D. or D.O.	Tested by ABIM; registered by the state; ACLS certification
Electrocardiograph Technician	3 months	certificate OJT	Optional

CAREER NAME	YEARS OF EDUCATION AFTER HIGH SCHOOL	DEGREE OR DIPLOMA	TESTED BY: REGISTERED BY:
Cardiac Technician R.C.T. or C.C.T.	1 years (3 quarters)	certificate	Optional
Cardiovascular Technologist	2 years (5 quarters)	A.A.S.D. in cardiovascular technology	(Certification depends on speciality)
Vascular Technologist	Previous health career plus seminar or OJT	certificate	—
Electroencephalo-graphic Technologist R.EEG.T.	2 years	Associate or Applied Science Degree or certification after hospital program	ABRET (optional)
Echocardiographic Technician	2-year community college academic program, a hospital program, or 6-month preceptorship training program	AAHD or certificate	(Optional)
Neurologist (M.D. or D.O.)	12 years: 4 yrs. college 4 yrs. medical school 4 yrs. postgraduate work	M.D. or D.O.; certificate in neurology	Tested by ABPN; registered by the state

Key to Abbreviations:
   ABRET: American Board of Registration of EEG Technologists
   ABIM: American Board of Internal Medicine
   ACLS: Advanced Cardiac Life Support
   ABPN: American Board of Psychiatry and Neurology
   AMA: American Medical Association
   A.A.S.D.: Associate of Applied Science Degree
   C.C.T.: Certified Cardiac Technician
   D.O.: Doctor of Osteopathy
   M.D.: Medical Doctor
   OJT: on-the-job training
   R.EEG.T.: Registered Electroencephalographic Technologist
   R.C.T.: Registered Cardiac Technician

●   ●   ●   ●

▶ JOB AVAILABILITY

Opportunities in the field of biometrics are good. The U.S. Department of Labor estimates that the demand for EKG technicians will increase 24 percent through the 1990s and more for those technicians with advanced skills. The demand for EEG technologists is estimated to be 57 percent through the year 2005.

▶ SKILLS

In a hospital setting, some tests must be available twenty-four hours a day, every day of the year. To ensure a group of staff who can carry out emergency procedures on all shifts, some hospitals train respiratory therapists to perform EKGs.

Skills learned include tests to measure heart function, identify structure and function of the heart and blood vessels, measure brain waves, and calculate nerve conduction. Each tech learns resuscitation procedures to support life in a cardiac arrest and safety measures to protect patients with grand mal seizures. Often, skills are performed in stressful situations since biometric techs report to all hospital emergencies. Other skills include learning updated computer programs that accompany testing instruments and caring for equipment.

Pulse taking is the most basic test done on the cardiovascular system, Figure 2-4. Counting the pulse includes measuring the rate, rhythm, and strength of the heartbeat. Each pulse "throb" represents one heartbeat, one arterial "ripple" every time the heart beats. Characteristics of the pulse are indicative of the person's condition.

The *electrocardiograph (EKG)* is a graphic tracing of the electrical activity of the heart. A penlike instrument draws a graph on special paper as electrical currents move through the heart muscle. Heart damage can be identified by comparing the abnormal pattern with a normal pattern.

The *Holter monitor* is a twenty-four-hour electrocardiograph. The patient wears five electrodes and a portable tape recorder for twenty-four hours. A diary of activities is simultaneously recorded. The test determines irregular heartbeats and patterns and associates those with the activity at the time the irregularity occurred whenever possible.

An *exercise tolerance test (stress test)* is done by a physician assisted by a tech to determine the heart's response to various levels

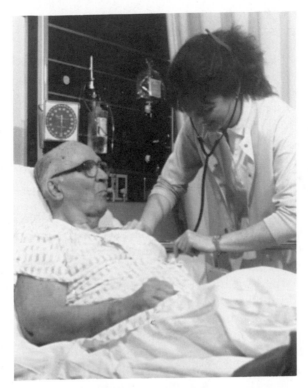

FIGURE 2-4. Pulse taking.

of exercise, Figure 2-5A. The patient walks on a treadmill while the heart and blood pressure are monitored. The treadmill gradually increases in speed as does the patient's physical activity. Depending on the patient's endurance, the physician may prescribe an exercise program, medication, or further testing.

An *exercise tolerance test with thallium* is a stress test plus an intravenous injection of a radioactive substance named thallium, Figure 2-5B. This substance circulates through the blood vessels in the heart muscle. The concentration is measured with a scanner immediately after the exercise session and again when the heart is at rest. The physician compares the resulting scans for blood distribution in the heart muscle during exercise and when the patient is at rest.

Ultrasound is a type of examination that uses sound waves to detect normal and abnormal structure and function of a body part. Sound waves travel from the machine to the part of the body to be studied, bounce off the structures, and return to the machine. The returning sound waves create a picture of those structures on the

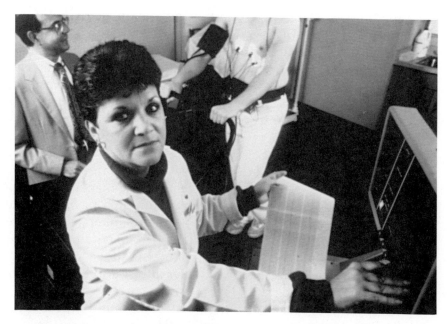

FIGURE 2-5A. *Checking leads before monitoring an exercise tolerance test.*

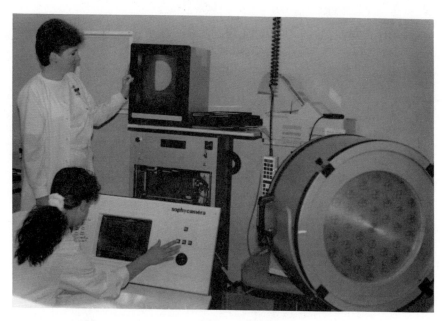

FIGURE 2-5B. *Scanner to trace thallium after a stress test.*

computer screen. The use of sound waves is particularly helpful in locating abnormalities of blood flow and problems with blood vessel structure. It can detect plaque disease, arteriosclerosis, and aneurysms. Ultrasound tests are named according to the technique used or the part to be studied—echocardiograph, Doppler ultrasound (Figure 2-6), and duplex scanner. Ultrasound is especially effective in detecting blood vessel function (blood flow through the vessels), whereas arteriography (X ray of arteries) is effective in detecting blood vessel structure.

An *echocardiograph* is a test that uses sound waves to visualize the heart and valves. Sound waves travel from the machine, bounce off the heart, and return to the machine, forming a picture on the screen. The waves show the size of the heart's chambers. During the test, heart motion is recorded on videotape so it can be later reviewed to determine how well the heart functions. Also, the machine prints an image of the heart on paper. A Doppler ultrasound test is always done with an echocardiograph, Figure 2-7.

A *Doppler ultrasound* is a test that uses sound waves with amplification. The purpose is to detect the flow of circulation in blood

HOW THE DOPPLER PROBE WORKS

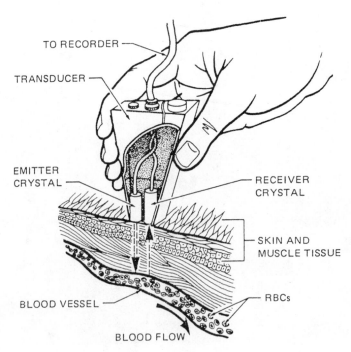

FIGURE 2-6. *Doppler ultrasound.*

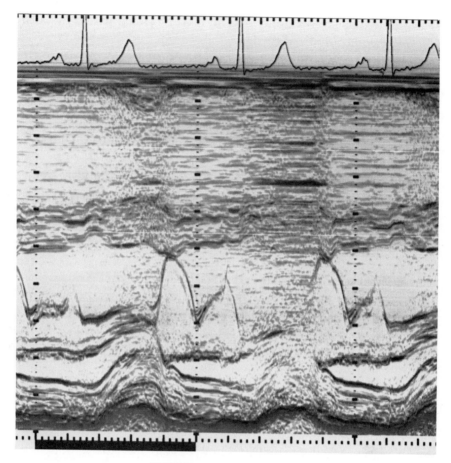

FIGURE 2-7. *Echocardiograph.*

vessels that are close to the surface of the body. Sound waves are sent toward a blood vessel where they bounce off blood cells as they pass through the vessel then return to the Doppler instrument where they are amplified. The presence of sound indicates that blood is flowing through the vessel. Lack of sound indicates that there is no blood flow through the vessel. The reason for the lack of circulation cannot be determined by this test.

A *duplex scanner* combines echo images (sound waves) and the pulsed Doppler technologies to make a picture of blood flow in a vessel. The test shows blood flow and obstructions to blood flow in an artery or vein. In a vein, the test can show blood clots. In an artery, the test can show the presence of disease that impedes blood flow. It can also show blood flow through a replacement vessel after surgery.

It is the actual sound generated by the Doppler instrument that generates a permanent record.

An *electroencephalograph (EEG)* is a graph of electrical impulses produced by brain activity. These brain waves are recorded by a special electronic apparatus, the electroencephalograph machine. Each part of the brain produces an electrical wave that has a distinctive rhythm and form. Variations in rhythm or shape of the wave indicate changes in brain activity. Reasons for those changes are determined by the physician.

An EEG measures how the nerve cells of the brain function. It does not measure thinking ability or intelligence. Electrical impulses do not pass through brain cells. There is no electrical shock to the brain. The EEG can be compared to the electrocardiograph for the heart because both tests measure the electrical activity of the part. An EEG does not show structure; the CAT and MRI scans show structure.

A *nerve conduction velocity test (NCV)* measures the speed of a stimulus as it travels along the pathway of a peripheral nerve. Electrodes are placed along the nerve's pathway followed by the application of a small burst of electricity. The electrodes pick up the speed of the electrical signal, and the machine automatically computes it.

Nerve conduction velocity tests are performed by an EEG technologist and interpreted by the neurologist. They are used to diagnose peripheral neuropathy, carpal tunnel syndrome, degenerative diseases, and nerve disuse. They are also used to evaluate nerve function following injury.

In *evoked potential (EP) tests*, certain nerves are stimulated and the response of the brain is measured. Evoked potential tests are divided into three groups: brain stem, visual, and somatosensory. In visual EPs, a person looks at a flashing pattern or light, and the optic nerve is studied. In brain stem EPs, an auditory signal is given through headphones, and the auditory nerve is studied. Brain stem EPs are used to diagnose auditory tumors, damage after injury, multiple sclerosis, nerve disease, and peripheral nerve tumors. In somatosensory EPs, a signal is applied along the peripheral nerve to be studied, and its response by the brain is recorded. EPs are usually performed by an EEG technologist and interpreted by a neurologist.

3
Communication Disorders Department

▼

OBJECTIVES

After completing this chapter, you will be able to:
- Define department goals
- Explain the difference between speech-language pathologists and audiologists
- Describe several careers within this department
- Identify required education and credentials for each career
- Understand the skills performed in this department

▼

TERMS

Function:
  Hearing
  Language
  Speech

Conditions:
  Aphasia
  Cleft palate
  Dysphonia
  Hearing loss

Paralysis
Stroke
Stuttering
Traumatic brain injury

Treatments:
  Artificial larynx
  Esophageal speech
  Voice prosthesis

▶ INTRODUCTION

Speech is the production of sounds with meaning. Speech is the result of a complex process involving the coordination of respiration, phonation (voice), and muscle movement for articulation. Voice quality and articulation are characteristics of the speech process.

Language is the meaning of sound. Sounds make words; words have meaning, Figure 3-1. Specific words are spoken to indicate specific things and thoughts. Understanding the meaning of specific words/sounds is an important part of the communication process.

Audiology is the science of hearing. It relates to the perception of sound and the degree to which sounds are heard. Speech is a two-part process consisting of speaking and listening. Children learn to speak by imitating the sounds they hear. Later, they discover that certain sounds mean certain things.

Audiologists determine if patients hear sound. Speech-language pathologists determine if patients understand the spoken word. Without the capacity to speak and hear, ordinary conversations cannot take place and oral directions usually cannot be followed effectively. People who cannot speak, hear, or understand can be lonely and may withdraw from society. They may feel like they are

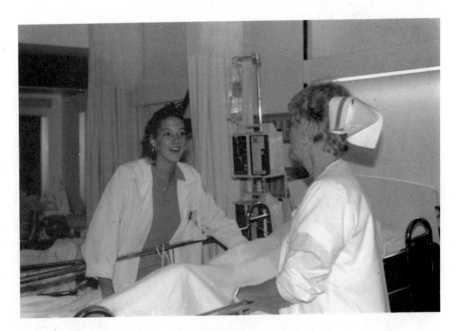

FIGURE 3-1. Words have meaning.

not a part of the world around them. Both speech and hearing disorders can be caused by physical or emotional problems.

Patients may have been born with a speech or hearing problem or a physical disability with its accompanying communication disorder. Language disorders may occur as a result of an accident, illness, surgery, loud sounds, or medications. An accident can cause a traumatic brain injury that may result in dysphonis. A stroke is an illness that might result in brain damage to the speech center and cause aphasia. Cancer of the larynx may result in the voice box being surgically removed, so the patient may need to learn to communicate by burping air through the mouth to make sounds called esophageal speech. Loud noise experienced at some rock concerts or on some job sites can result in damage to the middle ear and ultimately cause deafness. Some medications that are required for treatment of a disease such as antibiotics can cause damage to the auditory nerve and result in deafness. So hearing loss can be acquired at any age.

► GOALS

The goals of the communication disorders department are to identify and treat speech, language, and hearing problems, and provide counseling and guidance on social adjustment needs.

► CAREER HIERARCHY

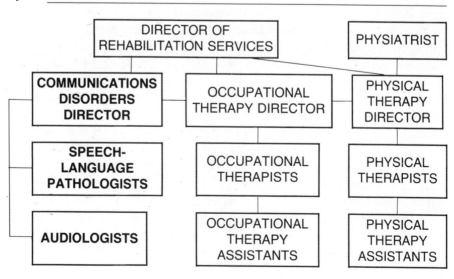

▶ CAREER DESCRIPTIONS

Speech-language pathologists and audiologists work together closely on the rehabilitation team. Though both careers relate to communication, differences occur in specialization, goals, job skills, diagnostic methods, and treatment techniques. Treatments depend on factors such as a client's age, medical diagnosis, physical or emotional problems, attention span, motivation, level of consciousness, and ability to cooperate. Both speech-language pathologists and audiologists work with persons of all ages.

Employment opportunities include hospitals, clinics, offices, school systems, speech and hearing centers, universities, research centers, and private practice. A doctoral degree is required to teach in most universities. Audiologists work to test, treat, and prevent hearing problems. Some work in government and industry in the specialty of dealing with noise pollution. They do research on the effects of environmental noise on hearing. The job market for both speech-language pathologists and audiologists is good but more limited than other health care professionals because of fewer available positions.

Work hours are usually during the day, 9:00 A.M. to 5:00 P.M. Occasional evening or Saturday hours may be needed to meet with family members.

Career advancements include supervisory and director positions in large departments of language disorders, lateral moves to other institutions, or indepedent contracting for services.

Job satisfaction comes from making a difference in peoples' lives. Both speech-language pathologists and audiologists know that the quality of their patients' lives is better because of them. Gratification comes from being creative and using ingenuity. It also comes from observing improvements in patients' conditions and finding the variety of cases seen each day to be pleasantly challenging.

Speech-language pathologists are often called speech pathologists. They help persons with disorders of voice, fluency, articulation, language, and swallowing. These problems can be the result of strokes, degenerative diseases (Parkinson's), cancer of the larynx, vocal nodules, abuse of the voice, accident or injury to the brain or the muscles of speech, or syndromes apparent at birth (cerebral palsy or Down syndrome.) A major portion of their work involves persons who stutter or have a cleft palate, facial paralysis, or speech and language problems due to a stroke or autism.

Speech-language pathologists assess patients to identify problems with producing sounds, pronouncing words, selecting words, and understanding words. They assess by reviewing records, observing patients, talking with them, and examining the mouth. They determine the extent of disability and evaluate solutions. During the assessment process, they look for answers to certain questions: Is the spoken word understood? Can thoughts be expressed in words? Are words spoken that are not intended? Are only sounds uttered, with no understandable words? Do tongue and facial muscles work appropriately?

Speech pathologists evaluate voice for quality, pitch, volume, and resonance. The quality of the voice may be hoarse or nasal, the pitch may be too high or too low, the volume may be too loud or too soft, and the resonance may be hypernasal or hyponasal. The muscles used in speech may be hypertense or hypotense. Speech may be precise or slurred.

They develop treatment plans and confer with patients to set goals. They often work with family members to teach methods of treatment and counsel them in ways to convey information when communication problems exist. They counsel patients who are lacking in self-esteem because of abnormal speech patterns. Speech-language pathologists work with the whole patient, not just the muscles that affect speech.

Speech-language pathologists work with methods that involve communicating by instruments. Voice synthesizers are available for the person whose larynx has been removed. Electronic devices that speak phrases can be used to express ideas and requests after a head trauma. To activate this apparatus, the patient pushes the appropriate button with a head control device and the computerized voice speaks. For example, "I'm cold" and "I need some water." Research into the causes of speech problems and in development of electronic and computerized instruments is ongoing.

Desirable personal characteristics include creativity and innovation. Since speech-language pathologists produce individual treatment plans that reflect the uniqueness of each patient and his or her special needs, they blend methods and treatments that have worked for others. They need to learn from their experiences and be considerate and honest with their patients.

Patience is another desirable attribute. Because change may come about slowly in this field, they need to be pleased with appropriate increments of progress, even if they are necessarily small. Self-confidence, a sense of humor, and enjoyment of the work are other assets.

Audiologists assess patients to identify problems in hearing. They operate precise electronic instruments to detect hearing deficits and to evaluate the degree of hearing loss. They confer with physicians to determine treatment. They fit patients with electronic devices to improve hearing and offer instruction in the use and care of these devices. Hearing loss can be from causes such as a birth defect, disease, medication, brain injury, accident, or excessive noise.

Audiologists must pronounce test words accurately and present information clearly. They need to be aware of available electronic hearing devices and, based upon audiometric test findings, select the most effective device for the individual problem. Some patients benefit from several meetings for guidance counseling on the social effects of hearing loss. Some situations require family interaction.

Desirable personal characteristics include the ability to work with precise instruments and painstakingly perform hearing tests. Audiologists need good problem-solving skills and motivation to keep up with current trends. They need insight into patients' feelings and the sensitivity to provide counseling and guidance.

► EDUCATION AND CREDENTIALS

CAREER NAME	YEARS OF EDUCATION AFTER HIGH SCHOOL	DEGREE OR DIPLOMA	TESTED BY: LICENSED BY:
Audiologist (M.A.,CCC-A) or (M.S., CCC-A) or (Ph.D. or D.Sc.)	7 years: 6 years school plus 9 months clinical fellowship	Master's degree in audiology or Doctor's degree in audiology	Certification by ASHA and state license
Speech-Language Pathologist (M.A.,CCC-SLP) or (M.S.,CCC-SLP) or (Ph.D. or D.Sc.)	7 years: 6 years school plus 9 months clinical fellowship	Master's degree in speech-language pathology or Doctor's degree in speech-language pathology	Certification by ASHA and state license

Key to Abbreviations:
  A: Audiology
  ASHA: American Speech-Language-Hearing Association
  CCC: Certificate of Clinical Competence
  M.A.: Master of Arts degree
  M.S.: Master of Science degree

SLP: Speech-Language Pathologist
Ph.D.: Doctor of Philosophy degree
D.Sc.: Doctor of Science degree

●   ●   ●   ●

▶ JOB AVAILABILITY

The U.S. Government Bureau of Labor statistics estimate that there will be a 34 percent increase in available positions for audiologists and speech-language pathologists by the year 2005.

▶ SKILLS

To help patients gain or regain the communication skills of speech and hearing function, speech-language pathologists and audiologists assess patients, review records, confer with physicians and other health team professionals, and develop treatment plans and goals mutually acceptable to the patient and health care worker. In speech pathology, skills and treatments center around oral function. In both speech pathology and audiology, motivation and selection of appropriate mechanical assistance are important factors in patient care.

Exercise of face, throat, and tongue muscles may increase functional ability and allow proper pronunciation of speech syllables, words, and sentences, Figure 3-2. Specific exercises develop muscle coordination so speech is clearer. Exercise of the tongue and mouth muscles is the basic treatment for patients with cleft lip and palate.

Overarticulation is an exercise to improve the speech of stroke victims. Overemphasizing mouth movements while reading phrases aloud hastens the return of controlled movement to muscles affected by the stroke. Patients are encouraged when they see the drooping mouth muscles move more precisely. Their motivation increases and often carries over to exercising their weakened arm and leg. Facial muscles improve more rapidly than the muscles of the extremities.

Motivation is a force from within that pushes a person to make an effort to act, Figure 3-3. It springs from a personal need or desire. It cannot be given to someone or forced upon someone. It must come from within the person.

Motivation is the key to continuing the effort to improve speech. Because patients need to do the exercises for improvement, they

FIGURE 3-2. *Proper pronunciation is important.*

FIGURE 3-3. *Motivation is a driving force.*

must feel the need or desire to do them. Often, patients become discouraged because they do not see immediate improvement from their efforts. The speech pathologist tries to rekindle that fire of enthusiasm, that spirit of wanting to continue to try, that desire to improve. It is not an easy task.

The speech pathologist points out to patients each small increment of progress. After a stroke, facial paralysis may cause drooping and lack of control of one side of the mouth. Patients want their smile to return immediately and become discouraged when it does not return quickly. The speech pathologist highlights small improvements that occur after exercise. Checking the number of teeth that show on each side of the mouth when trying for a full smile before exercise is one example. Then after exercise, the speech pathologist checks the number of teeth that show on each side of the mouth in a full smile. More teeth show on the droopy side after the exercise. Pointing out such progress encourages and motivates patients so they are more willing to cooperate with the exercise program. Motivation comes from seeing small differences, and then struggling to make the next improvement.

Family members are encouraged to be a part of the rehabilitation team. They are with the patient in the home setting after the patient is discharged from the hospital. The family can continue the treatment plan. They are taught to encourage patients to do facial exercises before meals. That effort, in combination with the action of chewing, increases the speed of recovery of the oral muscles.

Selection of appropriate devices is a specialty of speech-language pathologists and audiologists. They recommend the best method of communication and provide appropriate training. There is an electronic device that shows change in voice pitch. Changing the pitch of the voice may prevent polyp formation on the vocal cords. There are compact amplifiers with attached microphones to make sound louder if a patient does not have a hearing aid. A voice prosthesis can be surgically implanted to help speech production after a laryngectomy. An artificial larynx held against the neck can provide an external source of sound after a laryngectomy.

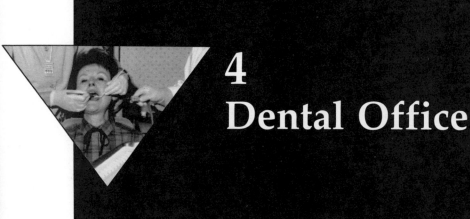

4
Dental Office

▼

OBJECTIVES

After completing this chapter, you will be able to:
- Explain the goals of the dental office
- Describe each career associated with dentistry
- Identify required education and credentials for each career
- Describe the skills performed in this office

▼

TERMS

Oral Hygiene:
    Calculus
    Plaque
    Tartar
    Floss

Problems:
    Caries
    Gingivitis
    Periodontitis

Restorations:
    Filling
    Inlay
    Crown
    Partial plate
    Dentures

► INTRODUCTION

Dental offices provide tooth care, oral hygiene, diagnostic services, and preventive measures to people of all ages. Patients are instructed in the care of the mouth, teeth, and oral appliances. Details of potential and existing conditions are presented and discussed with patients. Solutions to oral problems are reviewed and agreed upon. Treatments are performed to preserve the natural teeth and maintain alignment or straighten teeth.

There are many areas of practice in dentistry. Most dentists are general practitioners. Some dentists specialize in orthodontics, oral surgery, periodontics, and pedodontics. When specialties are selected, required educational programs and board exams must be completed before dentists are licensed as specialists. Areas of practice are clearly defined. Specialists do not perform procedures that general practitioners perform. General practitioners may perform special procedures if specific educational requirements are met.

► GOALS

The goals of the dental office are to **care for and preserve** natural teeth and periodontium, **provide prosthetics** when necessary, and **educate the public** about oral health and hygiene to prevent tooth decay and periodontal disease, Figure 4-1.

► CAREER HIERARCHY

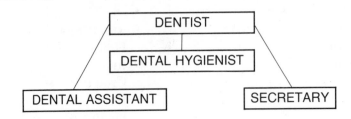

► CAREER DESCRIPTIONS

Though all careers in the dental field relate to care of teeth and maintenance of oral hygiene and health, areas of specialty and

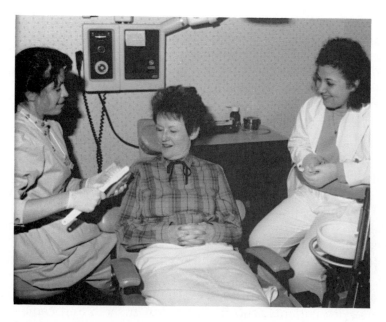

FIGURE 4-1. The goals of those in the dental office are to care for and preserve teeth.

educational programs differ. Roles and responsibilities vary with the type of specialty and position of the worker.

Employment opportunities are many and varied. In spite of the use of fluoride that has brought about a decrease in the number of dental caries, dental office visits have increased for prophylactic care. Job opportunities will continue to increase. Since people live longer, they require more dental work in their lifetime.

Most dental professionals work in private practice offices. Others work in hospitals, clinics, health maintenance organizations, research laboratories, school systems, and public health agencies. Some dental professionals work in the military services, correctional facilities, the Peace Corps, and with the World Health Organization. Some work as sales representatives for dental product manufacturers. With advanced training and education, options include teaching in universities, clinics, and vocational schools.

Work hours in an office setting are usually Monday through Friday with some hours on Saturday. Most offices work daytime hours, some have evenings hours. There are few emergencies in the dental field. Most people wait until a weekday morning to call the dentist, even when they have a toothache. When patients have had facial traumas that involve broken teeth or crushed jaw bones, a dentist may be contacted.

Career advancement occurs when duties are expanded, or a dental assistant returns to school to become a dental hygienist, or a dental hygienist attends dental school. Otherwise, in the field of dentistry, careers vary with a job change. Opportunity to advance to supervisor and administrator does not exist in most job sites.

Desired characteristics include a friendly manner, consideration of others, and communication skills. Since dentists and hygienists work inside the mouth with fine instruments and accompanying delicate parts, good vision, manual dexterity, and coordination are helpful. Good grooming, meticulous personal hygiene, and ability to maneuver effectively in small spaces are positive attributes. Attention to detail is particularly important when carrying out safety precautions with X-ray machines and following infection control procedures.

Job satisfaction comes from having a unique body of knowledge, performing procedures that are needed and appreciated by patients, relieving pain, and solving dental problems. It is rewarding to work with patients who care about their teeth and come to the office to maintain their oral health. Another source of job satisfaction is immediate feedback from a skilled performance. Patients often comment that they feel better after the cleaning procedure. Also, the congenial atmosphere of the office adds to job enjoyment.

Special biomedical hazards that dental workers need to consider include possible exposure to viruses that causes AIDS and hepatitis. Since the emergence of AIDS, workers who come in contact with blood or saliva wear protective clothing to avoid becoming contaminated with disease-producing viruses. Most dentists and their assistants wear gloves; some wear goggles during procedures that require drilling/preparing, extracting, and suctioning. Dental workers need to carefully handle instruments that have been in patients' mouths. Procedures related to cleaning and sterilizing dental instruments need to be precisely followed. A hepatitis vaccine is currently available; no vaccine is available against AIDS. Other hazards include exposure to mercury and radiation.

Dentists graduate from dental school with the basic training that is required for all dental specialties. Though most dentists remain in general practice, some choose to enter special fields. General practice is geared to the care and cleaning of the natural teeth, hygiene of the mouth, and prevention of decay. Preservation methods include education of patients in techniques to minimize tooth decay and plaque formation and maximize the health of gum tissue. If the nerve in a tooth becomes infected, endodontists remove that infected nerve and pulpal tissue inside the tooth to prevent bone infection and tooth removal. If the natural teeth cannot be saved, oral surgeons remove them, and dentists fit artificial teeth into the mouth. These artificial teeth may be bridges, partial plates, or dentures. If teeth are broken, the remaining stubs are filed down and capped. When teeth become so decayed that only weakened shells remain, crowns may be made to fit over them.

Dentists assess the health of the mouth and teeth through inspection, X-ray review, and hands-on examination. Fillings and crowns are checked to be sure there is no decay underneath. Cavities are filled/restored and restorations replaced as needed. Bridges, partial plates, and dentures are inspected for cracks and loose parts. If these appliances need to be replaced or a crown needs to be made, an impression of the mouth is taken and a model made that is sent to a dental laboratory. There the dental technician makes a plaster model of the mouth and the specific appliance or crown.

Dentists also solve the problems of toothaches and gum infections. They identify the cause and prescribe conservative treatment to save the tooth. If conservative therapy is not successful, a root canal or extraction may be necessary. Sometimes special treatment of the gums is necessary. The procedures of root canal and gum treatment are referred to specialists.

Orthodontists are dentists who specialize in straightening teeth. They assess patients by observation and extensive measurements and by taking panoramic radiographs and cephalometric radiographs. Impressions of the teeth and plaster models are made to study the articulation process. It may be necessary to extract some teeth if there are too many or if they are too big for the mouth. Bands are placed on or around teeth and wires attached to shift them into the desired position. This process takes from two to three years. When teeth have been realigned, a retainer is made. It is worn to prevent teeth from shifting back to their previous positions after braces have been removed.

Oral surgeons are dentists who specialize in extracting teeth. This procedure is usually done in the office setting using local or general anesthesia. If an extensive procedure is anticipated, such as extracting all the teeth, it may be done at the hospital. The most common procedure done by the oral surgeon is the extraction of wisdom teeth. They also remove extra teeth and some oversized teeth so that those remaining can be realigned.

Endodontists are dentists who specialize in performing root canals. That is, they remove the infected nerve and pulpal tissue from the tooth's center to prevent bone infection and tooth loss. The dentist then restores the tooth.

Periodontists are dentists who specialize in treating gums and supporting structure around teeth to prevent loss. The most common reason for loss of teeth is periodontal disease, often caused by gum infection called periodontitis. Periodontists also treat gums that have receded from chronic irritation or inflammation (gingivitis), often caused by plaque and tartar buildup. As gums recede, teeth become loose. Wiggly teeth cannot be used to chew. If the gum treatment does not result in tightening the wiggly teeth, these teeth need to be extracted so they don't fall out during sleep and cause choking. Patient education about gum disorders and instruction in continuing flossing treatments at home is essential to prevent more gum erosion and future tooth loss.

Pedodontists are dentists who specialize in the care and treatment of children's teeth. This includes education and measures to prevent caries and disease. Pedodontists care for baby teeth and permanent teeth. They work with patients from birth through adolescence. They are especially helpful with thumb-sucking children. They try to prevent the teeth shifting that often results from this activity.

Dental hygienists work under the direction of a dentist. They do all aspects of assessment and oral hygiene. They take patients' histories, asking about diseases and medications to determine possible effects on the condition of the mouth, teeth, and gums. They inspect the mouth for cavities, cracks in teeth, and loose fillings, bridges, or crowns. They examine the mouth for gum disease, open sores, and cancerous tissue. They clean the teeth, removing plaque and calculus deposits from above and below the gum line. They X-ray teeth, then mount and scan the films for caries and potential decay. They teach patients proper oral care and diet for good oral health. They explain the effects of smoking on the oral cavity. They teach brushing and flossing techniques for plaque control. They may apply fluoride treatments and place temporary appliances and fillings in the mouth. They mix dental cements, prepare restoration materials, take impressions, and pour study models. They remove sutures, smooth and polish new amalgam fillings, and document findings and treatments.

Dental assistants work under the direction of dentists and dental hygienists. They position patients in dental chairs and prepare equipment for use. They take and develop X rays, mount films, and obtain records. They document the condition of teeth as instructed by the dentist or dental hygienist. They set up instrument trays and suction saliva and spray from the mouth while the dentist or hygienist is working on the teeth. They prepare restoration substances, dental cement, and material for impressions, take impressions, and trim models. They clean, sterilize, and maintain equipment and order supplies. They answer phones, make appointments, work with billing, and post accounts. In some offices, their duties are expanded to handle equipment and assist dentists and hygienists as they work with patients.

Dental laboratory technicians work in technical laboratories making appliances, Figure 4-2. They do not work directly with patients. They receive instructions, impressions, and study models from dentists. They make plaster models, bridges, partial plates,

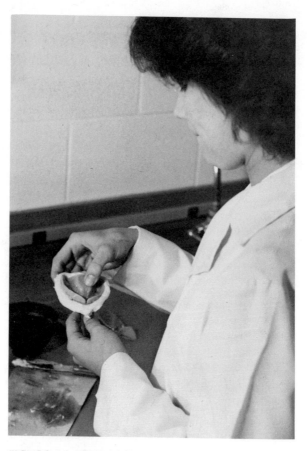

FIGURE 4-2. Dental laboratory technicians do not work directly with patients.

dentures, crowns, inlays, space maintainers, and orthodontic appliances. They work with a variety of materials and tools to make these appliances. Certification is offered in five specialty areas: crown and bridge, ceramics, partial dentures, complete dentures, and orthodontics.

▶ EDUCATION AND CREDENTIALS

CAREER NAME	YEARS OF EDUCATION AFTER HIGH SCHOOL	DEGREE OR DIPLOMA	TESTED BY: REGISTERED BY:
Dentist (D.D.S. or D.M.D.)	8 years: 4 yrs. college 4 yrs. dental school	Doctor of Dental Science or Doctor of Dental Medicine	National board exam by Dental Commission during school plus regional boards by Dental Examiners' Commission or state dental boards after graduation and licensed by the state
Orthodontist (D.D.S.)	10 years: 4 yrs. college 4 yrs. dental school 2 yrs. postgraduate training	Same as dentist	Same as dentist plus regional boards in orthodontics and registered by the state
Oral Surgeon (D.D.S.)	11 years: 4 yrs. college 4 yrs. dental school 3 yrs. postgraduate training	Same as dentist	Same as dentist plus regional boards in oral surgery and registered by the state
Endodontist (D.D.S.)	10 years: 4 yrs. college 4 yrs. dental school 2 yrs. postgraduate training	Same as dentist	Same as dentist plus regional boards in endodontics and registered by the state

CAREER NAME	YEARS OF EDUCATION AFTER HIGH SCHOOL	DEGREE OR DIPLOMA	TESTED BY: REGISTERED BY:
Pedodontist (D.D.S.)	10 years: 4 yrs. college 4 yrs. dental school 2 yrs. postgraduate training	Same as dentist	Same as dentist plus regional boards in pedodontics and registered by the state
Periodontist (D.D.S.)	10 years: 4 yrs. college 4 yrs. dental school 2 yrs. postgraduate training	Same as dentist	Same as dentist plus regional boards in periodontics and registered by the state
Dental Hygienist (LDH)	4 years or 2 years	B.S. degree in dental hygiene A.A.S.D. in dental hygiene	Written and practical national board exams by ADAJCNDE and licensed by the state
Dental Assistant (CDA)	1 year: (4 quarters) or On-the-job training	A.A.S.D. in dental assisting certification	Certification exam by Dental Assisting National Board (optional)
Dental Laboratory Technician	2 years: (7 quarters)	A.A.S.D. in dental laboratory technology	Certified exam by National Association of Dental Laboratories (optional)

Key to Abbreviations:
  AASD: Associate of Applied Science Degree
  ADAJCNDE: American Dental Association Joint Commission on National Dental
          Examinations
  CDA: Certified Dental Assistant
  D.D.S.: Doctor of Dental Science
  D.M.D.: Doctor of Dental Medicine
  LDH: Licensed Dental Hygienist

● ● ● ●

▶ JOB AVAILABILITY

The U.S. Bureau of Labor statistics estimate additional positions of 35 percent in the dental field in general and 41 percent for dental hygienists.

▶ SKILLS

Most dental workers spend their time with patients. Dental technicians are the exception. Technicians work in a laboratory setting and do not have patient contact. Skills vary according to the education level of the worker and job responsibilities.

Job skills include visual inspection, diagnostic testing, cleaning, and tooth preparation for restoration procedures. Other activities include extracting, crowning, bridge or brace application, root canal work, and gum restoration. Preparation of materials for diagnostic or therapeutic procedures, tissue and nerve injection to numb the work site, administration of general anesthetic agents, and monitoring vital signs are other tasks performed. Dental workers take mouth impressions, make study models, and prepare temporary appliances. Plaster models, dentures, crowns, bridges, and inlays are made in the dental laboratory.

Oral prophylaxis includes cleaning, scaling, and polishing skills with hand instruments, ultrasonic scaling equipment, and air-driven handpieces. The removal of plaque and tartar from teeth plus flossing help to keep gums healthy and prevent tooth decay. Patient instruction in these techniques is important so that good oral hygiene is continued between dental visits. Applying topical fluoride gel to aid in reduction of caries is another procedure used on children eighteen years of age and younger.

X-ray procedures vary with the type of specialty and purpose. Bitewing X rays are the small films that are placed in the mouth and held in place by the patient biting down on the cardboard film cover. A panoramic radiograph is a rectangular shaped X ray showing a continuous view of the whole jaw and teeth structures. The patient's head is positioned in a stabilizing device and remains still throughout the procedure as the X-ray machine moves around the jaw to visualize the structures. Protective procedures to prevent exposure of other body parts to X rays are skills that ensure the safety of the patient and worker.

Restoration describes a group of procedures that includes drilling and scraping to prepare teeth for filling, capping, inlays, crowns, and root canal work. These procedures involve manual dexterity, coordination, and good vision. Knowledge of tooth structure and treatment options is essential. Evaluation of drill-bit sizes and equipment choices are pivotal to professional technique.

Placing and removing permanent and temporary dental structures are other skills used in the dental office. *Applying bands and wires* is a basic procedure for teeth straightening. After the orthodontic braces are removed, a retainer is made and placed into the mouth to maintain teeth alignment.

Making crowns, inlays, bridges, partial plates, and full dentures involves working with gold, porcelain, ceramics, acrylics, and metals. Crowns are made to cover and support. Inlays are made to restore seriously decayed and weakened teeth. Bridges, partial plates, and full dentures are made to replace missing teeth. These parts and prostheses are made by dental technicians in laboratories. They are created from teeth and mouth impressions that have been taken by dentists and sent to the dental laboratories with written instructions.

5
Dietary Department

▼

OBJECTIVES

After completing this chapter, you will be able to:
- Explain department goals
- Understand the principles of nutrition
- Explain how dietary needs are assessed
- Describe each career in this department
- Identify required education and credentials for each career
- Describe the skills performed in this department

▼

TERMS

Nutrients:
    Carbohydrate
    Fat
    Protein
    Vitamins
    Minerals

Metabolism

Special diets

▶ INTRODUCTION

The principles of nutrition are the basis of dietetic plans for individuals, communities, and educational programs. Nourishment is essential to life and to the healing process. Good eating habits promote healthy living, Figure 5-1. Well-balanced diets include a daily intake of the basic four food groups. Moderate-sized portions help to control weight.

When health problems occur, modifications in dietary intake may need to be made. People with diabetes need to eliminate intake of concentrated carbohydrates such as sugar. People with high blood pressure need to decrease the intake of sodium. People who have gastrointestinal surgery may need to eat different foods, in a different consistency, and in a different pattern than they did before their surgery.

Dietitians work with other health care professionals and community groups to provide nourishment, nutritional programs, and instructional presentations to benefit people of all ages with a variety of health conditions.

FIGURE 5-1. Good eating habits promote healthy living.

FIGURE 5-2. *Serve attractive and nutritious food.*

Digestion of foods takes place in the gastrointestinal tract. The digestive system is the usual route for food to be ingested and processed by the body. When the system is diseased or affected by medical conditions, when certain organs are removed, or when the body cannot tolerate food because of symptoms, the body cannot ingest and process food as before. Other routes of ingestion and other forms of nourishment must be found to bring nutrition to the body if life is to be sustained.

▶ GOALS

The goals of the dietary department are 1) to **obtain, prepare, and serve flavorful, attractive, and nutritious food** to patients (Figure 5-2), family members, and health care workers; and 2) to **educate** patients and family members about diet and its effect on enhancing the healing process, maintaining health, and preventing illness or the recurrence of illness.

▶ CAREER HIERARCHY

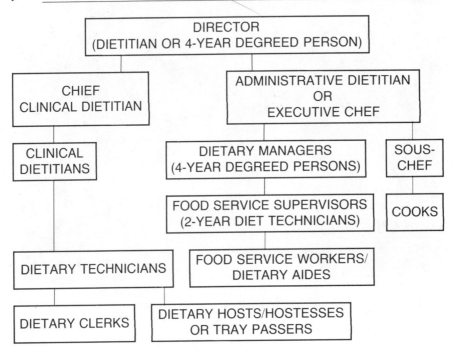

▶ CAREER DESCRIPTIONS

In a health care facility, dietary needs are assessed and planned by registered dietitians. Meals/snacks are then prepared and served by dietary workers under the direction of an administrative dietitian or executive chef and/or food service manager. Dietary technicians assist registered dietitians and may work as food service managers. Job responsibilities depend upon the nature of the employing institution, department organization, and job title of the worker.

Employment opportunities include hospitals, nursing homes, clinics, schools, universities, day-care centers, retirement centers, research centers, business and industry, Armed Services, government, international food organizations, and private practice. Hospitals are the largest employer of registered dietitians. The **job market** is good for all dietary workers.

Work hours vary according to the facility. In a hospital or nursing home, the dietary department functions 365 days a year on the day and evening shifts. Usually, dietitians work day shift; dietetic technicians and dietary assistants work day and evening shifts. In

community, business, independent practice, and education specialties, work hours are during the day, Monday through Friday.

Career advancements for dietitians include supervisory positions and directors of departments in their chosen specialty. With a
master's degree, dietitians can work in education, research, and
public health agencies.

Personal and professional qualities to be successful in this field
include the ability to accomplish detailed tasks, understand science-
related concepts, and develop nutritional care plans based on individual and group needs. Other characteristics include a keen interest
in people as individuals, and a desire to teach.

Job satisfaction comes from being respected members of the
health care team and from contributing to the well-being of others. It
comes from having a unique body of knowledge and meeting the
challenge of planning and providing therapeutic nourishment. Professional fulfillment also comes from the effect of teaching the
principles of nutrition and the correlation of dietary intake with
physical condition. Often, that teaching results in increased patient
compliance with physicians' diet recommendations, which ultimately results in increased comfort and the extension of life.

Registered/licensed dietitians may also be called *nutritionists.*
They have studied biological sciences, food, how food elements are
processed by the body, and the relationship between food elements
and the body's needs. They are uniquely qualified to interpet the
nutritional needs of various groups depending on age, gender,
activity, and illness. Through education and planning, they promote
health maintenance, prevention of illness, and treatment of disease.
Dietitians choose a specialty area of professional practice. These
career paths include clinical dietitian, community dietitian, administrative dietitian, business dietitian, educator dietitian, and consulant
dietitian.

Clinical dietitians are a vital part of the health team in patient
care settings such as hospitals, nursing homes, and clinics. They
evaluate the relationship between nutrition and health status with
patient/family interviews, medical record data, and lab reports. They
develop individual plans to meet nutritional needs. These plans
include diets, nourishments, tube feedings, and education. Clinical
dietitians provide individual and group educational programs for
patients and family members about their nutrition and health, the
importance of nourishment in the healing process, and the role of
nutrition in the prevention of illness. Instructions may include the
effects of calorie, fat, protein, and sugar intake, principles of well-

Figure 5-3. Two age groups that concern clinical dietitians.

balanced diets, details of special diets, and methods of food preparation. If prepared foods or medical nutritional supplements will be purchased, nutritional content of those items will be included as well as information about where they may be purchased. Details of instruction will depend on the physician's orders and the patient's illness and ability to understand. Frequently, dietitians instruct family members who are responsible for preparing the patient's meals.

Clinical dietitians are concerned with the nutritional needs of people in all age groups (Figure 5-3)—from premature infants to the elderly—who are afflicted with a range of problems that impact on their nutritional status. Often, when patients need nourishment to heal and regain health, other factors prevent eating. Some patients cannot chew or swallow, consume anything by mouth, or have no appetite. Clinical dietitians plan ways to meet individual nutritional requirements by circumventing symptoms and illnesses. Clinical dietitians can specialize in certain areas such as nutrition support, cancer, diabetes, kidney disease, pediatrics, or gerontology. In addition to hospitals, they work in research labs and in private practice.

Community dietitians work with wellness programs and international health organizations. They adapt knowledge of food and nutrition to life-style and geographic areas. They coordinate nutritional programs in public health agencies, day-care centers, health clubs, and recreational camps and resorts.

Administrative dietitians are also called *management dietitians.*

They manage dietary departments in health care facilities, school food service programs, prisons, cafeterias, and restaurants. They oversee food preparation and service. They hire, train, direct, and supervise department employees. They develop systems for obtaining, preparing, and serving food. They are responsible for large-scale food planning and service.

Business dietitians serve as resource persons for the media. They work as sales representatives for companies that make nutritional supplements and tube feedings. They work for food-manufacturing companies. They work as marketing specialists in corporate public relations.

Dietitian educators teach in colleges, universities, and hospitals. They teach courses on nutrition and food service management systems. They relate biological sciences with food elements. They demonstrate the effects of proper nourishment with health maintenance, disease prevention, and treatment of illness.

Consultant dietitians work in private practice. They contract independently to provide nutrition services and educational programs to individuals, nursing homes, health care facilities, and industry.

Dietetic technicians work under the supervision of registered dietitians or managers, Figure 5-4. They are trained in writing regular and modified diets, nutritional screening, patient visitation, and food production and delivery. They supervise food production, visit hospitalized patients to obtain preferences, provide simple diet instructions, and work with dietitians to review menus and recipes. They need to be able to work well with others and follow directions accurately.

Responsibilities include ordering food items, processing orders to suppliers, and managing food storage. They can work in the dietary office, in the kitchen and with patients.

Job opportunities include hospitals, nursing homes, universities, industrial food service, catering services, restaurant chains, day-care centers, and community agencies. By continuing their education, they can become dietitians.

Dietary clerks work in the diet office. They enter data and record diet changes from the computer. They check menus against recent diet orders before tray assembly begins. They are responsible for tracking financial data, such as the number of meals served. They provide communication between the patient care units and the rest of the dietary department.

Executive chefs plan and direct the production of food for patient

FIGURE 5-4. *A registered dietician and dietetic technician.*

service, retail (cafeteria) service, and catering. A certified executive chef is credentialed by the American Culinary Federation. A *sous-chef* is an assistant chef.

Dietary managers are responsible for the direct management of a specific departmental function, such as retail (cafeteria), catering, or tray line. If an operation is large, there may be one or more food service supervisors to assist in directing the dietary workers.

Dietary workers prepare food and meal trays in the kitchen area, Figure 5-5. They work on the tray line, determining tray completeness and accuracy. They maintain the storage area for food supplies, practice sanitary procedures, and can identify food contamination situations. Dietary workers are trained on the job and can work in any commercial kitchen.

Dietary hosts/hostesses transport trays and deliver meals to patients. They distribute and collect menus and help patients complete selections. They promptly address patient needs and concerns regarding meal service.

FIGURE 5-5. Dietary workers preparing food.

▶ EDUCATION AND CREDENTIALS

CAREER NAME	YEARS OF EDUCATION AFTER HIGH SCHOOL	DEGREE OR DIPLOMA	TESTED BY: CREDENTIALED BY:
Registered Licensed Dietitian (RD,LD)	5 years: 4 years plus 6–12-month internship or AP4 program: 4 years plus 900 hours of supervised practice	B.S. in food and nutrition or Master's degree in food and nutrition or institutional management	Tested and registered by ADA; licensed by the state
Registered Licensed Dietetic Technician (DTR)	2 years	A.A.S.D. in dietetic technology	Exam/certification by ADA; licensed by the state
Certified Chef (CEC or CWC)	2 years	AD in culinary arts or hospitality management	Certification by ACF

CAREER NAME	YEARS OF EDUCATION AFTER HIGH SCHOOL	DEGREE OR DIPLOMA	TESTED BY: CREDENTIALED BY:
Cook (CC)	On-the-job training		Education and certification via ACF (optional)
Host/Hostess or Tray Passers	On-the-job training: core training. program plus hospitality training		
Dietary Clerk, Worker, Aid	On-the-job training	—	—

Key to Abbreviations:
 AD: Associate Degree
 A.A.S.D.: Associate of Applied Science Degree
 ACF: American Culinary Federation
 ADA: American Dietetic Association
 ADCA: Associate Degree of Culinary Arts
 AP4: Approved Practice for Dietitian Program
 B.S.: Bachelor of Science degree
 CC: Certified Cook
 CEC: Certified Executive Chef
 CWC: Certified Working Chef
 DTR: Dietary Technician Registered
 LD: Licensed Dietitian
 RD: Registered Dietitian

● ● ● ●

▶ JOB AVAILABILITY

The U.S. Bureau of Labor statistics estimate that job availability for registered dietitians and dietetic technicians will increase by 34 percent, 42 percent for cooks, and 34 percent for bakers through the year 2005.

▶ SKILLS

Skills utilized by dietary workers in a hospital setting depend on job title and certification. Clinical dietitians assess and meet dietary needs according to physicians' orders, nursing requests, or from an interdisciplinary specialty team. Administrative dietitians manage the dietary department and develop methods to evaluate and improve food and nutrition service systems. Dietetic technicians work with department employees and patients to record the diet history, identify food habits, develop diet plans, and supervise food preparation and delivery. Dietary workers/aids prepare food and assemble meal trays; diet clerks do clerical tasks related to menus and diet changes; and dietary hosts/hostesses deliver meal trays. Department activities center around department management, food service, assessing and meeting nutritional needs, and patient education.

Department Management

Administration of the dietary department involves identifying and accomplishing department goals, determining department policies and procedures, hiring and training workers, and scheduling work hours. Other tasks include planning and structuring studies to determine customer satisfaction and seeking ways to meet consumer needs more effectively.

Food Service

Food service involves the purchasing of food according to planned menus for patients and workers. Amounts must be sufficient to feed the clients but not enough to spoil. Supplies such as plates, cups, napkins, and meal trays are ordered according to need and the type of equipment used in the food service system. Some facilities use thermal cups and a hot-plate system.

Food service includes tray preparation, assembling food items, transporting, serving, and collecting meal trays. Other responsibilities involve the delivery of between meal nourishments and tube feedings. Quality of service and customer satisfaction are measured and changes made when necessary.

Meeting Nutritional Needs

Meeting nutritional needs entails the assessment of patients by registered/licensed dietitians to determine nutritional status and diet habits. Nutritional assessment begins with a medical record review for pertinent data, a patient/family interview, and calculation of calorie intake. It includes identifying how dietary intake affects the disease process and making a plan to encourage food intake to meet the needs of the body, promote or maintain health, and prevent recurrences. Accomplishing nutrition care plan goals involves education of and working with patients, family members, and other members of the health team, Figure 5-6. It also includes participation

FIGURE 5-6. *Work with the family to make good nutrition a reality.*

in patient-centered interdisciplinary team meetings, such as the stroke team or the oncology team. Dietary needs become evident in these meetings and follow-up visits are scheduled by dietitians.

Diet Instruction

Instruction in nutrition and diet is done with individuals, in small groups, and in large classes. Topics include special diets for conditions or diseases and nutrition for various age groups. Classes in weight-reduction diets, diabetic diets, and gerontology nutritional needs may be offered. Diet instruction includes the rationale for the diet, a listing of foods allowed/not allowed for the special diet, and planning a day's menu. Appropriate teaching materials, such as brochures and videotapes developed by qualified dietitians, are used for diet instructions. Simple diet instruction may be done by qualified dietetic technicians. Complex diet instruction is done by qualified dietitians.

6
Emergency Department

▼

OBJECTIVES

After completing this chapter, you will be able to:
- Explain department goals
- Discuss the various kinds of emergencies handled in an emergency department
- Describe several careers in this department
- Identify required education and credentials for each career
- Describe the major skills performed in this department

▼

TERMS

Problems:
Asthma
Cardiac arrest
Cerebral vascular accident
Congestive heart failure
Fracture
Hemorrhage
Laceration
Myocardial infarction

Diagnostic tests:
Arterial blood gases
Blood pressure

Electrocardiograph
X ray

Treatments:
Aerosol treatment
Blood transfusion
Cardiopulmonary
resuscitation
Cast
Suture
Intravenous fluids

▶ INTRODUCTION

Professionals who specialize in emergency care treat patients with traumatic injuries and sudden severe illnesses. They assess, diagnose, and treat the acutely ill patients who usually need immediate medical attention. Activities include resuscitation and stabilization of critically ill patients, then arranging for transfer to the nursing unit or facility that will best meet their needs. Patients who have had a heart attack may be taken to the cardiac care unit. Patients who have been severely burned, may need to be transported to a hospital with a burn unit. Those with minor ailments may be treated and released from the emergency care setting without being admitted to the hospital.

Patients come to an emergency care setting in a variety of ways. Some patients drive themselves to the emergency care setting and some are transported by family, paramedics, or flight crew. However they come, both patients and families are experiencing stress, especially if the illness is life-threatening.

▶ GOALS

The goals of an emergency care setting are to assess, diagnose, treat, and stabilize acutely ill patients as quickly as possible in a friendly and comforting environment and direct them to appropriate aftercare.

► CAREER HIERARCHY

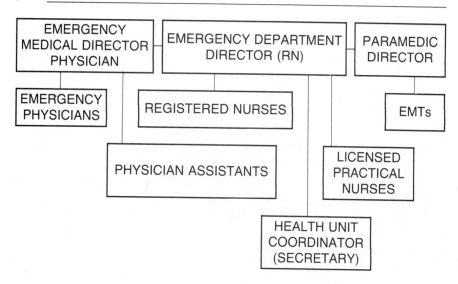

► CAREER DESCRIPTIONS

Professional workers who specialize in emergency care need to be prepared to minister to patients of all ages with a variety of conditions—from minor injuries to major trauma, from mild symptoms to cardiac arrest. They care for patients with all types of illness and accidents, some that are self-inflicted. Workers are often successful at saving lives; but sometimes patients die. Some emergency care professionals work in hospitals or freestanding emergency centers; others work outside the institutional setting, administering prehospital emergency care and transporting the victim to the medical facility.

After completing their basic educational programs, physicians and nurses who work in emergency care usually have had specialized training in caring for acutely ill patients. Advanced Cardiac Life Support (a course in cardiac monitoring) and previous work experience in a surgical intensive care or coronary care unit may be required to work in emergency care settings and on the helicopter flight team. The entire emergency medical technicians' course is geared to first aid training for suddenly acutely ill patients.

Job responsibilities vary according to the education and position of the workers and policies of the institution. In some hospitals, paramedics work in the emergency department when not responding to a rescue call. In some communities, they work out of the fire department and may also be fire fighters.

Some workers are permanently assigned to the emergency department, others come there when a critically ill patient arrives. Permanent workers include physicians with a specialty in emergency medicine, nurses, and health unit coordinators (secretaries). Medical centers may have a helicopter flight crew of doctors, nurses, respiratory therapists, and paramedics who work in the emergency care setting between rescue runs. Patient registration representatives help to obtain demographic information, initiate charts, maintain records, and arrange for hospital admission.

Workers who come to the emergency care setting when a critically ill patient arrives include an anesthesiologist, respiratory therapist, radiographer, medical laboratory technician, EKG technician, clergy, and social worker. Cardiologists, surgeons, and other specialists are called in as necessary.

Employment opportunities include hospital emergency departments, freestanding emergency centers, critical care transport services, private ambulance services, government agencies, pharmaceutical and manufacturer sales positions, home care, and industrial clinics. Other options include working in the operating room, clinics, law offices, and insurance companies. With an advanced degree, teaching and research may be options. Experience in emergency patient care serves as a background for positions on critical care nursing units, helicopter flight crews, and in surgery. Career opportunities for registered nurses, particularly those with critical care experience, are the broadest of all health careers. RNs are able to work with all age groups in all specialities. They can change their speciality and work in other cities, states, and nations.

The job outlook for all critical care workers is good.

Work hours vary according to the facility. Hospital emergency departments are usually open twenty-four hours every day of the year, Figure 6-1. Freestanding emergency centers may be open every day and evenings seven days a week. Workers can often schedule flexible hours, depending on the needs of the facility and their availability. Eight-, ten-, and twelve-hour shifts may be available, as well as four-hour periods during busy times. Paramedics may work the same schedule as fire fighters—on duty twenty-four hours, off duty forty-eight hours. Care givers may need to rotate to evening and night shifts and work weekend hours and holidays in a twenty-four-hour facility. Positions in education and industry usually offer daytime work hours.

Career advancements include supervisory or department director positions. With further education, a worker with emergency care experience can move into other positions. A paramedic or practical nurse may become a registered nurse, perfusionist, or a physician's or surgeon's assistant.

Desired personal characteristics include possessing a calm, kind demeanor; a friendly, reassuring manner; and a capacity for problem solving. Emergency care workers need to work well in stressful situations, be adaptable, give directions, take directions, and be prepared to help patients and family members cope with tragic situations. Other desirable qualities include dependability, skill in resuscitative measures, and ability to communicate effectively both verbally and in writing, Figure 6-2.

Nurses need confidence, leadership and teaching skills, ability to make fast and responsible decisions, good interpersonal skills, and ability to interact with many different types of people and personalities.

Paramedics need physical fitness—the ability to lift (about) 150 pounds with the assistance of one other person. Other attributes include the ability to communicate diplomatically with patients, family, and bystanders. Paramedics need a crisp appearance in a stainfree uniform. Both verbal skills and appearance are interpreted by patients and observers as indicative of the quality of care that will be given. Some paramedics keep a spare uniform at work in case the

FIGURE 6-1. Emergency rooms never close.

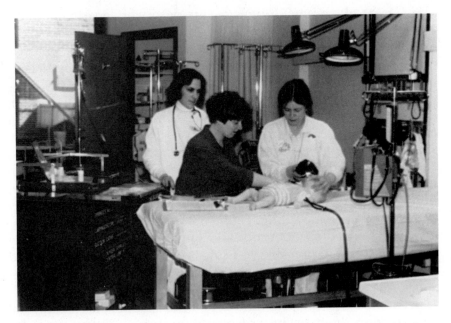

FIGURE 6-2. Effective communication is never more necessary than in an ER situation.

one being worn becomes spattered with blood or street soil. Leadership is another quality that is important in the field. Each paramedic needs to be able to take charge of the situation, make good decisions, go ahead with treatment of the victim, and prepare for transport. In a triage situation or when there are multiple victims, paramedics must lead or work alone.

Job satisfaction comes from feeling effective in easing suffering, calming fears, stopping a disfiguring process, stabilizing conditions, and saving lives. Making sound decisions under stress, the good feelings from helping people who are severely ill and fearful, and the variety of daily activities contribute to job gratification.

Personal safety is a concern for emergency care workers because of handling patients' blood and body fluids. Workers need to wear protective clothing in situations where they might contact body fluids.

Emergency care physicians are doctors with special training in emergency medicine. They lead the emergency team and work with team members to diagnose and treat patients. Physicians assess patients, order diagnostic tests, interpret test results, identify illnesses, and develop treatment plans. Because of severe illness and the unstable nature of patient conditions, these steps may need to be done in minutes. Physicians must recognize when to call in specialists, identify the need for hospitalization, and give discharge directions to those who do not need hospitalization. Physicians also determine the need for transfer to another facility and the best mode of transportation—ambulance or helicopter. Physicians explain the diagnosis and treatment plan to patients and families. They may be employed by the facility or by an agency that contracts with the facility to provide physicians.

The *registered nurse* coordinates the patient care and personnel in the emergency department. In most cases, this is the first person to see the patient upon their arrival. The nurse must obtain a medical history from the patient and/or family, including current medications and any drug allergies. In this setting, it is imperative for the nurse to do a fast and accurate initial assessment of the patient to determine the acuity level. If the nurse feels that the patient needs to be seen by the physician immediately, it is the nurse's responsibility to seek out and notify the physician immediately of the patient's condition. In the event that the physician is unable to see the patient immediately, it is the nurse's responsibility to initiate treatment. This may include starting intravenous fluids, drawing blood, applying oxygen, and anticipating any tests or treatments the physician may want to perform.

Nurses who work in the emergency department are responsible for coordinating all aspects of patient care, Figure 6-3. They not only carry out the physician's orders but must anticipate needs, make suggestions to the doctor, and intervene on the patient's behalf. The physician and nurse work together as a team.

Nurses monitor vital signs, provide physical comfort, administer medications, help patients to understand the diagnosis and treatment plan, instruct patients in aftercare, and work with physicians to identify other health team members who may be consulted. Nurses seek the identity of unknown patients, strive to locate family members, and arrange for hospital admission or transport to another facility.

Emergency Medical Service (EMS) is the system of rescue workers. There are several levels of emergency medical service technicians based on the length and content of the educational program. There is an EMT—A, EMT—I or EMT—D, and EMT—P. Some programs are full-time and some are part-time. Programs vary from six hundred to fifteen hundred hours of instruction and experience. The student must have practice in certain emergency care situations before program completion. In addition, an EMT must have a good driving

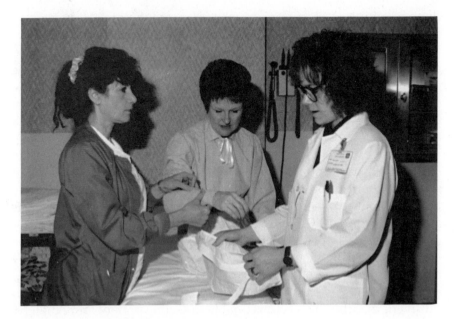

FIGURE 6-3. *Coordinating the health care team is one of the nurses's responsibilities.*

record. A conviction of driving while under the influence of alcohol (DWI) is grounds for refusal to admit a student into an EMT program and can cause the dismissal of an EMT from the emergency squad.

The *emergency medical technician—ambulance (EMT—A)* has basic training in emergency care. These workers are qualified to drive an ambulance, do CPR, and assist paramedics in the field, Figure 6-4. Technicians are trained in first aid, administer oxygen, and apply mast trousers. They can work for a private ambulance company or a municipal government after passing a civil service examination. They transport stable patients from hospital to nursing home or from hospital to diagnostic testing sites. In some geographic areas, this level is being phased out of existence because more education is desirable.

The *EMT—Intermediate (EMT—I)* or the *EMT—Defibrillation (EMT—D)* receives more in-depth training. These technicians work with more unstable patients, administer oxygen, apply mast trousers, perform the more advanced procedures of starting intravenous fluids and adminstering defibrillation. They are employed by fire departments and municipal governments in a rescue ambulance.

The *EMT—Paramedic (EMT—P)* has the most education in this category. These technicians act as the eyes, ears, and hands of the

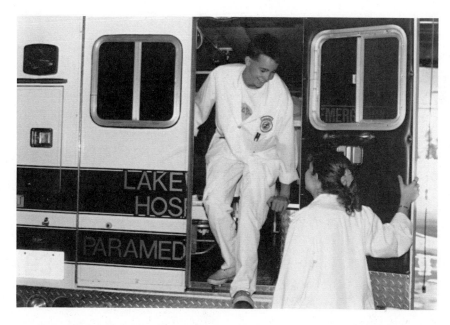

FIGURE 6-4. Emergency medical technicians (EMTs) are an important part of the ER team.

physician in the field. They administer treatments for life-threatening emergencies—the same tasks as the emergency care physician would do. They administer oxygen (Figure 6-5), apply mast trousers, start intravenous fluids, defibrillate, plus administer medications. They have a thorough knowledge of first aid, quickly assess situations and extent of illness or injury, follow definite protocols to stabilize patients on the scene, treat conditions that need immediate attention, convey information and receive direction from the emergency care setting over a two-way radio, then transport to a medical facility.

Members of the *flight crew* include physicians, registered nurses, and EMT—Ps who travel by helicopter to airlift a patient to a designated location. They may have to rescue a patient from an automobile accident in a remote area not accessible to an ambulance, or from the scene of an accident to a distant hospital. Or a patient may need to be transferred from one hospital to another in the least amount of time. Before the flight team is activated, both the medical crew and the pilots must approve the flight.

The medical crew members need to determine the feasibility of the rescue effort. To make that decision, they need an assessment

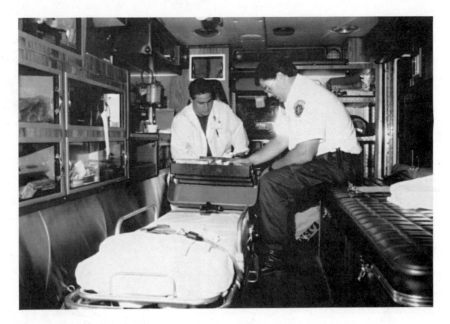

FIGURE 6-5. The EMT—P (emergency medical technician—paramedic) is the eyes, ears, and hands of the physician.

of the situation and patient condition from the emergency workers on the scene. After the medical crew decides that the assignment is appropriate, the pilots are consulted. They are responsible for determining if weather conditions are safe for flight. If the pilots decide that flight is possible, the team is on the way.

Upon arrival, the medical team helps the on-site workers prepare the patient for flight. In the field, at an accident site, the patient is transported as quickly as possible with stabilization efforts conducted in flight. If the patient is in a hospital, the flight team helps the hospital workers stabilize the patient before preparing for transport. A physician or EMT—P, two nurses, and one respiratory therapist may all fly in the helicopter with one or two patients.

▶ EDUCATION AND CREDENTIALS

CAREER NAME	YEARS OF EDUCATION AFTER HIGH SCHOOL	DEGREE OR DIPLOMA	TESTED BY: REGISTERED BY:
Physician (M.D. or D.O.)	11 years: 4 years college 4 years medical school 3-year program of residency in emergency medicine	B.S. M.D. or D.O.	National boards: 3 parts; state registration; Emergency medicine boards (written & oral); ACLS; ATLS; PALS
Registered Nurse (RN)	2, 3 or 4 years: 2 years 3 years 4 years	A.A.S.D. in nursing Diploma B.S.N.	State board of nursing; ACLS
Licensed Practical Nurse (LPN) (LVN)	1 year	Diploma	State board of nursing; BLS; pharmacology certification
Emergency Medical Technician— Ambulance (EMT—A)	13 weeks	Certificate	Ambulance state certification; CPR required
Emergency Medical Technician— Intermediate (EMT—I) or (EMT—D)	1½ years: 2 quarters plus EMT—A (9 months) same as EMT—I	Certificate or diploma if hospital program	State certification; written and practical administered by NREMT; and Basic Life Support required. EMT—I plus defibrillation
Emergency Medical Certification Technician— Paramedic (EMT—P)	3 years: 9 months for paramedic plus 2 years: EMT—P plus assoc. degree	A.A.S.D. in emergency medical technology	State administered by NREMT; and ACLS required

Key to Abbreviations:
ACLS: Advanced Cardiac Life Support
A.A.S.D.: Associate of Applied Science Degree
ATLS: Advanced Trauma Life Support

BLS: Basic Life Support
B.S.: Bachelor of Science
B.S.N.: Bachelor of Science in nursing
D.O.: Doctor of Osteopathy
EMT: Emergency Medical Technician
EMT—P: Emergency Medical Technician—Paramedic
LPN: Licensed Practical Nurse
LVN: Licensed Vocational Nurse
M.D.: Medical Doctor
NREMT: National Registry of Emergency Medical Technicians
PALS: Pediatric Advanced Life Support
RN: Registered Nurse

● ● ● ●

▶ JOB AVAILABILITY

Job availability is good for all workers in emergency care. The U.S. Bureau of Labor statistics estimate that emergency medical technologists—paramedic positions will increase 24 percent, registered nurse positions will increase 44 percent, and licensed practical nurse positions will increase 42 percent through the year 2005.

▶ SKILLS

Workers need training in emergency skills before going to work in an emergency care setting. **Assessing** patients' conditions quickly, **diagnosing** the illness accurately, **initiating a plan of action** to stop the disease progression, **stabilizing** and **treating** conditions, and **observing** the beginnings of recovery are the skills used by workers in this setting. The keys to this process are *speed* and *accuracy,* because lives often depend on swift intervention.

Emergency skills need to be practiced so that workers are ready to perform them effectively when a patient arrives. When paramedics are transporting a patient to the hospital, they may radio a patient's symptoms and traumatic injuries so workers can prepare to perform necessary skills. In a freestanding emergency care setting, separate from a hospital, workers may need to learn more skills because there are fewer disciplines at that facility.

Cardiopulmonary resuscitation (CPR) is the skill of providing oxygen and pumping blood when the heart and lungs are not functioning. Most patients who receive CPR after a witnessed cardiac or respiratory arrest survive with their mental capacities intact.

Defibrillating is the procedure that "shocks" the heart with an electrical charge. It is done to change the heartbeat from an irregular rhythm to a regular rhythm.

Cleansing and *bandaging* wounds, *suturing* lacerations, and *casting* fractured bones are other skills utilized in the emergency care setting. Physicians, paramedics, surgeons' assistants, and physicians' assistants suture wounds according to the policies of the facility.

Taking, interpreting, and documenting vital signs are essential skills in the emergency care setting, Figure 6-6. Temperature, pulse, respirations, and blood pressure readings indicate if patients' conditions are stable, improving, or deteriorating. Reporting changes in these signs may be lifesaving.

Inserting an intravenous needle is an essential skill that is done to draw blood or administer intravenous fluid and medication directly into the bloodstream. In some patients, the procedure is difficult because of arteriosclerosis, small veins, or collapse of venous circulation that may occur if the blood pressure is very low or absent. It is also difficult if the patient is unable to hold the arm still. This is often the situation with a baby, small child, or confused adult.

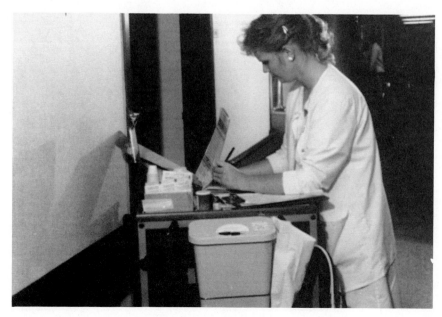

FIGURE 6-6. Documenting vital signs.

Planning for patient safety is a skill needed to protect the patient from events that could cause injury. The patient's identity is confirmed by the identification wristband applied upon arrival. Side rails are used to prevent falling from the high, narrow treatment carts; signal cords are used to indicate that help is needed; and special procedures are followed to ensure administration of safe, compatible blood transfusions.

Triage, handling large numbers of patients in a community disaster, is a skill performed by workers in a hospital emergency department. If a plane crashes, a bus accident occurs, or an apartment building burns, large numbers of patients would be transported to the hospital for assessment and treatment. Each hospital has a disaster plan to handle such events. Though it rarely occurs, workers need to be thoroughly schooled in triage techniques. They need to practice sorting and directing "patients" to appropriate treatment areas so that real patients would be effectively and efficiently treated if such an event should happen.

Communication skills, to comfort, support, and educate patients and family members and to inform other professionals, are also necessary, Figure 6-7. Accurate and adequate written communication is essential to providing adequate care and preventing error.

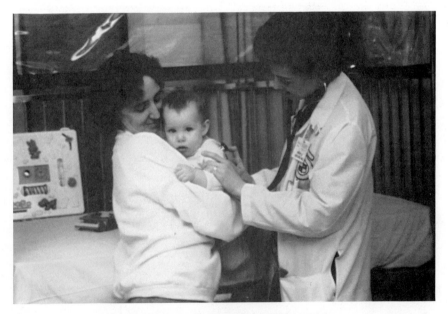

FIGURE 6-7. Communication is important.

Confidentiality is the skill that guarantees patients' privacy. Workers cannot explain to one patient about another patient, or talk to friends or to members of the press about patients' conditions or facts surrounding an event. Workers cannot disclose the circumstances of an automobile accident or mention any information about injured victims.

7
Medical Laboratory Department

OBJECTIVES

After completing this chapter, you will be able to:
- Explain department goals
- List the common tests performed in the medical laboratory department
- Describe the specialties in this department
- Identify required education and credentials for each career
- Describe the skills performed in this department

▼

TERMS

Sections:
Blood Bank
Chemistry
Cytology
Hematology
Histology
Immunology
Microbiology
Pathology

Serology
Urinalysis
Virology

▶ INTRODUCTION

The medical laboratory provides vital information that serves as a guide to physicians for diagnoses, treatment, monitoring disease progress, identifying effectiveness of treatment, and establishing a health maintenance regime. The process that fosters accurate results of clinical studies includes careful preparation and examination of specimens, precise performance of clinical tests, and thorough study and interpretation of the condition of tissues and body fluids, Figure 7-1. In addition, the laboratory issues compatible and safe blood and blood products for transfusion.

The laboratory is divided into sections. These divisions are made according to speciality and size of the hospital and laboratory. In every section, specific tests are done by workers with special training. Some tests are done manually; some are done on specifically designed instruments that are maintained by laboratory personnel.

Tests ordered by physicians are conducted in clinical laboratories. Large institutions may have research laboratories as well.

FIGURE 7-1. Careful examination of specimens.

▶ GOALS

The goals of a medical laboratory are to **report accurate test results** of body substances and tissues, to **issue compatible, safe blood** and blood products for transfusion, and to **determine a cause of death** by tissue exam and autopsy.

▶ CAREER HIERARCHY

```
┌─────────────────────────┐        ┌──────────────────────┐
│ ADMINISTRATIVE DIRECTOR │────────│   MEDICAL DIRECTOR    │
└─────────────────────────┘        └──────────────────────┘
            ┌──────────────────────────────────┐
            │   CHIEF MEDICAL TECHNOLOGIST      │
            └──────────────────────────────────┘

┌──────────────────────┐   ┌──────────────┐   ┌──────────────────┐
│  CYTOTECHNOLOGIST     │   │   MEDICAL    │   │   PHLEBOTOMIST   │
└──────────────────────┘   │TECHNOLOGISTS │   └──────────────────┘
                           └──────────────┘
                                ┌──────────────────────┐
                                │     HISTOLOGIST;     │
                                │    HISTOTECHNICIAN    │
                                └──────────────────────┘

┌──────────────────────────────────────┐
│  MEDICAL LABORATORY TECHNICIANS       │
└──────────────────────────────────────┘
┌──────────────────────────────────────┐
│  MEDICAL LABORATORY ASSISTANTS        │
└──────────────────────────────────────┘
```

▶ CAREER DESCRIPTIONS

Medical technologists and technicians are essential workers on the health care team. Roles and responsibilities vary according to the size of the laboratory and the facility, types of tests performed, specimen collection techniques, complexity of testing instruments, availability and sophistication of computer programs, and method of reporting test results.

Responsibilities include the daily calibration of instruments, careful monitoring of test results, and quality control procedures to be sure each instrument is functioning accurately. Definite steps must be followed on each instrument before patient specimens are run. In large laboratories, tests are performed on automated computer-driven instruments. In small laboratories, tests may be manually run. Chemistry, biochemistry, and microbiology are the basic courses in medical laboratory programs.

Laboratory personnel work more with specimens of body tissue, secretions, and excretions than they do with patients. Contact with patients includes drawing blood samples, receiving specimens from outpatients, and assisting physicians to obtain tissue specimens. Blood samples are usually drawn by phlebotomists, laboratory technologists, and laboratory technicians. Specimens of body secretions and excretions are usually obtained by nursing personnel. Tissue specimens are obtained by physicians. Laboratory personnel interact with health care professionals. Lab results are reported to physicians and nurses.

In small laboratories, medical technologists perform all tests. In large laboratories, technologists specialize in one or two sections. These sections may be Blood Bank, Chemistry, Hematology, Immunology, Microbiology, Serology, Urinalysis, or Histology and Cytology.

Employment opportunities for medical technologists include hospitals, clinics, physician offices, government agencies, research institutions, and pharmaceutical companies. Mobile laboratories take technologists into patients' homes. Other jobs include blood and organ donor banks, zoological settings, sperm banks, water treatment plants, government epidemiology labs, veterinary offices, and crime labs. Another employment opportunity is product development and marketing for companies that manufacture home testing kits and lab equipment.

Work hours vary with the institution and position. In a facility where acutely ill patients are treated, the laboratory operates 24 hours a day, 365 days a year. Full-time and part-time positions are available, sometimes on flexible schedules, depending on the needs of the facility and availability of personnel.

Career advancement includes section managers in large laboratories and supervisory positions in smaller facilities. An advanced degree in a biological science or education can lead to positions in teaching and research.

Desired characteristics include an aptitude for science, detail, and accurate and independent work. Other qualifications include the ability to operate complex equipment, calibrate instruments, run computers, and do scientific calculation. In addition, one needs the ability to strictly adhere to technical procedures and aseptic technique, work under pressure, and perform in emergency situations.

Good vision and fine dexterity are needed to manipulate tissues, cells, and bacteria and to see minute gradations of color.

Job satisfaction comes from doing an essential job well. Professional fulfillment comes from knowing that the lab plays an important part in patient care and treatment. Because of the precise work of laboratory professionals, disease-causing bacteria are isolated and identified, medication is recommended, medication treatment plans are evaluated, disease progress is monitored, life-threatening levels of toxins are perceived, and abnormal cells are recognized.

Personal safety is a concern of laboratory workers because they work with body fluids and tissues that contain disease-producing bacteria and viruses. Careful technique is the key to handling contaminated materials without becoming infected, Figure 7-2.

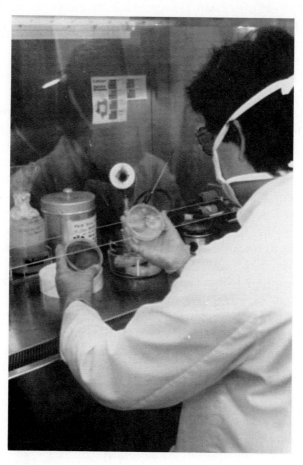

FIGURE 7-2. Personal safety is of prime importance.

The *administrative director* can be degreed as a medical technologist and often has a doctor's or master's degree in a medical specialty. This person is responsible for the quality of specimen preparation, accuracy of test results, and correct reporting of those findings throughout the laboratory. He/she is also responsible for the business or financial aspect of laboratory operations.

A *pathologist* serves as the *medical director* of the laboratory. The pathologist is a medical physician or osteopath physician who specializes in the study of the nature, cause, and development of diseases and the structure and function of normal and abnormal body cells. This specialty includes detecting cellular misfunction, abnormal structure, and the extent of disease progress. This is a serious responsibility because a patient's treatment is often based on pathology findings. If a pathologist reports that malignant cells are present, a certain type of surgery and medical therapy may be carried out. If a pathologist reports that no malignant cells are present, a more conservative surgery and medical plan may be carried out. Inaccurate cellular studies can result in a cancer growing and spreading. Pathologists need to be knowledgeable in both anatomical structures and clinical analysis of specimens.

Other responsibilities may include directing the clinical laboratory, monitoring quality-assurance studies, research, analysis of statistical data, and consideration of treatment strategies. Pathologists also perform autopsies to examine organs and tissues and establish a cause of death. Pathologists work in hospitals, medical schools, government, and private industry.

Medical technologists prepare and examine specimens of tissue, fluids, and cells. Under the supervision of a pathologist, these technologists determine the presence of abnormalities and diseases. They perform complicated chemical, microscopic, and automated analyzer/computer tests. They know the clinical significance of test results. Areas of specialization include microbiology, chemistry, blood bank, hematology, and immunology. The medical technologist is qualified to advance to a supervisory position.

Medical laboratory technicians work under the supervision of pathologists or medical technologists (Figure 7-3), and do the same tasks that are performed by medical technologists. They prepare tissue specimen slides for examination, perform cell counts, and run urinalysis. They draw blood samples from patients and perform tests in the hematology, serology, and bacteriology sections. They maintain supplies and equipment and keep up records.

FIGURE 7-3. *A medical technologist supervising a lab technician.*

Phlebotomists or *venipuncture technicians* are trained to draw venous blood samples. They process some blood samples and perform clerical duties.

Cytotechnologists work with pathologists in screening cells from tissue scrapings and body fluids for abnormalities, especially those changes that indicate cancer.

Histologists or *histotechnicians* prepare tissues for microscopic exam. The technician's findings are reviewed and confirmed by a pathologist. Before studying cellular changes, the technician may review the patient's medical record to learn about factors that impact on changes in body cells. These factors sometimes effect cellular patterns and cause diseases. These factors include family medical history, personal medical history, and special information such as type of work; smoking, eating, and drinking habits; symptoms; and treatment program.

EDUCATION AND CREDENTIALS

CAREER NAME	YEARS OF EDUCATION AFTER HIGH SCHOOL	DEGREE OR DIPLOMA	TESTED BY: LICENSED BY:
Certified Pathologist (M.D. or D.O.)	13–15 years: 4 yrs. college 4 yrs. medical school 2 yrs. postgraduate 3–5 yrs. pathology training	M.D./O.D.	National certification by American Board of Pathology and Licensed by the state as M.D. or D.O.
Medical Technologist (MT)	5 years: 4 yrs. college plus 1 year internship	B.S. in medical technology or chemistry, biology, or other science	Certification from National Certification Agency for Medical Laboratory Personnel; licensure or registration required in some states
Blood Bank Technologist (MT, AABB)	6 years: Same as for MT plus 1 year training in a certified program in the Specialty of Blood Bank (SBB)	B.S. plus certificate	Certification by AABB
Chemistry Technologist (MT)	5 years: Same as for MT with specialty in chemistry		
Hematology Technologist (MT)	5 years: Same as for MT with specialty in hematology		
Immunology Technologist (MT)	5 years: Same as for MT with specialty in immunology		

CAREER NAME	YEARS OF EDUCATION AFTER HIGH SCHOOL	DEGREE OR DIPLOMA	TESTED BY: LICENSED BY:
Medical Laboratory Technician (MLT)	3 years: 2 yrs. college and 1 yr. internship	A.A.S.D. in medical laboratory technology	Certification exam by ASCP; licensure or certification required in some states
Cytotechnologist (CT, ASCP)	5 years: 4 yrs. college plus 1 yr. internship	B.S. in biology or chemistry	Certification exam by ASCP
Histologist Histotechnician (HT, ASCP)	1 year	Certificate	Certification exam by ASC
Phlebotomist; venipuncture Technician	10 weeks or 2 quarters of On-the-job training	—	Certification exam by IAPS

Key to Abbreviations:
AABB: American Association of Blood Banks
AASD: Associate of Applied Science degree
ASCP: American Society of Clinical Pathology
B.S.: Bachelor of Science degree
CT: Certified Technician
CMT: Certified Medical Technician
D.O.: Osteopathic Doctor
HOE: Health Occupations Education in high school
HT: Histology Technologist
IAPS: International Agency of Phlebotomy Science
M.D.: Medical Doctor
MT: Medical Technologist
NCAMLP: National Certification Agency for Medical Laboratory Personnel
SBB: Specialist in Blood Bank

●　　　●　　　●　　　●

▶ JOB AVAILABILITY

The U.S. Department of Labor estimates a 24-percent increase in job openings to the year 2005 for medical technologists and technicians. The estimated increase in laboratory positions is less than some other health care careers because of automation and because physicians order fewer lab tests than in the past in an effort to control health care costs without jeopardizing patient care.

▶ SKILLS

Tasks performed by medical technologists and technicians vary according to the section in which they work. Both manual and computer techniques are learned during training, Figure 7-4. After training, they can specialize in certain sections depending on the size of the lab and job availability. Training is a continuous process because of scientific discoveries, advances in technology, and new equipment.

There are many computer-driven automated analyzers available in the marketplace. Laboratory workers learn to use instruments purchased by the facility, Figure 7-5A. If instruments malfunction, techs repair them, use backup equipment, or run the lab tests manually.

Blood Bank (Immunohematology) is the only section of the clinical laboratory that issues a product. All other sections prepare and test specimens and issue reports. Skills include identifying the patient, drawing the blood sample, determining the blood type, screening for antibodies, obtaining safe blood for transfusion, and ensuring compatibility by cross matching donor and patient blood.

Another task is the drawing and storing of autologous donations, i.e., obtaining blood from people who prefer to receive their

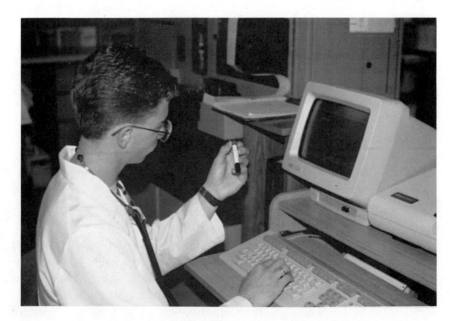

FIGURE 7-4. *Computers have found their way into the lab.*

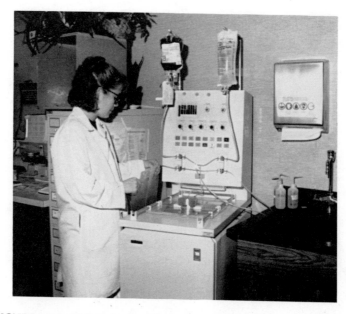

FIGURE 7-5A. Cell washer machine concentrates blood cells for transfusion.

own blood (if needed) when they undergo surgery. Another form of autologous transfusion is the salvaging of blood during surgery and returning those blood cells to the patient. This process can only be carried out in certain types of surgeries. The sterile solution that was suctioned from the operative site is taken to the lab and spun down (Figure 7-5B) to remove excess liquid and concentrate the cells. It is then transfused into the patient's veins. Though some cells are damaged in the process, the danger of contracting a disease from an unknown donor is eliminated. This may also be done with some postoperative wounds, usually knee and hip.

Preparation and permanent storage of all records associated with transfusions administered in the facility is another task entrusted to the blood bank. These records include information about donors and recipients. If an illness later develops in a donor, transfusion recipients can be traced, informed, and treated.

Other tasks relate to prenatal work. An expectant mother's blood is typed to determine the Rh factor. When the baby is born, a blood sample is drawn from the umbilical cord and tested.

In *Hematology,* whole blood is tested to determine the number and quality of blood cells. Some blood cell counts are done with an electric counter. Another part of the blood cell identification is done by preparing glass slides to view blood cells under a microscope.

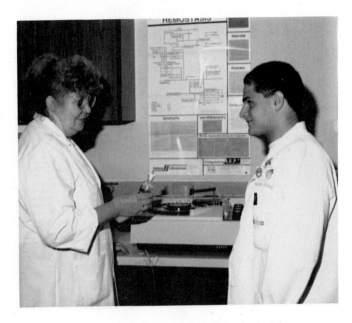

FIGURE 7-5B. On-the-job training in the lab.

These tests indicate if the patient has enough blood or needs a transfusion. They indicate if infection, mononucleosis, leukemia, or anemia is present. An expectant mother's blood is routinely tested to avoid anemia. Often, life-saving treatment is based on test results from this section.

In *Chemistry,* the blood serum is tested to measure the levels of organic and inorganic components, enzymes, and electrolytes. Essential elements like potassium can be life-threatening if too much or too little is present, Figure 7-6.

In *Microbiology,* various body fluids are studied to determine the presence of disease-producing microorganisms. Specimens are inoculated onto culture media where microorganisms grow in the incubator. Throat cultures are tested for strep, sputum specimens for tuberculosis and pneumonia, and urine cultures for bladder or kidney infections. Organisms are then isolated, identified, and tested to determine the most effective antibiotic medication.

In *Cytology,* tissue scrapings and liquid specimens are prepared to identify changes in cell structure, size, color, cytoplasm, and nuclei. Cancer is the most common type of abnormal cell detected. Cells from tissue scrapings, saliva, sputum, urine, and needle aspirations are all studied in this section. The Pap smear, cells from the uterine cervix, is the most common test done in this section. Speci-

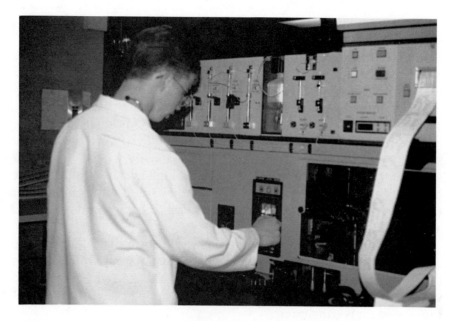

FIGURE 7-6. *The chemistry section of the lab.*

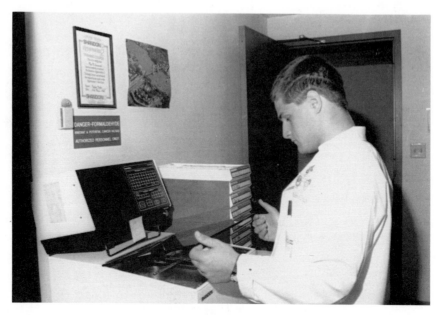

FIGURE 7-7. *Tissue stained and mounted for microscopic examination.*

men cells are smeared on glass slides and contrast stains added (sometimes) before the slide is viewed under the microscope.

In *Histology*, tissue from a solid organ is cut, stained, mounted, and prepared for microscopic examination, Figure 7-7. If the tissue is obtained from a patient in the operating room, a "frozen section" is done for immediate analysis. This tissue is quickly frozen to make the slicing process more accurate. Like other specimens in Histology, the frozen tissue is placed in paraffin (wax) and sliced very thin. These shavings are fixed on glass slides, stained with special dyes, and studied under the microscope by the pathologist. Other tasks include maintaining the paraffin, reagents, and other stains and solutions for tissue preparation. Tissue from fine-needle biopsies and autopsies are also studied in this section.

Immunology/Serology/Virology is the section that identifies the ability of the body to resist pathogens by producing antibodies. In this section, tests are done to determine the body's response to viruses or allergy-causing agents. The efficiency of the human immune system is concluded.

Urinalysis is the section that examines urine for cellular and chemical content.

In *Pathology,* body organs and tissues are studied and autopsies are done by the pathologist.

8
Medical Office

▼

OBJECTIVES

After completing this chapter, you will be able to
- Explain department goals
- Recognize the various health professions that comprise a medical office
- Describe several careers in this department
- Identify required education and credentials for each career
- Describe the skills performed in this department

▼

TERMS

Diagnoses:
Asthma
Congestive heart failure
Emphysema
Hypertension
Peptic ulcers
Stroke

Procedures:
Chemotherapy
Electrocardiograph
Dialysis
Laser treatment
Shock wave lithotripsy
Radiation therapy
Vital signs

▶ INTRODUCTION

A medical office, clinic, or hospital preadmission testing department is a clean, pleasant place to work, Figure 8-1. Usually, patients who come to this work site are in more stable condition than those who are hospitalized. However, they do have concerns about their physical condition and implications of their illness. The atmosphere of the office depends on the people who work there and the nature of the care given.

Generally, medical doctors have a practice of regular patients who return over years for checkups and medication regulation. After repeated office visits, staff befriend patients, develop ongoing relationships with them, show an interest in patients' progress, and help them develop coping skills. With chronic illnesses, patients may visit the office frequently during the course of those illnesses.

Working in a surgeon's office is different from working in a medical physician's office. Patients visit a surgeon's office once before surgery and once after surgery, at a minimum. After those two visits, the office staff might never see those patients again. Also, there may be a "'hurried" feeling because the surgeon may be late coming from the hospital or be called away from the office for emergency

FIGURE 8-1. A medical office is a pleasant place to work.

surgery. Because of the nature of the work, a surgeon's schedule may be somewhat erratic. Immediate availability to operate on patients who need care without delay is a factor.

▶ GOAL

The goal of the medical office is to serve patients by facilitating the assessment, diagnosis, and treatment processes and by meeting their educational, emotional, and psychosocial needs in a friendly, supportive, professional atmosphere.

▶ CAREER HIERARCHY

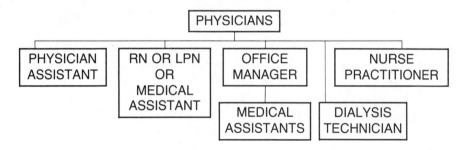

▶ CAREER DESCRIPTIONS

Careers in offices and clinics vary according to the type of medical specialty and the size of the work site. A large clinic will have more categories of professionals and more medical specialties than a small, one-physician office. It has become customary for physicians to form partnerships and share their practices. In these group practices, physicians with the same specialty establish a business relationship. Though physicians maintain their own patients, the partner physicians try to meet all the patients. Partner physicians share office space and workers, take turns being on call during evening and weekend hours, and relieve each other for vacations.

Office staff serve patients as well as physicians and try to make office visits as pleasant and expeditious as possible. Staff use careful techniques to maintain cleanliness, especially when handling blood and body fluids, because of the HIV virus and other infectious agents.

Employment opportunities depend on the career. Jobs are available in physician offices, clinics, hospital preadmission testing departments, and freestanding surgery or emergency care centers. The **job market** in office work is good, especially with keyboard skills and knowledge of medical insurance forms.

Work hours are usually Monday through Friday during the day, with some Saturday and evening hours. Offices may be open early morning to early evening, with fewer hours on Saturdays. Staff may work full-time or part-time. In some offices, staff members may be assigned to work with certain physicians. Their work hours then coincide with those physicians' hours. Wages in an office or clinic position may not be as high as in acute care settings because of daytime hours, no rotation of shifts or holiday work, and the stability of patients' conditions.

Career advancements are more lateral than upward. In a large clinic, moving into an administrative or teaching position may be an option.

Desired personal characteristics include being considerate, knowledgeable, personable, clean, well groomed, friendly, and eager to help others. Attributes include a positive attitude and the ability to be sympathetic, empathetic, patient, and tolerant. Even if patients come late to appointments, physicians are delayed, or it is past "quitting time," staff should never show irritation or speak sharply to patients.

Job satisfaction comes from being a part of a friendly and competent team that serves physicians and patients with cordial efficiency and sincere interest. It comes from mutual respect and the feeling of a job well done.

Physicians are either medical doctors (M.D.s) or doctors of osteopathy (D.O.s). Both M.D.s and D.O.s are called "Doctor," treat sick persons, and teach good health practices. However, doctors of osteopathy stress association between the muscles and bones of the body and the function of the organs. When treating patients, they use manual manipulation and palpation techniques in addition to traditional medical techniques.

Physicans obtain health histories, perform physical examinations, order and interpret diagnostic tests, diagnose conditions, prescribe medications, provide health instruction, and refer to other physicians and specialists as appropriate. They treat persons who are ill and injured, and teach health maintenance and prevention of illness.

Physicians specialize in one or two areas—internal medicine, family practice, general surgery, or other fields such as cardiology. They work in private practice, research, education, the military, veterans hospitals, public health and government agencies, school systems, or private industry.

Desirable personal characteristics include self-motivation, intelligence, clear thinking, and an aptitude for science. Physicians need to have good study skills, an interest in helping people, and the capacity to make good judgments under pressure.

Career advancement includes adding another specialty, learning more skills to serve patients, and becoming chief of their speciality or of the medical staff. Careers can expand to include teaching, scholarly writing, research, public speaking, and community projects. The job market is good.

Physician assistants work under the direction of physicians in clinics, offices, hospitals, and patients' homes. They do health screenings, physical exams, history taking, and may order laboratory tests. They identify initial diagnoses and initiate treatment plans according to guidelines. They confer with physicians and refer to specialists when appropriate. In rural areas, they may be the only health professional in the office or town. When questions arise, they contact the physician to whom they report for direction. If their educational program included surgical experience, they may do minor operations under local anesthesia and prescribe medication if allowed by state law and the state medical association.

Career advancement is more lateral than upward. Physician assistants can change offices or hospitals, move to a rural area or to a city, or work in clinics, nursing homes, or military service.

Nurse practitioners are registered nurses who specialize in a particular area of patient care, such as pediatrics or geriatrics. They care for more acutely ill patients and have more independence than do physician assistants, though they cannot order medication. They assess patients, order laboratory studies, carry out treatment plans, and make independent judgments. They contact physicians and refer to specialists when necessary. They are responsible for health teaching, and counsel patients and family members about illness and coping mechanisms.

Desired personal characteristics include creativity, innovation, independent spirit, clear thinking, a willingness to accept responsibility, and good decision-making skills. As with physician assistants, **career moves** are lateral rather than upward. The **job market** is good.

Dialysis technicians are registered nurses, licensed practical/ vocational nurses, or technicians who work with patients who have no kidney function and cannot make urine. Dialysis is a life-saving procedure for persons who would die without it.

Dialysis technicians are trained to care for a patient on the hemodialysis machine, also known as an artificial kidney. This procedure involves monitoring vital signs and observing that the patient's blood passes through the tubing on the machine and returns to the veins without mishap. Dialysis technicians monitor blood chemistry to determine if the treatment is effectively cleansing the blood of impurities and extra fluid. Dialysis treatments are usually done three times a week until a kidney becomes available for transplant or until the patient dies.

Some dialysis technicians make home visits to instruct patients in the technique of performing dialysis there. Family members may be taught in case the patient becomes unable to perform the procedure. Some patients may plug themselves into dialysis units at bedtime, allow the machine to run while they sleep, then unplug themselves and go to work in the morning.

Career advancement is lateral in dialysis work.

Job opportunities include hospitals, clinics, offices, and home care. Job availability is good.

Medical assistants are trained to work with physicians, physician assistants, and nurses in an outpatient area. They answer phones and schedule appointments, hospital admissions, and surgeries. They greet patients and help them prepare for a physical exam. They obtain and record health histories, vital signs, weight, and height. They test vision, draw blood, perform some lab procedures, and assist with physical exams and minor surgeries, Figure 8-2. They take X rays, obtain vital capacities, and do electrocardiograms for physician interpretation. They change dressings and do some treatments. They clean and sterilize instruments, straighten examining rooms, order supplies, and restock cabinets. They also work with the business aspect of office management. They handle correspondence, fax reports, process insurance forms, prepare bills, and post payments.

Job opportunities include offices, clinics, health maintenance organizations, and public health agencies.

Career advancements include becoming an office manager in a large office or clinic. Further advancement depends on obtaining a baccalaureate degree or a degree in another health field.

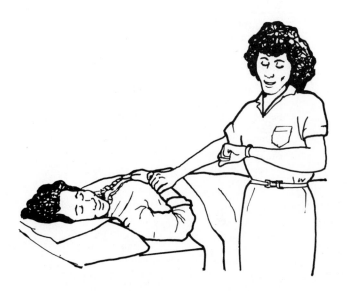

FIGURE 8-2. *A medical assistant takes vital signs and helps the physician with physical exams.*

▶ EDUCATION AND CREDENTIALS

CAREER NAME	YEARS OF EDUCATION AFTER HIGH SCHOOL	DEGREE OR DIPLOMA	TESTED BY: CREDENTIALED BY:
Physician (M.D.)	10 years minimum: 4 years college 4 years medical school plus 1 year internship 1 year residency in specialty	M.D. degree	Board exams by NBME and board exams by specialty organization and licensed by the state; (ECFMG exams are taken by graduates of foreign medical schools.)

CAREER NAME	YEARS OF EDUCATION AFTER HIGH SCHOOL	DEGREE OR DIPLOMA	TESTED BY: CREDENTIALED BY:
Physician (D.O.)	10 years minimum: 4 years college 4 years osteopathy school plus 1 year internship 1 year residency in specialty	D.O. degree	Exams by specialty plus licensed by the state
Physician Assistant (PA)	6 years: (usually) 4-year college degree* plus 2-year associate degree or *5 year minimum:	B.S. degree plus A.A.S.D. in physician assistant	Exam by NCCPA

*Applicant may be accepted to a physician assistant program with a two-year associate degree in another health field and minimum of one year significant health care work experience, instead of the four-year B.S. degree. Some programs have established a high school diploma as a minimum admission criterion.

CAREER NAME	YEARS OF EDUCATION AFTER HIGH SCHOOL	DEGREE OR DIPLOMA	TESTED BY: CREDENTIALED BY:
Nurse Practitioner (RN)	3–5 years: 2–4 yrs. registered nurse program plus 1 yr. practitioner program	Certificate	State certification required in some states plus RN
Dialysis Technician	Workshop on dialysis following RN or LPN program or OJT	Certificate	No specific licensure required beyond RN or LPN
Medical Assistant (CMA or RMA)	2 years	A.A.S.D. in medical assisting	No licensure required; optional certification after exam from AAMA or AMT

Key to Abbreviations:
  AAMA: American Association of Medical Assistants
  A.A.S.D.: Associate of Applied Science Degree
  AMT: American Medical Technologists
  CMA.: Certified Medical Assistant
  D.O.: Doctor of Osteopathy
  ECFMG: Educational Commission for Foreign Medical Graduates
  LPN: Licensed Practical Nurse

M.D.: Medical Doctor
MBME: National Board of Medical Examiners
NCCPA: National Commission on Certification of Physician Assistants
OJT: on-the-job training
PA: Physician Assistant
RMA: Registered Medical Assistant
RN: Registered Nurse

● ● ● ●

▶ JOB AVAILABILITY

The U.S. Department of Labor estimates that there will be an increase of job availability of 74 percent for medical assistants, 68 percent for medical secretaries, 54 percent for medical records technicians, 47 percent for receptionists and information clerks, 44 percent for registered nurses, and 42 percent for licensed practical nurses to the year 2005.

▶ SKILLS

Skills performed in an office or clinic are related to physician specialty. Electrocardiographs are done in a cardiologist's office; sutures are removed in a surgeon's office, Figure 8-3. Other factors that impact on skill performance are job descriptions, formal education and certification, experience, office policy, and state laws. Some states require that certain skills be performed by a specific worker category. They issue licenses to certify that practice, to protect the public against untrained persons administering care. Many skills are done by more than one worker category.

Scheduling appointments is an important skill that requires organization and good verbal communication techniques, Figure 8-4. Scheduling includes office visits, diagnostic test appointments, and registration for surgery. This is an important service to patients and it requires a certain knowledge base and an ability to negotiate. Patients may be too ill to wait for a long time to be seen by a physician or have a diagnostic test done. Understandably, patients may need to wait for a physician who is detained in an unplanned situation. But habitual poor scheduling technique may irritate patients and result in their seeking another physician.

Assessment is a skill practiced by all those who have patient contact, Figure 8-5. Physician assistants, nurses, medical assistants,

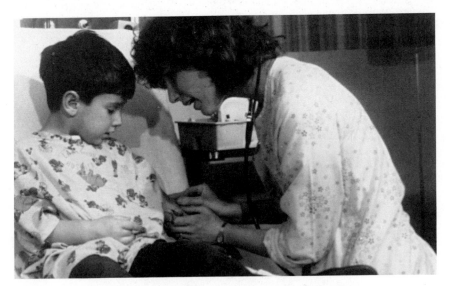

FIGURE 8-3. Sutures are removed in the surgeon's office.

FIGURE 8-4. Good telephone skills are an integral part of the medical office.

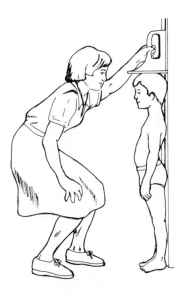

FIGURE 8-5. *Assessment skills also come into play.*

and physicians assess patients according to their ability and purpose. Staff members interview patients to obtain a health history, observe symptoms, notice physical appearance, take vital signs, and review lab work. Some staff members auscultate, palpate, document observations, arrange plans for treatment, and follow patients' progress.

Diagnostic tests are sometimes done in the office, Figure 8-6. For tests not done in the office, appointments need to be scheduled at the hospital or diagnostic center. Patients may need X rays, blood work, urinalysis, electrocardiographs, or pulmonary function and allergy tests in the office. The type of tests ordered will depend on patients' diagnoses and office specialty.

Treatments may be done in the office or clinic. Deep heat treatments, removal of skin lesions, chemotherapy, allergy shots, suture removal, dressing changes, dialysis, and cast removal can all be done in an outpatient area.

Providing needed medical equipment is another service that may be done by the office or a medical supply store. The physician, office staff, patient, and family members determine the need for special devices and adaptive equipment that would be beneficial and where it can be obtained. Contact lenses or glasses to improve vision may be dispensed by the office. Walkers, air mattresses, wheelchairs, and blood sugar testing instruments are usually dispensed by medical supply stores. Some equipment, such as an artificial limb, is made

FIGURE 8-6. *Diagnostic tests are sometimes done in the office.*

to order for patients. Other devices need to be fitted by specially trained salespeople or registered nurses and dispensed with extensive teaching and followup. These include a prosthesis after a mastectomy, and collection bags after ostomy surgery.

Processing insurance forms is a skill that is essential in every office in health care today. Different insurance companies have different forms, rules, regulations, and reimbursement guidelines. It is almost impossible for elderly patients to understand how to apply for payment or reimbursement, and nearly impossible for younger adults. In many offices, at least one worker is exclusively responsible for handling insurance forms. Other responsibilities may include preparing bills and posting payments.

Dialysis is the procedure that "cleanses" the blood of waste products and removes extra fluid from the body. The hemodialysis machine is called the "artificial kidney." Over a 4–6-hour period, blood is pumped through a semipermeable tubing that is immersed in a special saline-type solution. The chemical makeup of this solution determines how much of what electrolytes and waste products will be drawn out of the blood into the surrounding solution.

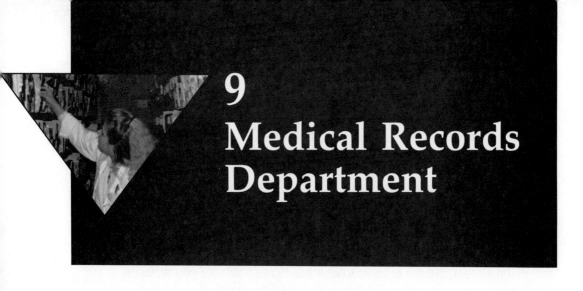

9
Medical Records Department

OBJECTIVES

After completing this chapter, you will be able to
- Explain department goals
- Explain the importance of documentation
- Describe each career in this department
- Identify required education and credentials for each career
- Describe the skills and activities performed in this department

TERMS AND ABBREVIATIONS

Terms:
Abstracting
Chart analysis
Coding
Confidentiality
Microfiche
Reimbursement

Abbreviations:
DRG
JCAHO
TD filing

▶ INTRODUCTION

The medical records department plays an important role in health care. Department activities include the coordination of all written information about every patient treated at the facility. Responsibilities include completing, sorting, compiling, analyzing, storing, and retrieving patients' records, Figure 9-1. Other activities involve coding information for insurance company or government agency reimbursement and assembling statistics about illnesses and treatments.

Each time a patient is treated at a medical facility or physician's office, that care is recorded, Figure 9-2. This documentation includes diagnosis of the illness, care and treatment administered, medication prescribed, and health maintenance instruction. All information must be documented before the record is permanently filed. The completed record is then stored according to a specific universal system so it can be retrieved when needed. Implementation of the storage and retrieval system is a major activity in the medical records department.

Other activities performed by workers in the medical records department include assigning a unique number to each new patient, copying chart forms for legal correspondence, and analyzing charts.

FIGURE 9-1. Retrieving a patient's record

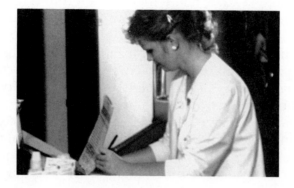

FIGURE 9-2. Recording care given a patient

The transcription service and monitoring the utilization of services are other department functions.

▶ GOALS

The goals of the medical records department are to **manage information, identify optimum reimbursement** for patient care, and **maintain confidentiality** of patient data.

▶ CAREER HIERARCHY

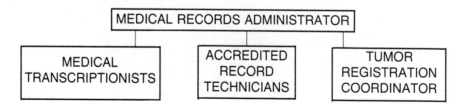

▶ CAREER DESCRIPTIONS

Medical records personnel work more closely with information than with patients. The roles and responsibilities of medical records workers are determined by education and experience. There are two educational programs available: registered record administrator and accredited record technician. In small departments or physician offices, technicians will be expected to perform all duties related to the completion, storage, and retrieval of a record (Figure 9-3), and coding and indexing diagnosis and treatments. In large departments, technicians specialize.

Working hours vary according to the facility. In a hospital where acutely ill patients are treated, medical records are retrievable 24 hours per day, 365 days a year. Full-time and part-time positions are available during the day and evening shifts. Some night shift positions are available in large facilities. In a physician's office, registered record technicians work when the office is open—usually day shift, Monday through Saturday. Technicians who work for insurance companies can negotiate their working hours according to mutual need.

Employment opportunities include hospitals, clinics, physician offices, research centers, nursing homes, and government agencies.

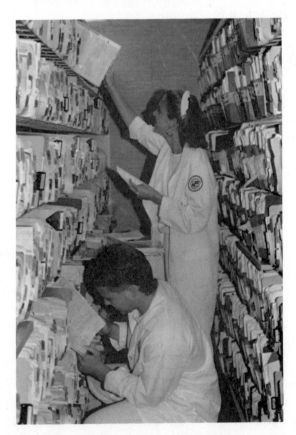

FIGURE 9-3. Retrieving patient records, adding forms, and refiling

Other opportunities include law firms and insurance companies. Because of technological advances and requests for patient information, the **job market** is good.

Career advancement depends on education and availability of positions. There are few director positions available. A change in facility or in type of work may be necessary for a career advance.

Desired personal characteristics include organizational skills, precision with paperwork tasks, ability to function independently, verbal and written communication skills, and accuracy with detailed work. Recognizing the importance of the medical record and taking pride in being a part of the information management system are other characteristics.

Job satisfaction comes from doing the work well; servicing patients, physicians, and the facility; being a part of the health team; and gaining the respect of peers and other professionals. Medical records personnel interact with physicians, nurses, attorneys, insurance people, administrators, and other professionals.

The *registered record administrator* is responsible for all functions of the medical records department. These functions include planning and implementing the system for completing, analyzing, storing, and retrieving patients' charts. Functions also include providing statistical data to plan future patient care, support research, and plan services. Also, the director facilitates timely billing for reimbursement, reviews bed utilization, and monitors quality of care. Directors ensure the confidentiality of patient information. Other areas of responsibility include the supervision of medical transcription services, microfilming of patient records, obtaining and coding the final diagnoses for all inpatient and outpatient visits, and securing maximum reimbursement.

The registered record administrator needs to manage effectively and work well with people. The ability to make decisions quickly and with good judgment is important. Other characteristics needed are organizational skills and the ability to complete large volumes of work, delegate duties effectively, determine priorities, and work under pressure.

Accredited record technicians carry out all skills in the department according to facility guidelines. They maintain patient confidentiality. Though they can complete all tasks in the department, they usually specialize in certain skills, depending on the size of the department. Skills include coding diseases and surgeries on the medical record according to the ICD-9-CM classification system and UHDDS definitions and assigning a DRG through computer data entry. Obtaining paper reimbursement for the facility is assured by identifying the correct DRG assignment. Technicians help physicians to interpret guidelines of regulatory agencies, and participate in the utilization review process and quality assurance analysis.

Registered record technicians need to have a high degree of accuracy, attention to detail, initiative, judgment, discretion, and understanding of the confidential nature of their work. Good organizational skills and the ability to complete a large volume of work with little supervision are important qualities. The ability to work effectively with the medical staff, members of other departments, and medical records coworkers is another vital characteristic. Also, it is helpful to type well enough to work with a CRT terminal.

Medical transcriptionists type data that has been dictated on an audiotape recorder system by physicians, Figure 9-4. This data consists of history and physical exam summaries, surgery reports, consults' findings, pathology studies, and radiology reports. Medical transcriptionists need to concentrate for extended periods at a word processor, listen and interpret recorded reports with accuracy, spell medical terms accurately, and produce a perfectly typed report with reasonable speed. A word processor is used to facilitate the typing process.

Utilization review coordinators are responsible for performing the work prescribed by the utilization review committee. Utilization

FIGURE 9-4. *Medical transcription of a doctor's notes*

review coordinators critique inpatient records for justification of admission and extended stay, based on quantitative analysis of the patient's record. This process includes the assistance of a physician advisor whenever a medical judgment must be made. Responsibilities include identification and referral of potential length-of-stay problems and report potential problems to the social service department. Also, utilization review coordinators monitor reimbursement and denial actions and report them appropriately, gather statistical data, and carry out preprocedure certification activities according to policy.

Medical record coding personnel classify (code) the names of diseases and surgeries identified on medical records according to the ICD-9-CM classification system and UHDDS definitions. This procedure is done upon admission, concurrently as requested, and upon discharge. Coders assign DRGs through computer data entry to the maximum reimbursement justified, based on services received by the patient. Another coding system used is CPT. This is required by some third-party payers for ambulatory surgery procedures. As with DRGs, there is a fixed amount of reimbursement assigned to these payment groups.

Tumor registration coordinators report all cancer cases according to the guidelines designed by the American College of Surgeons' Commission on Cancer. Other responsibilities include entering statistical data so that reports can be developed to compare regional and national cancer statistics. Participating in quality assurance studies is another form of reporting cancer data.

▶ EDUCATION AND CREDENTIALS

CAREER NAME	YEARS OF EDUCATION AFTER HIGH SCHOOL	DEGREE OR DIPLOMA	TESTED BY: REGISTERED BY:
Registered Record Administrator RRA	4 years	B.S.	Licensed by AMRA
Accredited Record Technician ART	2 years	A.A.S.D. in medical record technology	Licensed by AMRA
Medical Transcriptionist AMT	9 months	Competency Award	Certified by AMT (optional)

CAREER NAME	YEARS OF EDUCATION AFTER HIGH SCHOOL	DEGREE OR DIPLOMA	TESTED BY: REGISTERED BY:
Tumor Registration Coordinator ART	2 years	A.A.S.D. in medical record technology	Licensed by AMRA and can be certified by ACS

Key to Abbreviations:
    B.S.: Bachelor of Science degree
    A.A.S.D.: Associate of Applied Science Degree
    ACS: American College of Surgeons
    AMRA: American Medical Records Association
    AMT: American Medical Transcription
    ART: Accredited Record Technician
    RRA: Registered Record Administrator

● ● ● ●

▶ JOB AVAILABILITY

Job availability is excellent for medical records positions. The U.S. Bureau of Labor statistics estimate a 54 percent increase in available positions to the year 2005 for medical records technicians.

▶ SKILLS

Chart analysis is the process of reviewing a medical record to be sure that all information, reports, and signatures are present and conform to the standards of the Joint Commission for Accreditation of Hospitals Organization (JCAHO). The record is arranged in a specific order, missing information (deficiencies) identified, and problems or unusual cases reported to the department director. Completed records are stored (Figure 9-5); incomplete records are filed in a specific area and appropriate persons are notified to document deficiencies. Charts must be completed within a specified time from the date of patient treatment. If charts are not completed within the specified time, the facility can lose its license to treat patients.

Statistics gleaned from the analysis process include data on deaths and types of surgical cases.

Transcription is the process that transforms the spoken word into typewritten copy. Usually, physicians have access to a recording system throughout a facility by dialing a certain number on the

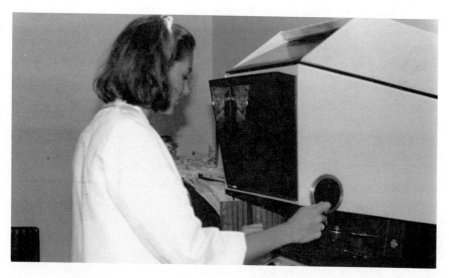

FIGURE 9-5. *Completed records are sometimes stored on microfiche.*

telephone. Information, such as a summary of illness or the details of surgery, can be dictated onto the audiotape system. A transcription-ist receives the audiotaped information through a headset, types it, then erases the audiotape. This typed report is placed in the medical record and a copy sent to the physician's office.

Chart tracking is the system used to locate a medical record that was stored using the TD filing system. Whenever a patient is treated in the health care system, a written record is generated, completed, and filed. That record is forever accessible. When a patient again becomes ill, all previous records can be retrieved and used as reference by the treating physician. This function of chart tracking occupies much of a worker's time. Because of short hospital stays, there is a large volume of documents that must be completed, stored, and retrieved.

Records are stored for approximately five years in hard copy (on paper), then transferred onto microfiche, a photographing process. Each page of the medical record is photographed on tiny film. The resulting strips of film are stored in plastic holders, like a page in a photo album. This microfiche is stored forever and the paper copy is destroyed.

Another important function to both the patient and the institu-tion is the *reimbursement process* for services rendered. Every health care consumer hopes that the fees for services rendered by the physician and hospital will be paid for or "covered" by a health insurance policy. This is not an automatic process. It is a complicated process, conducted by the medical records department. The system consists of *precertification, abstracting,* and *coding,* followed by submission to third-party payers.

Some surgical procedures are required to be preapproved by insurance companies before the procedure is performed. This ensures that insurance carriers will cover the cost. This process is called *preprocedure certification.* The medical records department assumes the responsibility of contacting some carriers, particularly Medicare, to assure coverage. Many insurance carriers require the patient to call and gain permission before the procedure is performed, particularly if hospitalization is required.

Abstracting is the process of reviewing medical records to gather data related to the hospital and to gather facts for physicians. This information is entered into the central register. From this central register, data is gathered for statistical purposes. Some examples of the reports written from this data are: the number of patients admitted to the hospital with a stroke during the previous year; the number of patients between twenty and thirty years of age who had their gallbladder removed during a particular year; the most common cause of death of persons between certain ages.

Coding is the process used by the technician to identify the primary diagnosis and the principal procedure performed on the patient in the treatment of illness. The names of the diagnosis and procedure must be verified by the attending physician. The medical records technician locates the Diagnostic Related Group (DRG) from a book listing all groups. That DRG is entered into the computer. The computer then codes the information based on the data entry. In other words, each diagnosis is assigned to a group of similar diagnoses and each of these groups is assigned a code according to the ICD-9-CM guidelines. Each code is assigned a sum of money. That is the amount of money sent to the facility as payment for the care of the patient. The medical records technician works with the data to obtain optimal reimbursement for the hospital. The agencies that use the coding system to determine reimbursement are the federal government (Medicare and Medicaid), Blue Cross, and other private insurance companies. Coding is a vital function of the medical records department. It is the determining source of income for the facility. If maximum reimbursement is not obtained, a hospital might not have sufficient operating money and will close.

Utilization review is the process that monitors the use of hospital beds to ensure the medical necessity of hospitalization. The system was developed to contain health care costs. At that time, studies were done to determine the average number of days patients were hospitalized during a particular illness. Insurance carriers then assigned that average number of days to each diagnosis. Usually, that is the number of days that an insurance carrier will "cover" or pay for when patients are hospitalized. Depending on the facility, patients may be responsible for paying for additional days of hospital stay over that set number.

This system of utilization review requires daily monitoring of the use of hospital beds. This is concurrent utilization review. That is, for all currently hospitalized patients, statistical data is kept on the number of days and types of illnesses. To do this, a medical records department worker logs how each hospital bed is being utilized every day. These facts are compared with the number of days allowed or covered by insurance carriers. When the number of days is near the maximum, the physician is notified. The physician then decides if the diagnosis has changed, if it is appropriate to apply to the insurance carrier for an extension of hospitalization, or if it is time for discharge.

To ensure accuracy and honesty in data reporting, representatives from Medicare regularly visit hospitals to review charts. This is called retrospective utilization review of medical records because the patients have already left the hospital.

Valuable information and statistical data are gleaned from the process of utilization review. Often, information is needed from Medical Records for workmen's compensation and disability cases. Persons who claim injury are responsible for proving the extent of injury by verification on the medical record. Because of patient confidentiality, Medical Records follows strict guidelines before releasing any records. Other statistical data is shared with the state's peer review organization.

Correspondence is another important responsibility of the medical records department, Figure 9-6. Hundreds of requests for data come into the department each month. A few examples include requests from health care insurance companies, attorneys, other physicians, other hospitals, and employers. Requests also come from insurance carriers for disability verification and liability claims. Clarifying the legitimacy of each request, gaining patients' permission for the release of information, and processing each request are painstaking tasks. Care is always taken to protect the confidentiality of each medical record.

FIGURE 9-6. Correspondence is a responsibility of the medical records department.

Quality assurance is the process of studying the delivery of health care as it relates to patient satisfaction, safety, comfort, and successful outcome. It is an important part of a caregiving institution. Through statistical analysis of illnesses, accidents, and occurrences, patient care and safety can be improved. Medical Records is an important source of statistical data for that review. Ultimately, the delivery of health care improves because of these studies and the resulting corrective actions.

Consultative services are offered to physicians for their information and their committee reports. This data can be helpful for many reasons. For example, data can show that new equipment is needed to improve medical practice. Also, data can illustrate health trends in the community. The department helps physicians interpret guidelines of new documentation requirements that are periodically revised by institutional accrediting and regulatory agencies. Certain documentation can only be provided by the physicians.

Standards of documentation dictated by institutional accrediting and regulatory agencies are strictly adhered to by the medical records department. These agencies include federal, state, and local governments; Joint Commission on Accreditation of Hospitals Organization; Department of Health and Human Services; the state department of mental health; and the state health department. New policies from these agencies are reviewed and the system is modified to meet those new standards. A health care facility must be accredited by agencies designated by the U.S. government to be reimbursed with Medicare and Medicaid moneys. Accreditation is based on the ability of a facility to meet guidelines for patient care. This care must be documented on the medical record to be verified. Though verification of documentation is a time-consuming process, it is the only way to show that care was delivered. The system was established to protect the public from substandard and unsafe facilities.

Tumor registry is a central data bank that accumulates information about cancer in specific geographical areas. All cancer cases are reported to this central data bank. Treatments and follow-up survival rates are also entered. Comparative analysis can be done related to city, state, and national data. The tumor registry is approved by the American College of Surgeons' Commission on Cancer and serves as a source of statistical data.

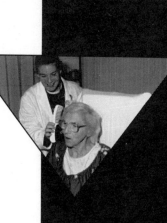

10
Mental Health Department

OBJECTIVES

After completing this chapter you will be able to
- Explain department goals
- Recognize the difference between normal and dysfunctional feelings
- Describe each career in this department
- Identify required education and credentials for each career
- Describe the skills performed in this department

TERMS

Classifications of Disorders:
    Addictive
    Anxiety
    Mood
    Personality
    Psychosis

Symptoms:
    Agitation
    Confusion
    Depression
    Hallucination
    Paranoia
    Tremors
    Withdrawal

▶ INTRODUCTION

Mental health and mental illness are states of mind that are influenced by several factors. These factors relate to feelings of well-being and the ability to control behavior, maintain emotional balance, cope with problems, and function in society. Mental health is jeopardized when one of these factors becomes a negative influence on the state of mind.

A state of mind can change because of a physical condition, illness, emotional stress, environmental factors, food and chemical intake, and mental disorders. There is a range of mental states within each disorder that extends from normal to extremely dysfunctional, Figure 10-1. Some conditions that can range from normal to dysfunctional are anxiety disorders, mood disorders, psychosis, personality disorders, and addictive disorders.

NORMAL FEELINGS	EXTREMELY DYSFUNCTIONAL
• Anxiety before tests or before a job interview	• A fear that immobilizes the person and (s)he does not leave home.
• Grief and sadness	• Severe depression with suicide attempt
• Ability to distinguish reality from nonreality	• Hearing voices, seeing objects
• Personality idiosyncrasies, such as shyness	• Sociopathic behavior
• Compulsions with no negative consequences	• Addictive problems with major or even life-threatening consequences

People in the normal group commonly experience mild symptoms of distress or imbalance sometime in their lives. But they cope with those periods in their lives, keep their symptoms under control, and continue with their lives.

In the extreme, these disorders can cause persons to become dysfunctional. Persons in this group cannot cope with their lives or manage their behavior. With some disorders, persons may be unsafe

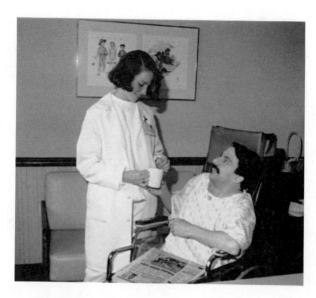

FIGURE 10-1. *There is a wide range of states of mind.*

to themselves or to others. In this case, hospitalization may be necessary for a time.

Addictive behavior is conduct that is carried out in a compulsive manner despite the negative consequences that result. When one family member is addicted, all family members experience the effects. They alter their ways of thinking, feeling, and behaving to cope with the stress caused by the addiction. When addictions are thought about, being hooked on alcohol or drugs generally comes to mind. But there are many addictions. Workaholism, sexual addictions, and gambling are examples. Each addiction involves a loss of control over the chemical or behavior and a progressive deterioration of the health of the addict and those close to him/her.

People with behavior disorders or personality disorders live in the community and appear relatively normal. But they are troublesome to themselves, to their family members, and to society.

There is a wide range of treatments: reading self-help books, attending special interest groups, walk-in clinics, psychotherapy, hot lines, emergency centers, and hospitalization. Medication may be prescribed by physicians to relieve stress, elevate mood, level out mood swings, or regain control of aggressively hostile behavior.

It is normal to seek counseling to improve the quality of life, improve relationships, and lessen stress. Some patients seek counseling when they or their family members recognize that their

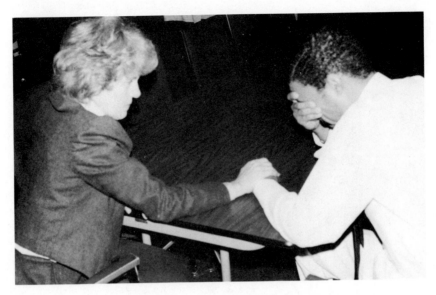

FIGURE 10-2. *Stress is a normal part of life.*

behavior is not manageable. This recognition frequently comes about because of the intensity of the symptoms, e.g., extreme fears, hostile actions, or threats of suicide.

Mental health workers often counsel healthy people because of stress-related problems and personal tragedies, Figure 10-2. Loss of a job, death of a loved one, end of a romance, or the process of divorce are normal stresses in life. Individual, family, and group counseling are conducted by mental health professionals for self-improvement.

Behavior disorders and mental illness can become evident in young children. More attention is being given to behavior disorders of youth in schools and in communities.

▶ GOAL

The goal of the mental health department is to **provide a safe, therapeutic, interactive environment; intensive counseling; and participative activities** for patients who have mental, emotional, and psychosocial problems.

▶ CAREER HIERARCHY

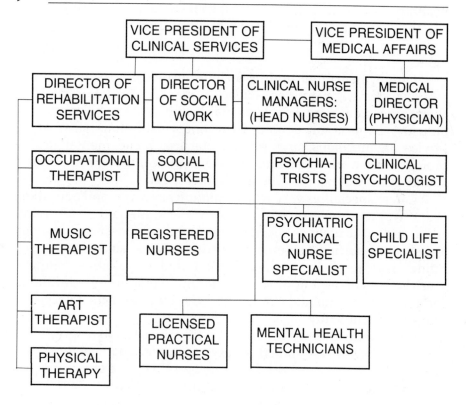

▶ CAREER DESCRIPTIONS

There are many careers associated with mental health. While some careers involve years of schooling, the study of psychology, and practice in patient counseling, a few involve only on-the-job training.

Mental health professionals interact with people of all ages, degrees of illness, self-awareness, and stress levels. Some patients may be members of the same family—battered children, abusive parents, and depressed elderly may all need counseling simultaneously. There are a variety of acuity levels. Some patients are functional, live at home, and work full-time. Some patients are severely ill and repeatedly return to therapy and hospitalization. Some experience severe stress and may need assistance only once in their lifetime. Recovery can require only minimal intervention (a few visits to a counselor) or may require ongoing help over years. Mental health professionals help patients regain contact with reality, manage their behavior by developing healthy coping skills, recapture feelings of well-being, and interact positively with their environment.

Employment opportunities include hospitals; outpatient clinics; school systems; government agencies; mental retardation centers; child, adolescent, and family mental health centers; business and industry; chemical abuse clinics; correctional institutions (jails); social service organizations; and private practice. Some mental health professionals work in research where they deal more with animal studies than with people. The **job market** is good.

Career specialties vary with community agencies and education of the worker. Some mental health workers specialize in specific areas, such as acutely ill hospitalized patients, counseling in homeless shelters, suicide hot lines, rape crisis centers, substance abuse, eating disorders, behavior modification, and sexual abuse. Others specialize in counseling of school children, community education, and prevention of mental illness. Workers can change their specialty area without difficulty.

Work hours depend on the type of facility and job responsibilities. Many facilities are staffed twenty-four hours a day, every day of the year. Personnel can work full-time, part-time, or a few hours per month. Shifts vary from a few hours to twelve hours a day. Some mental health professionals have established their own counseling practice and set their own working hours.

Career advancement depends on the education of the worker and the area of interest. Promotion to a management position in a patient care facility, municipal setting, or national organization is possible with an advanced degree. Entrepreneurship is fostered in the mental health field both on the job as well as with independent projects.

Job satisfaction comes from helping needy people and from making a difference in their lives, from determining effective treatment methods and evaluating results. Gratification comes from helping clients solve problems so they can effectively straighten out difficult situations. It also comes from guiding patients to make sound decisions about their lives and relationships. Other sources of satisfaction are providing a safe, therapeutic environment and using innovative and problem-solving techniques to help patients help themselves. Mental health workers are challenged by the variety of situations that occur every day.

Desired personal characteristics include inner strength. Mental health professionals see many undeserved and deplorable situations. They see pain and hardship that must be faced and dealt with realistically. To be successful, they must have the patience to counsel rather than direct, sensitivity and empathy, and insight into thought processes.

Safety of the patients, families, and staff is always at the forefront for the mental health worker. Professionals remain alert for hazards and opportunities for accidents and injuries.

Psychiatrists are physicians. They graduate from medical school, then specialize in the diagnosis and treatment of mental illness. Physicians direct patient care. They diagnose patient illness, prescribe medications, interact with family members, and administer treatment.

There are several forms of treatment. The two most common are 1) prescribing medication for the psychiatric symptoms, and 2) psychotherapy, i.e., meeting regularly with patients to talk about symptoms and concerns, determining the cause and identifying coping mechanisms. Another form of treatment is electroshock therapy—passing an electrical charge through the brain. Another is psychoanalysis, an in-depth study of thoughts, feelings, and behavior.

Most psychiatrists are in private practice, counseling patients in an office setting. Some work in research, private industry, government, or school systems.

Clinical psychologists have studied psychology. They work with patients to help them understand their needs and how those needs can be met. They help patients to identify their strengths and abilities. They help patients to set goals. They guide patients to channel their energies into productive, acceptable, goal-directed behaviors. Their guidance helps decrease patients' stress levels and increase their coping mechanisms. They interact with patients and families to increase communication and improve relationships. They **cannot** prescribe medication or admit patients to hospitals. If these measures are necessary, the patient must be referred to a psychiatrist.

Some psychologists work in market research to discover motivational factors that influence human behavior. Some work in clinical research to investigate the effects of physical, emotional, and social factors on human behavior. Some develop questions and administer aptitude and intelligence tests. Some work in laboratories to perform controlled experiments. Some work in industry and some counsel in private practice.

Social workers consult with individuals and families to identify concerns that relate to interaction with family members and the community. These include homelessness, lack of income, and abusive home settings. Social workers often contact community agencies to help find solutions.

Social workers help people of all ages, from newborns to the aged adult, Figure 10-3. They find foster homes for abused and abandoned infants and advise families about nursing homes for the confused and agitated elderly. They conduct group therapy sessions with cancer and rape victims. They work with individuals, groups, and government agencies to prevent and manage the social problem of homelessness. They help plan and develop health and recreation services. They counsel people on housing, welfare, pregnancy, abuse, abortion, and coping with death and dying. They locate agencies to help those with specific needs, like emergency housing and clothing after a house fire.

Social workers are employed by social agencies, hospices, hospitals, government agencies, correctional institutions (jails), human resource departments, religious organizations, and research organizations. Some are in private practice.

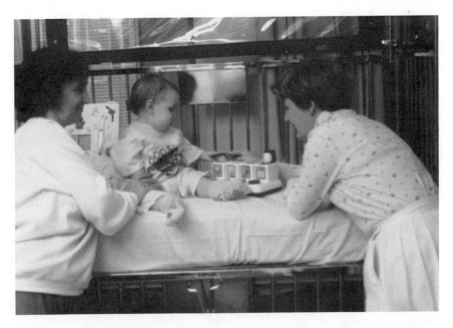

FIGURE 10-3. *Social workers help people of all ages.*

Occupational therapists help patients increase their independence by helping them perform activities of daily living. They structure therapy to increase confidence and skills. Some activities relieve anger, frustration, and antisocial behavior; some change compulsive behavior.

Psychiatric clinical nurse specialists are registered nurses who have a master's degree in psychiatric care. They work with patients, family members, and nursing staff to bring about the most effective treatment plan to help patients resume responsibility for self. They teach workers about crisis intervention techniques and have experience and expertise in handling difficult patients. They teach programs, such as stress reduction, in the community to encourage mental health. They serve as consultants within a clinical facility to patients, families, and professional persons outside the psychiatric unit.

Registered nurses work in a variety of settings in the mental health field. In a hospital setting, they spend the most time with patients and their family members. Upon admission, nurses initiate care plans based on assessment and the medical diagnosis. Goals are mutually set with patients. During the day, evening, and night shifts, that plan is carried out. Patients expect a safe environment, understanding, and consistent guidance throughout their hospital stay and course of therapy. This is primarily provided by nurses, who are with the patients twenty-four hours a day. Nurses listen to patients' concerns and discuss options for behaviors and thoughts. They work with patients to identify precipitating factors that trigger unmanageable thoughts and behaviors. Nurses structure social activities, group therapy, and interactions on the unit; supervise activities of daily living; and maintain a calm and safe environment. They document progress and response to therapy and administer medications ordered by the physician.

Licensed practical nurses assist registered nurses in carrying out the care plan. They supervise patients during activities of daily living, talk with them, and help them communicate their feelings and thoughts. They document progress and response to therapy and administer medications ordered by the physician.

Most practical nurses work in hospitals and nursing homes. Some work in private homes, clinics, and office settings.

Mental health technicians work directly with patients under the direction of the registered nurse. Technicians carry out the care plan, listen to patients, and help to clarify their thoughts and feelings, Figure 10-4. They confer with other professionals on the mental health care team.

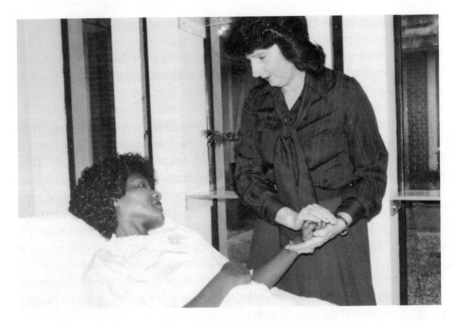

FIGURE 10-4. Above all, technicians listen!

Mental health technicians are employed in hospitals, mental health clinics, mental retardation facilities, nursing homes, and day-care centers. Some work in private homes.

Psychiatric aides work as assistants to the nurses or mental health technicians. They help with physical care and feeding tasks. They sit with patients who may be frightened of being alone. They escort patients on "off unit" privileges approved by physicians.

They are employed in hospitals, clinics, and chronic care settings.

Art therapists work with patients of all ages to help them express feelings and emotions through a variety of projects. Patients express themselves through color choices and the type of art project selected. Art therapy is especially effective with children. Often, they can draw pictures depicting their feelings more easily than they can express those feelings in words. Art therapy is also effective for adults whose traumatic experiences may be too painful to relate in words.

Music therapists work with patients who have physical, emotional, and developmental handicaps. Generally, patients who benefit from occupational therapy and psychiatric therapy would also benefit from music therapy. In music therapy, music acts as a tool to facilitate therapeutic changes. For example, language-delayed preschool children or brain-injured adults may sing and vocalize but not talk. In this case, music therapy is a precursor to language. Physically handicapped patients might learn to play an instrument to increase strength in a broken arm or improve finger dexterity. This type of work draws on knowledge of music, psychology, and physiology.

Child life specialists help children in health care facilities adjust to whatever is happening to them. This professional talks to children about going to surgery, explains what to expect, and accompanies them there. Included in the role are listening to children's ideas and fears and knowing what kinds of things worry them. Then they talk about these ideas and fears. Play therapy is utilized to allow children to act out their fears under the guidance of the child life worker. Play therapy reduces stress and helps children accept the pains and discomforts of illness and the separation from family during hospitalization.

Chemical dependency counselors assess persons for alcohol and other chemical dependencies, intervene in crisis situations, develop therapeutic plans, facilitate group therapy, conduct relapse prevention programs, and refer to community resources and other professionals as appropriate. Counseling of family members and significant others, discussion of cause, effect, and recovery issues, and knowledge of treatment centers, aftercare, and outreach programs are other areas of expertise.

▶ EDUCATION AND CREDENTIALS

CAREER NAME	YEARS OF EDUCATION AFTER HIGH SCHOOL	DEGREE OR DIPLOMA	TESTED BY: REGISTERED BY:
Psychiatrist (M.D. or D.O.)	12 years: 4 yrs. college 4 yrs. medical school 1 yr. internship 3 yrs. residency	M.D. or D.O. Certification	Boards exams by ABPN; state license
Clinical Psychologist (Ph.D.)	8 years	Ph.D. in clinical psychology	Board exams by ABPP; state licensed or certified

CAREER NAME	YEARS OF EDUCATION AFTER HIGH SCHOOL	DEGREE OR DIPLOMA	TESTED BY: REGISTERED BY:
Social Worker (ACSW) (LISW or LSW)	6 years 8 years	Master's degree in social service Ph.D. in social service	ACSW is national accreditation; exam given by NASW; state licensure required in some states. LISW granted with M.S. and two years clinical experience; LSW granted with M.S.; indicates less than two years clinical; supervision required
Occupational Therapist (O.T.R.)	4½ to 6 years: 4 years plus 6–9 months internship 5 years plus 6–9 months internship	B.S. in occupational therapy or B.S. in another field plus Master's degree in OT	AOTA national exam and state registration same as above
Psychiatric Clinical Nurse Specialist (RN)	6 years	Master's degree in psychiatric nursing	Exam by state board of nursing and licensed by the state
Registered Nurse (RN)	2 years 3 years 4 years	A.A.S.D. in nursing Diploma in nursing B.S. in nursing	Exam by state board of nursing and licensed by the state (same for all RNs)
Licensed Practical Nurse (LPN)	1 year	Diploma in practical nursing	Exam by state board of nursing and licensed by the state
Mental Health Technician	2 years	Associate of Arts degree	Licensed by the state
Psychiatric Aide	On-the-job training or brief course in vocational school	— Certificate	— —

CAREER NAME	YEARS OF EDUCATION AFTER HIGH SCHOOL	DEGREE OR DIPLOMA	TESTED BY: REGISTERED BY:
Art Therapist	6 years: 5 years college plus 1 year clinical training	B.F.A.	Board certification examination
Music Therapist	4½ years: 4 years school plus 6 months internship	B.M. in music therapy	Board certification available from AAMT and NAMT (both grant registration)
Child Life Specialist	6 years	B.A. in early child development or psychology and M.S. in child life specialist	Certificate from child life certifying commission (optional)
Certified Chemical Dependency Counselor (CCDC)	4 years: 2 years work experience* 2 years (4000 hours) precepted counseling experience	Certificate	State certification by CDCCB, Inc. (oral and written exams)

*Applicants may substitute years of education and training for qualifying work experience, but not for the precepted experience.

Key to Abbreviations:
AAMT: American Association for Music Therapy
ABPP: American Board of Professional Psychology
ABPN: American Board of Psychiatry and Neurology
ACSW: Academy of Certified Social Workers
AOTA: American Occupational Therapy Association
B.A.: Bachelor of Arts degree
B.F.A.: Bachelor of Fine Arts
B.M.: Bachelor of Music
B.S.: Bachelor of Science degree
CDCCB: Chemical Dependency Counselors Credentialing Board, Inc. (State)
D.O.: Doctor of Osteopathy
LPN: Licensed Practical Nurse
LISW: Licensed Independent Social Worker
LSW: Licensed Social Worker
M.D.: Medical Doctor
M.S.: Master's degree
NAMT: National Association for Music Therapy
NASW: National Association of Social Workers
Ph.D.: Doctor of Philosophy
RN: Registered Nurse

▶ JOB AVAILABILITY

The U.S. Bureau of Labor statistics estimate that job availability will increase 64 percent for psychologists, 44 percent for registered nurses, 42 percent for licensed practical nurses, 55 percent for occupational therapists, 34 percent for social workers, and 43 percent for nurses aides, orderlies, and attendants to the year 2005.

▶ SKILLS

Tasks in psychiatry involve **communication skills,** (Figure 10-5) **observation skills, quick thinking and good judgment, problem solving, assessing postdischarge needs, and evaluating capabilities of the elderly and disabled.**

Communication skills involve the ability to listen and hear what is being said. This is especially important in psychiatry because how

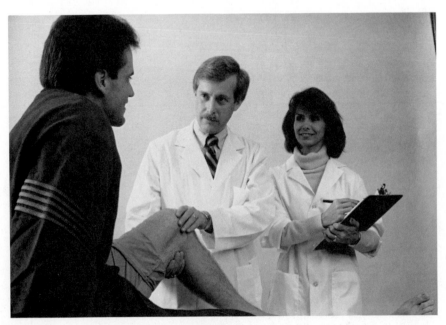

FIGURE 10-5. *Confidentiality is always important.*

something is said is often as important as what is said. Sometimes, what is said is not what is meant. This involves insight by the listener. Also, what is said may mean more than what the words convey. Communication also involves body language, facial expression, and tone of voice. Refusal to speak is also significant.

Evaluation of the written word is another facet. Patients sometimes write about feelings more truthfully than they talk about them. They may write threatening letters to someone or express bizarre ideas in writing.

Staff is responsible for documentation of treatment sessions and progress or regression of behaviors and thoughts. Suicidal thoughts and actions are important to report to appropriate staff members so protective measures can be taken.

As in all health care, confidentiality is important. No information about patients in a psychiatric setting is to be told to anyone other than staff working directly with those patients.

Good observational skills are also important. Behavior observed by the worker is often as important as what patients say. If an unanimated patient, who is slouched in a corner and facing the wall, responds "Fine" to the question "How are you?", it can be assumed that the response is not a true picture of how this patient feels about himself/herself.

Observations are important indications of how patients feel about themselves. Meaningful observations include body language, quality of interaction with others, choice of activities, and talking with imaginary people.

Quick thinking and good judgment are needed in psychiatry. Workers must anticipate patients' responses, thoughts, and actions. This involves an understanding of how an individual patient is thinking. Workers need to be alert to potentially hazardous behavior. They must make good decisions about measures to protect themselves, patients, and other workers in case someone's behavior escalates out of control.

Problem solving is constantly utilized in the field of mental health. Workers know when they can handle a situation and when to request help. Patient safety and a calm, therapeutic environment are foremost in mental health care.

Assessment of postdischarge needs is an important service rendered by social service workers and other professionals. Placement in an appropriate facility after hospital discharge may be a necessary step in the rehabilitation process.

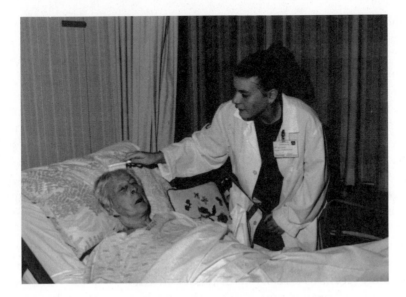

FIGURE 10-6. *Evaluation of ADL needs.*

Evaluation of an elderly person's functional status is done by nurses, social service workers, and other professionals on the geriatric team, Figure 10-6. The purpose of this assessment is to determine the ability to carry out activities of daily living safely. This will help to decide the mental status of the patient and what living accommodations will be in the patient's best interest.

Counseling is a skill that can be done with individuals, family members, and groups. Types of counseling are in-depth, cognitive, and eclectic. **In-depth** counseling is insight-oriented. The past is reviewed and studied to determine the connection between past events and current behavior. **Cognitive** counseling is an approach that focuses on current ways of thinking and behaving. The present is reviewed, problems identified, and coping strategies developed to modify behavior. **Eclectic** counseling is a combination of in-depth and cognitive. Some past events are reviewed, goals are set, and behavior is changed.

11 Nursing Department

▼

OBJECTIVES

After completing this chapter, you will be able to
- Explain department goals
- Relate the numerous roles of the nurse
- Describe each career in this department
- Identify required education and credentials for each career
- Describe the skills performed in this department

▼

TERMS AND ABBREVIATIONS

Concepts:
   Nursing process
   Health care team

Abbreviations:
   TPR
   BP
   VS
   PO
   NPO
   I&O

BR
BRP
HIV
AIDS

Others:
   Preoperative
   Postoperative
   Benign
   Malignant
   Terminal

▶ INTRODUCTION

Nursing is a caregiving profession that serves every aspect of human need. The process of nursing includes **assessing patients' conditions** through interpersonal communication, observation, physical exam and health history, and **identifying their needs** using problem-solving techniques based on scientific knowledge. After **developing a plan** to meet identified needs, the nursing process concludes with **implementing, evaluating, and adjusting** those measures to provide comfort, care, and education to help patients realize their full potential, Figure 11-1.

Nurses interact with patients, family members, and other professionals; coordinate patient care; and help move patients through the maze of the health care system. Nursing represents patients' interests and seeks the best and most effective care for them.

Nursing is a large and versatile career whose members are in demand. Employment is available to those with a current state license and acceptable skill performance. Nursing professionals, as in some other health careers, take continuing education classes to renew state licensure. Nursing positions are available in every state in the United States and in every country in the world.

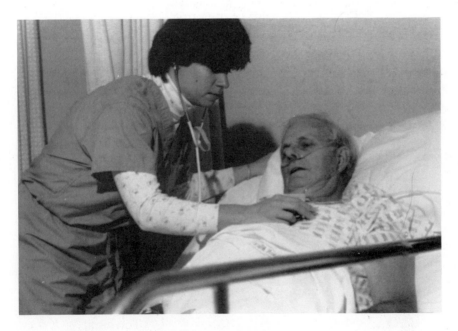

FIGURE 11-1. A nurse helps the patient realize his/her full potential.

▶ EDUCATIONAL LADDER

| RN WITH PH.D..
RN PROGRAM
PLUS
MASTER'S PROGRAM
PLUS
2 YEARS IN PH.D. PROGRAM | N.D.
BACHELOR'S DEGREE IN
NONNURSING SUBJECT
(4 YEARS)
PLUS
3 YEARS IN N.D. PROGRAM |

RN WITH MASTER'S DEGREE:
B.S.N./RN
PLUS
2 YEARS IN MASTER'S PROGRAM

REGISTERED NURSE:
 4 YEARS IN BACHELOR'S DEGREE
 3 YEARS IN DIPLOMA PROGRAM
 2 YEARS IN ASSOCIATE DEGREE PROGRAM

LICENSED PRACTICAL/VOCATIONAL NURSE:
 1 YEAR PROGRAM

NURSE ASSISTANT:
 75–120 HOURS IN PROGRAM

NURSE TECHNICIAN:
 A STUDENT NURSE,
 ONE-DAY ORIENTATION

HEALTH CARE ASSISTANT:
 ON-THE-JOB TRAINING

▶ EDUCATIONAL PROGRAMS

The career of nursing offers several educational programs consisting of academic and clinical experience. After introductory courses, patient care is integrated with academic courses.

Nursing programs may be offered as full-time or part-time. Some offer flexible day, evening, and weekend classes; some require an internship.

Nursing assistant, nurse's aide, **and** *home health aide programs* are offered in high schools, vocational schools, technical schools, nursing homes, and by the Red Cross. The program consists of a 75–120-hour training course over approximately four months and includes supervised clinical experience in a hospital or nursing home. Certificates are awarded to those who successfully complete the course, Figure 11-2. Passing a practical and a written exam is required to become certified in the state.

Practical nurse programs are offered by hospitals, technical schools, city school systems, and community colleges. Technical schools and hospital- and college-based programs cover one year full-time. City school systems and college-based programs may be taken in one year as a full-time student or in two years part-time. Graduates are awarded a certificate. Though there are program differences, all graduates of approved practical nurse programs are qualified to take the written state board of nursing examination to practice as a Licensed Practical Nurse (LPN) or a Licensed Vocational Nurse (LVN).

Professional nursing programs may be two, three, or four years in length when taken full-time. They are based in a variety of settings, such as colleges and universities, community colleges, hospitals, and

FIGURE 11-2.   *A nursing assistant certificate program class in session.*

technical schools. Another difference is the amount of college credit awarded to graduates at the end of the programs. Though there are differences in the number of years, locations, and amount of college credit awarded, all graduates of approved schools are eligible to take the same written state board of nursing examination to obtain state license and practice as a registered nurse.

Significant differences between the LPN and the RN programs, and between the two-, three-, and four-year RN programs are depth of knowledge; amount, depth, and expectations of clinical practice; and professional responsibility. Nurses with a B.S.N. degree have the highest academic (undergraduate) degree. They usually advance more rapidly on the career ladder and have more career options.

Associate degree programs are usually two years in length with full-time attendance. They are based in a community college, university, or hospital. The academic courses can be taken part-time or full-time. Clinical rotations may take place in several hospitals. At the conclusion of the program, graduates are awarded an associate degree in nursing (A.D.N. or A.A.S.N.) and have earned two years of college credit.

Diploma programs are three years in length when taken full-time and are usually based in hospitals. The first year usually consists of academic courses at a community college or university that can be taken full-time or part-time. The second and third years consist of clinical courses and patient care rotations in the "home hospital," if all services are available. At the conclusion, graduates are awarded a diploma and have earned more than one year of college credit.

In some states, diploma programs no longer exist as previously described. Instead, these programs have developed an affiliation with a community college's or university's two-year associate degree program. At the completion of this three-year, hosptial-based program, these graduates are awarded an associate degree (A.D.N.) and a diploma from the hospital. These graduates have more clinical experience than the two-year associate degree graduates but have earned only two years of college credit after the three-year program.

A *bachelor of science in nursing (B.S.N.)* program is a four-year degree program that is college-or university-based. After initial courses, patient care experience is integrated with academic courses. This program may have a "home hospital" that is associated with the university. Otherwise, affiliations are arranged with several hospitals. The four-year, full-time program is ideal because of the academic approach, consolidation of courses, time-sequencing of courses, and amount of college credit granted.

Some schools have a two-plus-two program. A registered nurse with an Associate of Applied Science Degree in Nursing (A.D.N.) can complete a bachelor's degree in nursing program (B.S.N.) with two additional years of full-time schooling.

Graduates of traditional two- and three-year programs may return to college to obtain a bachelor's degree, often spending more than two years in the process. However, time, money, study habits, and other responsibilities in life influence the decision of program selection. Some hospitals offer scholarships in return for nurses working there after graduation.

Advanced study in nursing leads to graduate degrees. Those degrees are Master's of Science in nursing (M.S.N.), Doctor of Philosophy in nursing (Ph.D.), and Doctor of Nursing (N.D.). These degrees require a bachelor's (undergraduate) degree, but not necessarily in nursing.

A *master's degree in nursing* usually takes two years in graduate school, longer if attendance is part-time. Candidates select a specialty and earn a degree in that area. For example, graduates may be awarded an M.S.N. in gerontology mental health, administration, oncology, or maternal or child health.

A *doctor of philosophy degree in nursing* requires a two-year program beyond a master's degree in nursing. Graduates of this program participate in research or teach nursing in college or university nursing programs and are awarded a Ph.D. in nursing.

A *doctor of nursing program* is three years in length. This program accepts candidates with a baccalaureate degree in a field **other than in nursing.** The goal of the graduates of this program is to work in administrative and community planning positions. For example, they work with federal or state government agencies, Veterans Administration, school systems, or community health planning commissions. Graduates of this program are awarded an N.D. degree.

Health unit coordinator programs (unit secretary programs) consist of on the job training, Figure 11-3. They are high school graduates who have completed at least one course in medical terminology. Keyboard or typing skills are helpful, but not required.

▶ GOALS

The goals of the nursing department are to plan and administer safe, comprehensive care to those in need of assistance and to help them achieve maximum potential and manage their illness. Other goals include health education, counseling, and disease prevention.

▶ CAREER HIERARCHY

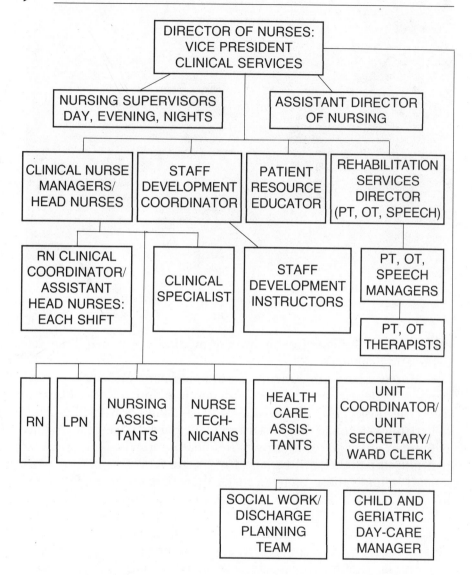

▶ CAREER DESCRIPTIONS

Nurses plan and provide direct patient care. They give care to those who are unable to help themselves and they show persons how to help themselves carry out the activities of daily living. For example, they feed, bathe, dress, and move patients into comfortable positions. They help patients stand, walk, and transfer from bed to

FIGURE 11-3. Health unit coordinators are trained on the job.

chair. They administer treatments and medications to help them feel better and heal faster.

Nurses plan with patients, family members, and social service workers to determine where to go when it is time for the patient to leave the hospital or extended care or rehabilitation facility. They help patients face sad diagnoses and make hard choices; they rejoice with them when status improves and health returns. Nurses realize that not all patients will be cured and return home. So they work toward helping these patients reach their maximum potential and live with residual conditions. They give compassionate care to those who will not recover and try to make those last days as comfortable as possible. They recognize death as a fact of life and know that a caring person at the bedside can provide solace at the end of life.

Nurses care for all aspects of those who come for assistance—including mental, physical, emotional, and spiritual needs. They recognize needs best served by others and refer those to appropriate members of the health care team.

Employment opportunities include many specialty areas of practice, such as medical, surgical, pediatrics, maternity, psychiatry, geriatrics, intensive care, cardiac care, emergency room, or operating room in a hospital facility, Figure 11-4. They work on helicopter rescue teams, in freestanding emergency centers, clinics, physician

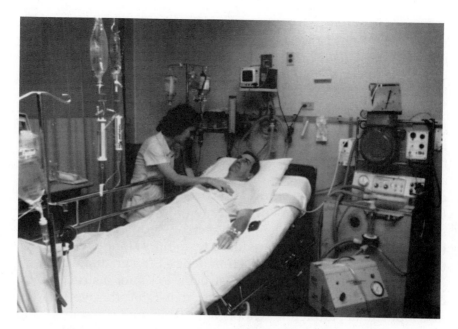

FIGURE 11-4. Nurses assess and care for critically ill patients.

offices, law firms, insurance, medical equipment and pharmaceutical companies, homes, public health agencies, schools, and rehabilitation centers. They work in shopping malls, on ocean liners, at summer camps, ski resorts, race tracks, drug detoxification centers, and jails. They work in the military, World Health Organization, Peace Corps, Vista, and for the Red Cross. They work in broadcast media and for magazines and newspapers. They teach, write, and develop health maintenance programs.

Some nurses are employed by a facility or agency; some practice independently and contract for services. Nurses work in every country in the world with people of all ages, from those in the womb to the very old. The **job market** for all positions in nursing is excellent.

Work hours depend on the job site and type of work. In hospitals, extended care facilities, inpatient rehabilitation facilities, and nursing homes, nursing staff are present twenty-four hours a day, every day of the year, during the day, evening, and night shifts. Offices and clinics are open day shift, five or six days a week, with some evening and Saturday hours. Home care hours are usually during the day on weekdays, but some patients need twenty-four-hour coverage every day.

Nurses may work full-time, part-time, or a few hours a week. They can work day, evening, or night shift any day of the year. They can work four days of ten-hour shifts (and have three days off a week). Or, they can work a few hours in the morning or evening during peak patient care periods. Some nurses are self-employed, working out of their homes and determining their own working hours.

Career advancement depends on education, credentials, and experience. **Career advancement for registered nurses** can be in the fields of administration, clinical practice, and education. In **administration,** advancement leads to a position of clinical nurse manager of a unit, supervisor, manager of a department, director of nurses, or director of the agency. In **clinical practice** with education beyond the B.S.N. degree, advancement leads to positions such as clinical specialist, nurse practitioner, midwife, nurse anesthetist, dialysis technician, flight nurse, organ donor team nurse, and enterostomal therapist. Advancement in **education** depends on graduate degrees. It can include moving from staff instructor to senior instructor or to director of the section, department, or school. Educators work in staff development departments, schools of nursing, and community and government agencies such as high schools and vocational schools.

Career advancement for LPNs includes positions as coordinators and supervisors in nursing homes and facilities for the mentally retarded. LPNs may make a variety of lateral moves to change facilities or areas of practice, but substantial career advancement depends on attaining education to become a registered nurse.

All nurses are capable of giving physical care to patients. With more education, the nurse's information scope broadens and knowledge deepens so that more job responsibility can be assumed and more job opportunities become available.

Career advancement for nursing assistants is dependent on additional education to become licensed practical nurses, registered professional nurses, or members of other medical careers.

Desirable personal characteristics include sensitivity to the needs of others, good verbal and written communication skills, clear thinking, sound decision-making skills, and reliable judgment. They need to perform calmly in stressful situations. Other characteristics include patience, friendly demeanor, and a sense of humor. They should speak kindly to persons who may be irritable and short-tempered, and take pride in their work and their profession.

Job satisfaction comes from caring for persons who cannot care for themselves and from showing others how to help themselves, Figure 11-5. It comes from making a difference in the lives of patients, family members, and coworkers. Other sources of satisfaction in-

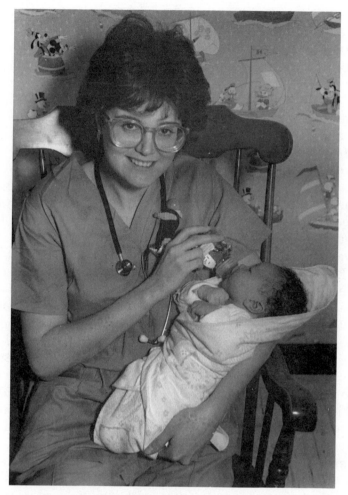

FIGURE 11-5. Evidently this nurse enjoys her work.

clude the challenge of using the problem-solving techniques and professional skills developed over years of study and professional practice. It comes from observing sick persons regain their health, from realizing the effectiveness of instruction, and from seeing patients develop adaptive skills to cope with the constraints of illness. Fulfillment comes from the sensitive, caring investment of self in the well-being of others, from the feeling of a worthwhile job done well, and from the respect of peers.

Personal safety is an issue in health care today. Nursing is considered a high-risk career because of association with patients who are sick with many kinds of diseases that may be contagious or infectious. To protect themselves and patients, nurses use body substance precautions (BSP) and other protective covers as indicated.

Health care assistants (nursing service technicians) are given an orientation to the facility, then trained on the job to help with patient comfort measures, position, and transport; to provide a safe, comfortable environment; and to obtain and deliver equipment. They keep the patient rooms and supplies tidy, straighten up the utility rooms, and clean and exchange equipment. This is not a formal educational program and certification is not required.

Nurse technicians are student nurses who help nurses assess, plan, carry out, and document patient care. Their role includes nourishment, hygiene, comfort and evacuation measures, and treatment needs. Nurse technicians perform the same role as the LPN but certification is not required.

Nursing assistants are state certified to care for patients' basic needs. They attend to patients' hygiene, comfort, nourishment, and social needs. They take vital signs (VS), measure intake and output (I&O), perform some procedures and treatments, change bed linen, help with ambulation and positioning, and transport patients to other departments, Figure 11-6. They monitor patients' well-being, observe physical and mental changes, and report those to the charge nurse.

Licensed practical nurses utilize the nursing process and identify and minister to identified patient needs. They give physical care, take vital signs, give medications, and hang and regulate tube feedings. In some states, with special training and in certain circumstances, they are permitted to hang premixed intravenous fluids, regulate flow, and discontinue this therapy with a physician's order. LPNs assess patients, carry out sterile procedures, and administer more complex treatments such as irrigations, suctioning, traceostomy care, neuro checks, and hot and cold applications. They document clear and descriptive notes regarding care and observations.

Registered nurses utilize the nursing process and carry out nursing skills to meet patient needs. They assess patient status, observe strengths, identify problems, determine possible solutions, implement the best solution, evaluate the effectiveness of the solution, and change the action plan if another solution would be more effective. Much of the problem solving and planning is done with patients, family members, and other professional staff.

After completing a basic RN program, additional education can lead to even more job opportunities. Some postgraduate programs grant certificates, some grant college degrees. Positions that require

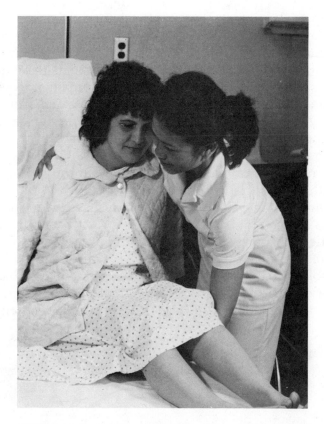

FIGURE 11-6. *Assisting patients in and out of bed is part of a day's work.*

education beyond the two-, three-, or four-year basic professional nurse programs are administrator of a health agency, director of nurses, instructor in a nursing school, staff development instructor, nurse practitioner, organ donor team nurse, enterostomal nurse, dialysis technician, flight nurse, nurse anesthetist, midwife, and clinical specialist.

Both RNs and LPNs are required to complete a certain number of educational hours to renew their state licenses in some states. Approximately twenty-four contact hours of classes must be attended every two years to comply with this regulation.

Health unit coordinators (unit secretaries, ward clerks) perform secretarial tasks on the nursing unit. They synchronize activities at the nurses station, serve as a resource to the nursing staff, schedule patient appointments, transcribe physicians' orders, obtain necessary equipment, manage incoming telephone calls, and communicate messages. Most tasks are performed to ensure that physicians' orders are carried out so that patient care will be prompt and accurate. Coordinators communicate with other departments to request tests, treatments, nourishments, and medications for patient comfort and rehabilitation. Using a computer, they enter data and order tests. In emergency situations, they call for appropriate assistance and facilitate patient transfer to an acute care setting. They greet patients and visitors, answer questions, and provide direction. They assemble charts for new patients, file reports, replenish forms, and graph vital signs on the medical record.

Employment opportunities are most available in hospital patient care areas on medical, surgical, intensive care, obstetric, pediatric, psychiatric, and emergency care nursing units, as well as in the medical records department, Figure 11-7. Other opportunities may be available in patient service areas in the radiology, biometrics, respiratory, occupational therapy, and physical therapy departments. Other job sites include nursing homes, outpatient clinics,

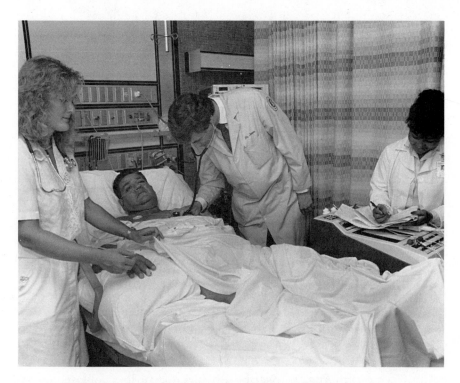

FIGURE 11-7. Employment opportunities are available in many areas.

physician offices, pharmaceutical companies, and research institutes. **Job outlook is good.**

Work hours depend on the facility and department. In patient care areas in a hospital, coordinators work day and evening shifts, seven days per week, including holidays. Few positions are available on night shift, but some rotation to day and evening shifts may be necessary. Part-time and full-time jobs are often available. In an office setting, work hours are Monday through Friday, with some evening and Saturday hours.

Career advancement may include teaching and supervising health unit coordinators within a department or facility. However, most moves are lateral. With additional education, a coordinator may become a health care professional, assume more responsibility, and give direct patient care.

Desired personal characteristics include a pleasant disposition, positive attitude, an aptitude for detail work, and the ability to concentrate and work accurately in the midst of interruptions, noise, and distractions. Other qualities include good communication skills, pride in workmanship, versatility, and ability to maintain a calm, friendly environment at the nurses' station.

Organization is especially necessary. The health unit coordinator needs to set priorities, rank tasks, and complete the most important first. Accuracy, conscientious effort, and acceptance of responsibility are other desirable attributes.

Job satisfaction comes from the smooth management of the nurses' station; completing detailed work accurately and promptly; serving professional persons, patients, and families in a positive, helpful way; and knowing that your work is greatly appreciated.

▶ EDUCATION AND CREDENTIALS

CAREER NAME	YEARS OF EDUCATION AFTER HIGH SCHOOL	DEGREE OR DIPLOMA	TESTED BY: CREDENTIALED BY:
Registered Nurse (RN)	2, 3, or 4 years:		Written exam by state board of nursing; state registration renewed every two years with CNE
	2 years	A.A.S.D. in nursing	
	or		
	3 years	Diploma; A.A.S.D. in nursing (few programs)	
	or		
	4 years	B.S.N. required	

CAREER NAME	YEARS OF EDUCATION AFTER HIGH SCHOOL	DEGREE OR DIPLOMA	TESTED BY: CREDENTIALED BY:
Clinical Nurse Specialist (RN)	6 years 4 years 2 years	B.S.N. M.S.N.	same as for RN plus certification in area of specialization (required in some states)
Nurse Practitioner (CRNP)	6 years: 4 years 2 years	B.S.N. M.S.N.	same as for RN plus certification in area of specialization (required in some states)
Licensed Practical Nurse (LPN)	1 year	Certificate	Written exam by state board of nursing; state license renewed every two years with CNE
Nursing Assistant or Home Health Aide (CNA)	75–120 hours (4 months)	Certificate	Written and practical exam; state license required
Nurse Technician (NT)	A student nurse in: 2d year of diploma program or 3d year of bachelor's program	—	—
Nursing Service Technician	On-the-job training	—	—
Nurse Anesthetist (CRNA)	7–8 years: 4 years college plus 1 year critical care experience plus 2–3 years anesthesia program	B.S.N. degree plus M.S.N. in anesthesia	Same as for RN plus exam for certification by AANA Council; Certification and State license

CAREER NAME	YEARS OF EDUCATION AFTER HIGH SCHOOL	DEGREE OR DIPLOMA	TESTED BY: CREDENTIALED BY:
Discharge Planning Coordinator (RN or ACSW)	4–6 years: RN or Social Worker	B.S.N. or Master's degree in social work	State board for RN; licensed in state (voluntary) exam for social worker (See Mental Health dept. chapter)
Child Life Specialist	(See Mental Health department chapter)		
Enterostomal Therapy Nurse (CETN)	8-week program (Must be RN to qualify for program.)	Certificate	National boards exam by IAET to attain state certification
Midwife (MSN, CNM)	2 years (Must be RN to qualify for program.)	M.S.N. in midwifery	National boards exam by ACNM to attain state certification
Health Unit Coordinator (Unit Secretary or Ward Clerk)	1 course on medical terminology (one quarter/semester) (keyboard knowledge is helpful)	High school diploma (usually required)	—

Key to Abbreviations:
A.A.S.D.: Associate of Applied Science Degree
ACNM: American College of Nurse Midwifes
ACSW: Academy of Certified Social Workers
B.S.N.: Bachelor of Science in Nursing
CETN: Certified Enterostomal Therapy Nurse
CNA: Certified Nurse Assistant
CNE: Continuing Nursing Education
CRNA: Certified Registered Nurse Anesthetist
CNM: Certified Registered Nurse Midwife
CRNP: Certified Registered Nurse Practitioner
IAET: International Association of Enterostomal Therapists
LPN: Licensed Practical Nurse
M.S.N.: Master of Science in Nursing
NT: Nurse Technician
RN: Registered Nurse

▶ JOB AVAILABILITY

Job opportunities are excellent for members of the nursing team. The U.S. Bureau of Labor statistics estimate that job availability will increase 44 percent for registered nurses, 42 percent for licensed practical nurses, 43 percent for nurses aides, orderlies, and attendants, 92 percent for home health aides, and 68 percent for medical secretaries to the year 2005.

▶ SKILLS

Nurses learn patient care skills during their basic nursing program. Although most nurses work directly with patients, some nurses have no patient contact. Basic nursing skills include, but are not limited to, the nursing process. Nurses develop skills to care for the physical, emotional, cognitional, and social needs of their patients.

The *nursing process* is a procedure that involves the skills of assessment, observation, communication, clear thinking, problem solving, decision making, therapeutic action, and revision of action plan. Nurses work with patients and family members to **identify problems** that can be helped by the efforts of the health care team.

The next step is to decide what to do about those problems. A problem may be physical, e.g., a sudden decrease in a patient's blood pressure (BP), or social, e.g., bulimia. With a decreased blood pressure problem, nurses determine the actions and then act. They give medication or intravenous fluid that effectively solves the blood pressure problem. With a bulimia problem, the patient must decide the actions and then act. Nurses may counsel, identify possible actions, or make a referral to another professional, but the patient must decide the actions and follow through to resolve the problem.

Sometimes the action chosen does not achieve the established goal, so other actions are tried. This is the process of nursing.

Physical care includes all the actions necessary to attend to the body's needs—cleanliness, toileting, nourishment, dressing changes, inserting tubes, using medical and surgical aseptic techniques, and doing treatments. While nurses are doing these tasks, they are assessing, observing, and teaching.

Physical care is only one nursing skill that nurses carry out to meet patients' needs of comfort and cleanliness, Figure 11-8. Bathing

FIGURE 11-8. Physical care is not the only nursing skill practiced by the nurse.

and bed making are actions that patients and family members see and associate with nursing. But much of what nurses do involves thinking, solving problems, teaching, and communicating with patients and other professionals. In addition to physical care, nurses attend to the emotional, cognitional, and social needs of their patients.

Emotional care relates to feelings. Nurses provide the opportunity for patients to express their feelings and give them emotional support during that process. Though nurses may not be able to solve every problem that worries patients, nurses often help put the worry into perspective. Patients may have worries related to their illnesses and associated treatments. For example, there might be anger or sadness associated with a diagnosis of cancer, fear of the prognosis, and hate for the fate that befell them. Though nurses cannot change the diagnosis or prognosis, they can listen to patients vent their feelings. They can encourage them to talk, offer alternative ways of thinking, and suggest ways to help accept the facts.

Cognitional care relates to the patients' need to know about their illness—what it means to their life, how to help themselves, and when they can expect to feel better. Patients who are newly diagnosed with diabetes may experience an emotional shock. Before they can intellectualize, they will need to deal with their emotions and accept the disease. Then, they will want to know exactly how the disease works, what it will mean in their life, about their diet, how to test their blood sugar level, about the effect of exercise, and about insulin injections. Nurses teach diabetic patients and families all facets of the disease, how to maintain health and prevent complications.

Social care involves patients' need to be cared about and accepted by family members, friends, and (when they are ill) health care workers. In the hospital, patients may not signal for medication to relieve pain when they are uncomfortable because they "don't want to bother the nurses." Nurses work closely with patients before and after surgical procedures that change body image. Otherwise, patients may have problems adjusting after mastectomy, limb amputation, or colostomy surgery because of the change in physical appearance. Another problem may be fear relating to social acceptance because they feel different.

Team work is important in hospital nursing, Figure 11-9. Two or three different shifts of nurses work every day with every patient. A change-of-shift report informs oncoming nurses about patients and

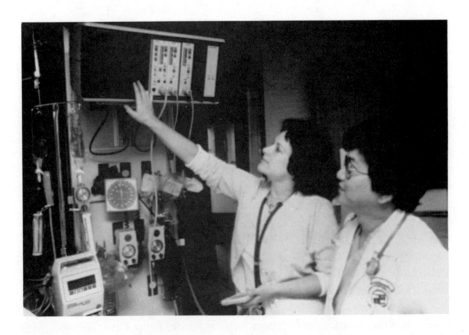

FIGURE 11-9. Team work is important.

their needs so they can be continuously addressed. That is one way the nursing team works together to carry out the nursing process, to care for those who cannot help themselves, and to teach patients how to help themselves.

Health unit coordinators work under the direction of registered nurses and perform skills in the categories of communication, physicians' orders, medical records, supplies, and organization.

Communication

Communication includes **interpersonal, telephone, and computer.** Interpersonal communication is reflected in attitude, facial expression, body language, and the tone and content of speech. The health unit coordinator influences the atmosphere of the nursing station. A receptive and pleasant atmosphere is the goal.

Unit coordinators are in telephone communication with many departments and offices. They answer incoming calls almost constantly. They "beep" physicians and personnel on the silent pager then deliver messages to the responder. Accurately taking and delivering telephone messages and responding to pages for busy staff are essential services. Maintaining a positive attitude and responding cordially to negative or angry callers are challenges of the job, achievements to be mastered, and skills required in this position.

The use of computers and fax machines in health care is becoming standard practice. Information is sent and received from nursing units to other departments, offices, and hospitals. Health unit coordinators enter data from physicians' orders into the computer terminal in their department. These messages are instantly transported to the terminal of the receiving department. With some computer programs, a nurse checks the accuracy of the unit coordinator's work before the computer sends entries. This procedure ensures that the nurse is informed of the new order and serves as a safety check to prevent errors that may be costly in patient comfort and in dollars. Lab results, pathology reports, and consult reports may be faxed to nursing units and to physicians' offices.

When information is received by the computer terminal on the unit, it is printed out, reviewed by the nurse, and posted in the medical record. To gain the coordinator's attention, an audible beep may sound when the fax machine begins to produce a copy.

Physicians' orders

Transcription of physicians' orders is the most important function of the health unit coordinator's role. This skill must be done accurately, Figure 11-10. If errors are made, procedures may be performed on the wrong patient, test results attributed to the wrong patient, medications ordered for the wrong patient, or departments may not be notified about tests to be performed. Orders that must be carried out immediately take precedence over other activities. In addition to notifiying departments of new treatments and medications that were ordered for patients, the coordinator follows up to see that the orders were carried out.

Medical Records

Medical records are permanent legal documents that serve as an account of patient care, treatment, and progress. The health unit coordinator collates a new chart for each newly admitted patient. Forms are stamped with an identification nameplate, organized into sections, and replenished as needed. The coordinator graphs temperatures on the chart and inserts reports from the laboratory, radiology, surgery, and consultation summaries. When the chart becomes too large to handle comfortably, the coordinator "thins" the record by removing some pages, then returns them to the record after patient discharge. The coordinator arranges pages in "discharge" order and sends the complete record to the medical records department for review and storage.

FIGURE 11-10. Accurate transcription is important.

Supplies

Health unit coordinators ensure that workers have the supplies they need to do their jobs effectively. Many facilities have developed a system of automatic stocking of sterile items from central service, linen from the linen room, forms from the print shop, and office supplies from the storeroom. If these supplies become depleted or if the unit's needs increase, the coordinator notifies the proper department and arranges delivery.

Organization

Organization is a skill that is crucial to the successful performance of the health unit coordinators' role. Activities often occur simultaneously, e.g., multiple incoming telephone calls, physician requests, nurses asking for a colleague to be paged, technicians needing requisitions, visitors waiting for assistance, and transport personnel requiring direction. Continuously straightening the desk area by putting charts away, filing reports promptly, and checking task completion contributes to increased accuracy and fewer errors. Using a memo pad to list messages and keeping it by the phone is an organizational technique. It helps to remind the coordinator of the information that callers require and reminds the coordinator to repage if someone does not respond to a page within a reasonable time.

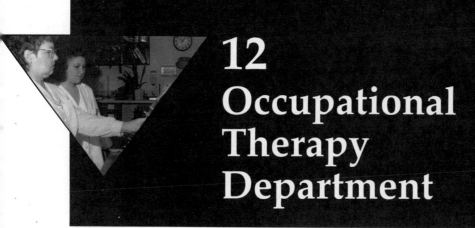

12
Occupational Therapy Department

▼

OBJECTIVES

After completing this chapter, you will be able to
- Explain department goals
- List the various reasons people need occupational therapy
- Describe each career in this department
- Identify required education and credentials for each career
- Describe the skills performed in this department

▼

TERMS

Activities of daily living (ADL)
Cognition
Perception
Sensation
Mobility
Disability
Handicap
Rehabilitation

159

▶ INTRODUCTION

Occupational therapy helps disabled persons become more confident and self-sufficient in carrying out activities of daily living. It enables them to learn or relearn the performance of basic skills that were interrupted by physical, mental, or emotional illness, traumatic injury, or congenital or developmental disability. In the occupational therapy department, job skill requirements are determined; also, training, retraining, and work-hardening programs are developed after work-related injuries. Basic life skills that are taught include bathing, dressing, food preparation, shopping, banking, and vocational activities. Job skill evaluations include testing for the necessary level of manual dexterity required to do a job, then determining if the those requirements can be met, Figure 12-1.

FIGURE 12-1. A test for arm dexterity and strength.

▶ GOALS

The goals of the occupational therapy department are to evaluate, diagnose, and treat persons with impaired function to enable them to achieve optimum living skills, prevent disabilities, and maintain health.

▶ CAREER HIERARCHY

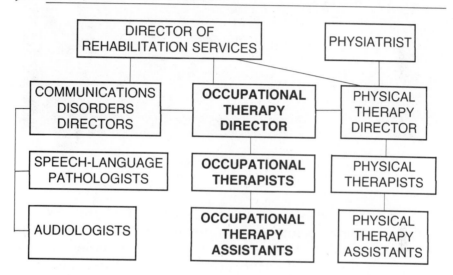

▶ CAREER DESCRIPTIONS

In the occupational therapy department, the assets and deficits of patients of all ages are assessed, patient potential is analyzed, and activities are set up to increase patients' ability to function and lessen limitations. Workers teach premature babies to suck. They treat children who are slow in development. They help stroke patients regain cognitive, perceptual, sensorial, and physical abilities. They interact with mentally ill persons to give them the confidence and the skills needed to return to family and work. They aid patients who have been weakened by the debilitating illnesses of emphysema and multiple sclerosis to organize their activities to conserve energy. They design, construct, and adapt equipment to help patients become more independent, Figure 12-2.

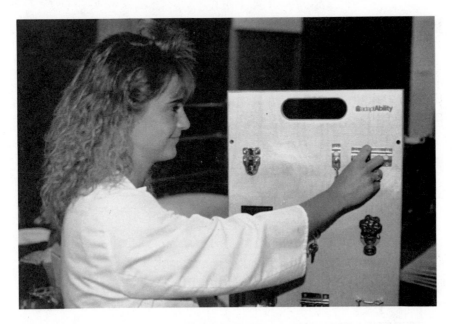

FIGURE 12-2. Equipment adaptation.

Occupational therapists determine the extent of problems and available strengths before planning treatment. They confer with other professionals and include patients in the goal-setting process. Occupational therapy assistants help carry out the treatment plan established by the occupational therapists.

Employment opportunities include hospitals, clinics, rehabilitation facilities, long-term care facilities, facilities for mentally retarded and handicapped persons, nursing homes, schools, camps, private homes, day-care centers, mental health facilities, government agencies, and community health centers. Occupational therapists can also work in private practice or with a group of physicians who specialize in a particular field. Areas of specialization include spinal cord injuries, mental retardation, strokes, hand injuries, and mental illness. Job availability is excellent.

Work hours are usually during the day, Monday through Friday, with Saturday hours in some facilities.

Career advancement for occupational therapists includes supervisor, section head, or director in a large department. Occupational therapy assistants can progress to occupational therapist positions with additional education. A master's or doctoral degree is needed to teach in colleges and universities.

Desired personal characteristics include an encouraging, supportive approach to patient care and a nurturing attitude toward people of all ages and backgrounds. Other assets include versatility, adaptability, and sensitivity to patients' needs and moods. Along with a good knowledge base in science, anatomy, muscles, and nerves, creativity and imagination are needed to develop unique treatment programs. Strength of purpose is needed to surmount the stress and frustration that result from unreached anticipated outcomes of treatment. Occupational therapy assistants need good communication, observational, and problem-solving skills; creative thinking; and the ability to follow directions.

Job satisfaction comes from being a part of the health care team with a special body of knowledge. It comes from a feeling of professional accomplishment and the ability to work independently with patients and family members. It comes from using creativity to develop a rehabilitation plan, serving as a resource to other professionals, teaching preventive measures, and helping patients regain maximum independence. Other sources of gratification are observing patients' progress, and taking pride in their continuing efforts to maintain maximum potential though it may be less than full function.

Occupational therapists interview and evaluate patients to assess strengths and weaknesses and to determine physical and mental abilities. They plan and direct activities specifically designed for patients with physical, mental, or emotional problems. They devise methods and treatment plans to prevent complications, increase independence, and adjust to residual deficits. They evaluate progress, work with patients to set realistic goals, and share insights into life changes as a part of the daily treatment regime. Therapists work with patients to develop or improve fine motor coordination, manual dexterity, and small muscle strength. They teach prevention of complications or deformity from existing medical conditions. They help patients adapt to temporary or permanent disabilities and function within those limitations.

Occupational therapy assistants work under the direction of the occupational therapist to carry out the treatment plan. They observe patients' tolerance, report improvements, document activities and progress, and work with the occupational therapist to upgrade and adjust patients' treatment plans. Other responsibilities include checking inventory and ordering supplies.

Occupational therapy aides/technicians help the therapists and assistants by carrying out some patient treatments, escorting patients, preparing project parts, and cleaning after arts and crafts projects.

▶ EDUCATION AND CREDENTIALS

CAREER NAME	YEARS OF EDUCATION AFTER HIGH SCHOOL	DEGREE OR DIPLOMA	TESTED BY: LICENSED BY:
Occupational Therapist (O.T.R.)	5 years: 4 years plus 6–9 months internship or 6 years: 5 years plus 6–9 months internship	B.S. in occupational therapy or B.S. in another field plus master's degree in OT	AOTA national exam and state licensure same as above
Occupational Therapy Assistant (C.O.T.A.)	2½ years: 2 years plus 6 months internship	A.A.S.D. in occupational therapy assisting technology	AOTCB national exam and state registration
Occupational Therapy Aide/Technician	1½ years: 12–14 months plus 6 months internship	Certificate	Vocational/technical schools

Key to Abbreviations:
AOTA: American Occupational Therapy Association
AOTCB: American Occupational Therapy Certification Board
A.A.S.D.: Associate of Applied Science Degree
B.S.: Bachelor of Science degree
C.O.T.A.: Certified Occupational Therapist Assistant
O.T.R.: Registered Occupational Therapist

● ● ● ●

▶ JOB AVAILABILITY

The U.S. Government Bureau of Labor Statistics estimate that there will be a 55-percent increase in job openings in occupational therapy to the year 2000.

▶ SKILLS

Occupational therapy skills are geared to strengthening fine motor skills, improving cognition, preventing complications, and training or retraining in job skills. Treatments are based on the assessment of strengths and deficits, medical diagnosis, age, general condition, ability to cooperate, type of surgery, and expected discharge dispostion. Treatment plans help patients overcome the restrictions of disability, adjust to residual limitations, and increase independence.

Assessment is the skill of interviewing, observing, and testing patients' physical and mental abilities. This process helps therapists determine deficits and needs. Then goals and treatment plans are designed and aftercare needs recommended. Assessment of patients' cognitive function, safety factors (using a stove), ability to organize thoughts (balance checkbook) and carry out steps of a task (preparing a meal), memory, problem-solving skills, and ability to manage medication may need to be evaluated before patients are discharged to a home setting, particularly if they live alone.

Techniques to prevent complications are planned, based on the medical diagnosis and assessment. Patients are taught methods of doing tasks to minimize damage to joints and tissues. Patients with arthritis can be taught to stand from a sitting position by pushing up with the flat of the hand without using the fingers. This method avoids pressure on the fingers and eliminates joint damage from this activity. Therapists design and fit splints and braces to support affected parts.

Activities of daily living (ADL) are skills that relate to self-care and the quality of life. The degree that these skills can be done alone makes the difference between dependent and independent living. Most adults want to be independent and feed, dress, and bathe themselves. Needing to ask for the help of others to accomplish basic tasks can result in feelings of worthlessness.

Therapists use their creative ability to develop methods and devise or provide special equipment to help patients achieve maximum independence. They teach mobility skills and plan activity schedules so that patients who have low energy levels can accomplish certain tasks.

Therapeutic activity planning is the skill of selecting appropriate games, arts, crafts, and social activities that facilitate adapting to existing handicaps, Figure 12-3. Activities are based on the patients' interests and physical and mental capacities. Some activities are used to increase organizational skills and concentration, ability to follow directions, and hand-eye coordination. Some activities may change compulsive behavior and decrease frustration. Also, they can be used to express feelings of accomplishment, particularly in a mental health setting. Art therapy is especially effective with children.

FIGURE 12-3. Finger exercises are therapeutic.

Exercise is another form of therapeutic activity that can be used to increase fine motor skills of fingers and arms. Activities such as "stair climbing" with fingers and playing catch with a large foam ball can improve dexterity and perception.

Motivational techniques are needed to help patients continue to strive for improvement. One technique is setting attainable goals, evaluating progress every day, and changing the goals as conditions progress or regress. Both therapist and patient need to guard against discouragement if improvement is slow or limited.

Job skill assessment and training are used with patients who have been hurt on the job. This assessment is done to determine if injured patients can return to their previous jobs or if training for new jobs may be necessary. Documentation from occupational therapy is often required before funds from disability insurance or workmen's compensation insurance can be distributed.

13
Pharmacy Department

▼

OBJECTIVES

After completing this chapter, you will be able to
- Explain department goals
- Relate the importance of prescribing medications
- Describe each career in this department
- Identify required education and credentials for each career
- Describe the skills performed in this department

▼

TERMS AND ABBREVIATIONS

Terms:
Unit-dose method
Prescription

Drug Classifications:
Narcotic/controlled
    substance
Analgesic
Antibiotic
Chemotherapy
Laxative

Tranquilizer

Abbreviations:
PO
IV
TPN
stat
asap
prn
D.E.A.

▶ INTRODUCTION

The hospital pharmacy provides essential services to patients, physicians, and nurses by preparing and providing prescribed drugs in a timely manner so they can be administered by nurses or taken at home by patients. The pharmacy serves as a resource for information on the effects of drugs and medications on the human body.

There are hundreds of chemical substances that affect the body or a disease process, Figure 13-1. If a chemical helps to slow a disease process or improves the body's ability to function, it is manufactured, packaged, and sold as a medication. When more than one medication is prescribed and ingested, a drug interaction may result. That is, the chemical makeup changes, producing effects on the body that were not intended. Drug interaction may involve food. Some food elements combine with medications and render them ineffective. Some drugs must be taken with food to prevent side effects. Pharmacology is constantly changing and expanding because of new discoveries in biochemistry and pharmacokinetics. Medicine and drug therapy are becoming more advanced and complex each year and pharmacists continuously study to keep up with these changes. Computers are helpful as a resource for drug data and are used as a support service for clerical tasks.

FIGURE 13-1. Literally hundreds of medications are available.

The pharmacy provides a clean work environment, uniquely free of bacterial and viral contamination in a hospital setting.

▶ GOALS

The goals of the pharmacy are to **prepare** and **dispense** prescribed medications safely and promptly; and to **advise** physicians, nurses, and consumers on the use, action, interaction, and side effects of prescription and nonprescription (over-the-counter) drugs and medications.

▶ CAREER HIERARCHY

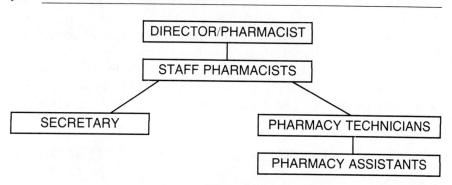

▶ CAREER DESCRIPTIONS

Job descriptions in the field of pharmacy vary according to the site of employment. Hospital pharmacists interact more frequently with nurses, physicians, and pharmacy staff than with consumers. Although consumer contact is more common in a retail store than in a hospital setting, hospital pharmacists are involved in outpatient education programs and homegoing-medication counseling for patients leaving the hospital.

Employment opportunities. Most pharmacists are employed in retail drug stores where they fill prescriptions and interact with the public. The majority of these stores belong to a chain; some are privately owned, often by the pharmacist. Pharmacists also work in hospitals, nursing homes, outpatient clinics, universities, government institutions, and in sales or research for pharmaceutical companies, Figure 13-2. A Doctor of Pharmacy degree is usually required for administrative, teaching, and research positions.

Pharmacy technicians are employed by hospitals, retail stores, nursing homes, and clinics. **Career advancement** depends on additional education or specialized training.

The **job market** is good for pharmacists and technicians.

Working hours. Many hospital pharmacies are open twenty-four hours a day, every day of the year. Most of the staff works on the day shift, fewer on evening shift, and least on night shift, reflecting the volume of medication orders that are processed on each tour of duty. Pharmacists can work varied hours, scheduling their work time to cover the needs of the pharmacy and their own personal goals.

Career advancements for pharmacists include becoming a hospital pharmacy director, a research supervisor, or an administrator in a pharmaceutical company. Other opportunities include buying a retail store or serving as program director in a government agency. Career advancement for pharmacy technicians and assistants requires further formal education or on-the-job training.

Desirable characteristics in pharmacists include an aptitude for science, especially math, organic chemistry, and biochemistry. They must have the capacity to do precision work, have good organiza-

FIGURE 13-2. Pharmacists are employed in many sectors.

tional skills, and strictly follow the Drug Enforcement Administration's (D.E.A.) guidelines. A good memory, a pleasant manner, and an interest in helping people are beneficial. The ability to verbally communicate ideas clearly and inspire confidence are other favorable assets.

Desirable characteristics in pharmacy technicians include an aptitude for detail tasks and routine procedures. They need to work well with people, have a positive attitude and a friendly manner, and take pride in their work.

Job satisfaction comes from providing essential services to patients, physicians, and nurses. Pharmacists gain job gratification from being a respected professional member of the health care team with a unique body of knowledge. Physicians, nurses, and the public look to them as resource people to identify properties of various medications as therapeutic agents. Pharmacy technicians gain satisfaction from assisting the pharmacists, interacting with professional people, and facilitating pharmacy services.

Safety is a concern for pharmacists when mixing chemotherapy solutions. Since these solutions are classified as hazardous materials, special protocols must be followed when mixing and delivering and when cleaning up spills. Also, certain procedures must be carried out if the chemotherapy solution accidently contacts the skin or eyes.

Pharmacists dispense drugs and medications prescribed mainly by licensed physicians and dentists, Figure 13-3. They continuously study the composition, action, interaction, and effect on the body of chemical compounds. They learn how to avoid interactions, but know antidotes if interactions occur. They act as consultants to physicians to ensure optimal drug use for particular conditions; advise patients about drug action, interaction, and side effects; and recommend some drug products and caution against others. They review patients' drug profiles and work with computers to identify safe drug interaction. They participate in patient care conferences and provide reliable labels and safe drug packaging. They develop methods and systems to process orders, deliver medications to nursing units in a timely manner, manage inventory control, communicate with professional persons, and educate patients and health care professionals. In a hospital setting, pharmacists have the added responsibility of overseeing the preparation of sterile products, primarily intravenous solutions. They mix chemotherapy solutions.

Pharmacy technicians work under the supervision of the licensed pharmacist. In a hospital, they routinely visit nursing units to deliver newly ordered medications and pick up new prescriptions (if

FIGURE 13-3. Pharmacists dispense drugs.

not ordered through the computer). They work with the unit-dose or other drug-dispensing system and replenish medication bins. In a unit-dose system, daily tasks include placing a twenty-four-hour supply of medications into each hospitalized patient's drawer in a "medication cart" designated for a specific nursing unit. Drugs are checked by a pharmacist before delivery to the nursing unit, where refilled drawers are exchanged for empty drawers. Upon return to the pharmacy, technicians credit drugs left in the patients' drawers.

Technicians enter the patient's drug history and diagnosis into the computerized patient medication record or onto the drug profile card each time a patient is admitted. These records/cards are updated each time a new drug is ordered, changed, or discontinued. Questions about orders regarding dose, route, or frequency are handled by the pharmacist with the physician or nurse taking care of the patient.

Technicians deliver controlled drug substances to the nursing units and obtain proper signatures. They assist pharmacists in completing documentation and maintaining records according to the Drug Enforcement Administration's regulations. They monitor the storage of medications according to manufacture recommendations. They inventory pharmacy stock and reorder when supplies are low.

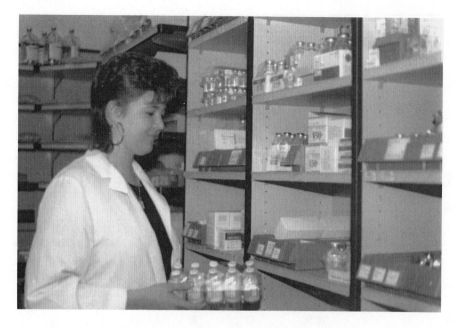

FIGURE 13-4. Assistants restock shelves as needed.

They review stock of standard medications on nursing units and resupply as needed.

Technicians mix and add medications to intravenous solutions under the laminar-flow hood to maintain sterility. They label each container carefully. Special solutions and chemotherapy agents are mixed by a pharmacist.

Pharmacy assistants check in orders, price items, maintain records, and restock pharmacy shelves, Figure 13-4. They have an aptitude for detail tasks and routine work.

► EDUCATION AND CREDENTIALS

CAREER NAME	YEARS OF EDUCATION AFTER HIGH SCHOOL	DEGREE OR DIPLOMA	TESTED BY: REGISTERED BY:
Registered Pharmacist (R.Ph.)	5 years plus 1500 hours internship (during three summers)	B.S. in pharmacy	State board of pharmacy exam and pharmacy law exam; licensed by the state

CAREER NAME	YEARS OF EDUCATION AFTER HIGH SCHOOL	DEGREE OR DIPLOMA	TESTED BY: REGISTERED BY:
Doctor of Pharmacy (Pharm.D.)	6 years+: plus 500 hours internship plus residency training program	Doctor of Pharmacy	State board of pharmacy exam and pharmacy law exam; licensed by the state
Pharmacy Technician	2 years	A.A.S.D. in pharmacy technology	none
Pharmacy Assistant	On-the-job training	none	none

Key to Abbreviations:
  A.A.S.D.: Associate of Applied Science Degree
  B.S.: Bachelor of Science degree
  R.Ph.: Registered Pharmacist

● ● ● ●

▶ JOB AVAILABILITY

Job availability is good for pharmacy workers. The U.S. Department of Labor predicts that pharmacist positions will increase 24 percent to the year 2005.

▶ SKILLS

Tasks performed in the pharmacy revolve around four categories: **management, distributive services, communication, and clinical/cognitive services.**

Management involves hiring staff, scheduling time, developing personnel policies, delineating roles and responsibilities, and developing safe, cost-effective systems for providing pharmacy services.

Distributive services involve systems of drug inventory, purchasing, dispensing, billing, delivery to nursing units, computer data entry, procedures for mixing intravenous solutions, storing and dispersing controlled drugs, and working with outpatient prescriptions, Figure 13-5.

Communication involves written and oral techniques. Written communication includes physician prescriptions, memos on proce-

FIGURE 13-5. *Distributive services.*

dures, incident reports on missing drugs or errors, ordering drugs and supplies, and developing patient and professional educational materials. Oral communication includes telephone calls between nursing units, physician offices, outpatients, and pharmacy; and verification and clarification of prescriptions. It also includes participation in team conferences, consulting services, interrelationships between pharmacy staff and nursing unit staff, and presenting patient and professional education through counseling and seminars.

Clinical/cognitive services involve reviewing patient medication profiles and screening for potential allergies, adverse reactions, and drug interactions. Monitoring patient therapy to ensure compliance and providing dosing information to assure optimal therapy are additional aspects of clinical services.

14
Physical Therapy Department

OBJECTIVES

After completing this chapter, you will be able to
- Explain department goals
- Differentiate activities from occupational therapy
- Describe each career in this department
- Identify required education and credentials for each career
- Describe the skills performed in this department

TERMS AND ABBREVIATIONS

Terms:
  Exercise:
    Passive
    Active
    Adduction
    Abduction
  Physical status:
    Fracture
    Arthritis

  Stroke
  Joint replacement

Abbreviations:
  ADL
  ad lib
  amb
  PT
  ROM

▶ INTRODUCTION

The physical therapy department specializes in helping patients regain strength in large muscle groups to improve mobility and function. The department helps patients regain flexibility, coordination, and functional independence from disabilities that impede normal activity. These disabilities may be new or old, acute or chronic, congenital or acquired, painful or not painful. They may have started slowly or suddenly and may be mild and temporary or severe and permanent.

Under the direction of patients' physicians, treatment and assistance are provided to those who are unable to move, have limited range of motion (ROM), have musculoskeletal pain or dysfunction, or have had surgery on bones or muscles. Patients may need physical therapy for muscle, nerve, or joint diseases, such as multiple sclerosis, stroke, and arthritis, Figure 14-1. Others have disabilities caused by spinal cord injuries, brain lesions, and musculoskeletal or neuromuscular problems. Babies needing physical therapy may have been born with physical defects, or children may experi-

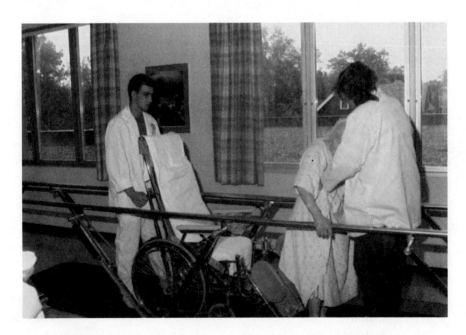

FIGURE 14-1. Physical therapy is needed for a variety of conditions.

ence developmental delays. Other patients have become disabled by illnesses, sports injuries, work-related incidents, or accidents.

Members of the physical therapy department are a part of the rehabilitation team. Others include representatives from the occupational therapy, speech therapy, nursing, dietary, and social service departments.

▶ GOAL

The goal of the physical therapy department is to help patients achieve their highest level of independence by increasing mobility and function through strengthening large muscles, reducing pain, and improving balance and endurance.

▶ CAREER HIERARCHY

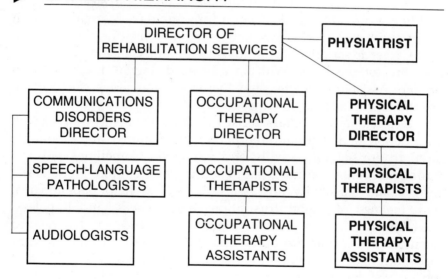

▶ CAREER DESCRIPTIONS

Physical therapists, physical therapy assistants, and physical therapy technicians work directly with patients to strengthen muscle tone, increase joint function, decrease pain, retrain muscles, stimulate nerves, improve balance, and regain strength. They work toward preventing complications of disuse, overcoming disabilities, and restoring physical health. This is done through an individualized plan of care developed by the therapist and carried out by the therapists, assistants, and technicians.

Employment opportunities include acute and chronic care hospitals, long-term care facilities, rehabilitation units, burn units, outpatient centers, school systems, home care, athletic facilities, and professional sport teams. They work in centers for mentally retarded and physically handicapped patients, and residences for the aged. The **job market** is excellent. There is a nationwide shortage of physical therapists. Unfortunately, there are relatively few programs to train them. As a result, entrance into a physical therapy program is highly competitive. Some programs require up to six hundred volunteer hours in a physical therapy department before application is considered.

Work hours in a hospital setting may be from five to seven days a week during daytime hours. Outpatient clinics, physicians' offices, and home care are usually open during the day, Monday through Friday, with some Saturday and evening hours.

Career advancements for physical therapists include supervisor and director positions. With an advanced degree, teaching is an option. Assistants can become therapists and aides can become assistants with additional education.

Desired personal characteristics include the ability to work well with people of all ages and temperaments. Courage and emotional strength are helpful to withstand seeing the sometimes sad and traumatic events that have happened to good people, Figure 14-2. Insight and sensitivity are assets needed to help patients deal with feelings of anger, frustration, helplessness, and hopelessness toward their disability. Tolerance, patience, and a relaxed manner are valuable attributes under the pressure of heavy work loads. Strength and stamina are needed because workers must stand most of the day, lift heavy equipment, and move and raise weighty extremities.

Job satisfaction comes from helping people achieve the highest level of independence possible. Gratification comes from seeing patients' efforts, physical improvement, and goal achievement. Making a difference in patients' lives and improving the quality of their lives is also rewarding. Job satisfaction comes from being a member of the rehabilitation team with a unique body of knowledge, and from

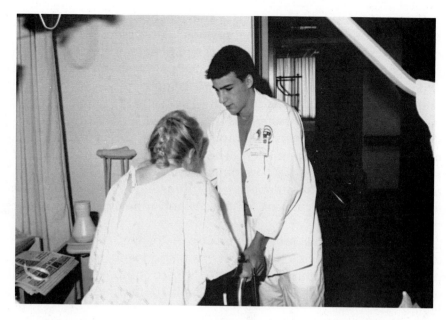

FIGURE 14-2. It takes courage and emotional strength to work with patients.

the comradeship of working with other professional persons to plan and achieve goals.

Safety measures to protect patients from harm is a high priority. Procedures for preventing falls, burns, pressure injuries, joint dislocations, and muscle strains are followed carefully.

Physiatrists are physicians who specialize in physical medicine and rehabilitation. They have studied methods of caring for patients with spinal cord injuries, brain lesions, musculoskeletal and neuromuscular problems, and sports injuries. They understand the relationship of exercise and its effect on bone, muscles, and circulation. They are knowledgeable in the principles of sports medicine and the psychosocial aspects of patients with disabilities. They meet with other rehabilitation team members to plan treatment, teach and counsel patients and families, and serve as a resource to staff. They may be employed by facilities to direct rehabilitation activities or serve in a consultant capacity.

Physical therapists review the records of new patients, interview them, assess their physical strengths, disabilities, and capabilities, and identify problems and needs. They set treatment goals with patients, develop the plan of care to meet those goals, administer treatments, and document therapy and progress. They monitor effectiveness of care, change the treatment plan as needed, and teach patients methods of self-help, safety factors, preventive measures, and rehabilitation strategies. Therapists encourage patients and point out realistic accomplishments.

Physical therapist assistants carry out patient treatment plans developed by the physical therapist and give direct patient care under professional supervision. They perform all major treatment procedures, including gait training; exercise; modalities of heat, massage, electrical stimulation, and ultrasound; and give home instruction. They document treatments and report progress to the therapist.

Physical therapy aides/technicians help therapists and assistants carry out selected treatments, transport and converse with patients, prepare equipment for use, clean equipment after use, order and obtain supplies, and answer the department telephone, Figure 14-3.

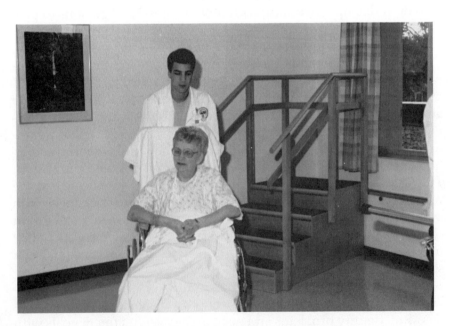

FIGURE 14-3. *Physical therapy aides transport patients.*

▶ EDUCATION AND CREDENTIALS

CAREER NAME	YEARS OF EDUCATION AFTER HIGH SCHOOL	DEGREE OR DIPLOMA	TESTED BY: LICENSED BY:
Physiatrist (M.D.)	13 years: 4 yrs college 4 yrs. medical school 1 yr. general internship 4 yrs. residency in physical medicine & rehabilitation	M.D. Certification	Certified by ABPMR and licensed by the state
Physical Therapist (PT or RPT)	5 years: 4 years school plus *Volunteer hours or	B.S. degree	National exam; state license
Sports Medicine**	6 years: 5 years school plus internship *Volunteer hours	Master's degree	

*Applicant must have 200–300 volunteer hours in a hospital physical therapy department before being accepted into a PT program. The number of hours is determined by the school.

**Sports medicine is a specialty of physical therapy. To gain this expertise, a candidate may spend a 6–8-week rotation in the sports medicine section of a physical therapy department during the basic PT program. Another option is to spend the internship of a master's degree program in exercise physiology in the sports medicine section of a PT department.

CAREER NAME	YEARS OF EDUCATION AFTER HIGH SCHOOL	DEGREE OR DIPLOMA	TESTED BY: LICENSED BY:
Physical Therapy Assistant (PTA)	2 years	A.A.S.D. in physical therapist assisting technology	National exam; state license
Physical Therapy Aide/Technician	On-the-job training or 1½ years: 12–14 months plus 6 months internship	— Certificate	— Vocational or technical school

Key to Abbreviations:
   A.A.S.D.: Associate of Applied Science Degree
   ABPMR: American Board of Physical Medicine and Rehabilitation
   B.S.: Bachelor of Science degree
   M.S.: Master's degree
   PTA: Physical Therapist Assistant
   PT: Physical Therapist

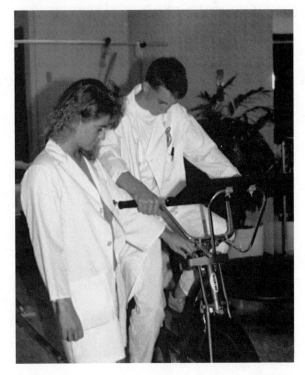

FIGURE 14-4. *Exercise is essential for joint motion and muscle strength.*

▶ JOB AVAILABILITY

The U.S. Government Bureau of Labor statistics project that the field of physical therapy will grow faster than the average. Positions for physical therapists will increase 76 percent and for physical therapy assistants and aides will increase 64 percent to the year 2005.

▶ SKILLS

Certain skills are required to help the patient regain strength, flexibility, mobility, coordination, and independent function. The type of treatments selected for each patient depends on age, physical and emotional problems, kind of surgery, strength, general condition, medical diagnosis, ability to help, degree of cooperation, presence of pain, and capacity to understand.

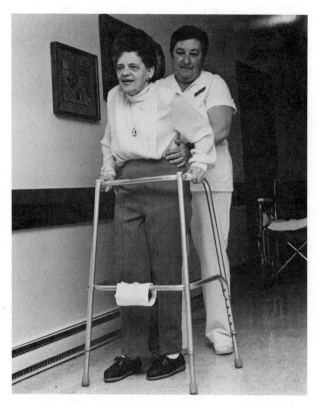

FIGURE 14-5. Learning to use a walker is also part of PT.

Kinds of therapy include exercise, massage, manual therapy, hydrotherapy, electrical, ultrasound, heat and cold, traction, and exercise machines. Some exercise equipment that may be used includes stairs, weights and pulleys, dumbbells, and stationary bicycle. If a muscle is very weak, moving the injured limb under water may be done. Therapists teach techniques of ambulation with walkers, crutches, canes, and sometimes with braces and artificial limbs.

Exercise is essential for the maintenance of joint motion and muscle strength, Figure 14-4. Active exercise is necessary to increase strength. Passive exercise keeps muscles pliant and joints mobile. The goal of exercise is to increase the strength, flexibility, and coordination of the muscles. Paralysis is caused by nerve damage, not muscle damage. Passive exercise will not return active motion to the part. Instead, it will maintain joint motion so that if motion does return, the patient will not have to overcome contractures. Facilitation techniques help stimulate muscle function.

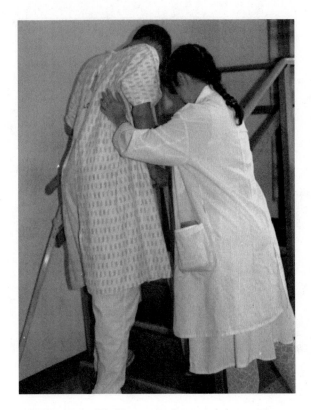

FIGURE 14-6. Climbing stairs is part of the exercise program.

A small **electrical current** is used to produce contractions. The goal of this treatment is to reeducate the patient in using weak muscles. Electrical currents are also very effective to reduce pain.

Gait training is used to teach patients to walk using whatever strength or restrictions they have. After hip or leg surgery, many patients are only allowed to put a little weight on the injured leg. The therapist teaches them to use a walker to protect the injured leg, Figure 14-5. After a stroke, many patients are unable to move one leg. The therapist teaches them to walk using a quad cane so they can protect the weak leg. The therapist uses parallel bars, walkers, crutches, and canes to teach patients to walk as independently as possible.

Massage is used to relax tight muscles and promote circulation.

Applications of heat increase circulation and relieve muscle tension. *Cold applications* decrease pain and prevent muscle swelling.

Mechanical traction mobilizes the spine and helps reduce pressure on pinched nerves.

Stair climbing, weights and pulleys, dumbbells, and stationary bikes are used to increase muscle strength and endurance, Figure 14-6.

Hydrotherapy can be used to decrease pain and increase ability to move muscles. It is also frequently used to cleanse open wounds.

Mobilization and stretching techniques are used to increase range of motion in joints after surgery or injury.

15
Radiology Department

▼

OBJECTIVES

After completing this chapter, you will be able to
- Explain department goals
- Define the major imaging techniques
- Describe each career in this department
- Identify required education and credentials for each career
- Describe the skills performed in this department

▼

TERMS

Diagnostic tests:
  X ray
  Ultrasound
  Magnetic resonance imaging
  Computerized axial tomography
  Cardiac catheterization
  Arteriogram

Treatments:
  Cobalt
  Radiation
  Angioplasty

▶ INTRODUCTION

Radiology is an essential department in every health care facility where patients come for treatment. Diagnostic and treatment procedures are both performed. However, only a few facilities have the special equipment needed to treat malignant diseases with radiation therapy.

Procedures done in the radiology department produce images that visualize bones, organs, and vessels of the body. This is accomplished by using X rays, sound waves, magnetic resonance imaging, and radioactive nuclear material, Figure 15-1. Most of these methods are enhanced by computer technology. Diagnosis of diseases can be made earlier and with more certainty because of the development of high-tech equipment. Treatment of diseases has changed because of new procedures that allow simultaneous viewing of internal structures with treatment strategies. Other treatment changes have occurred because of new discoveries and refinements in the use of radiation therapy as a tool to stop malignant cell growth.

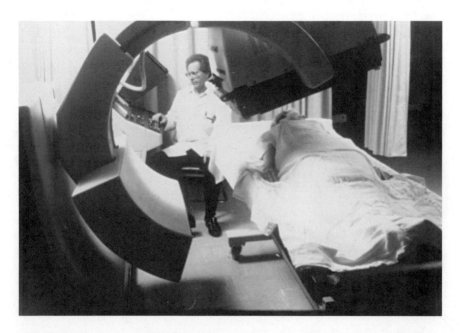

FIGURE 15-1. C-arm portable fluoroscope used in surgery when inserting a pacemaker.

▶ GOALS

The goals of the radiology department are to **produce images** of interior body structures for diagnostic purposes and to serve as a guide in the treatment of injury or disease. Departments that provide radiation therapy have the additional goal of **administering treatments safely** to control the growth of malignant cells.

▶ CAREER HIERARCHY

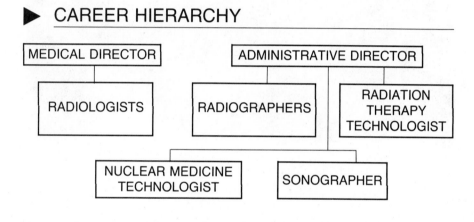

▶ CAREER DESCRIPTIONS

The roles and responsibilities of radiology professionals are determined by the education and experience of the staff, type of facility, policies of the department, and available equipment, Figure 15-2. There are several specialties in radiology. Radiographer is the basic educational program. Additional formal education can lead to a career as a radiation therapy technologist, nuclear medicine technologist, or sonographer. Other specialties that require additional on-the-job training are CT or CAT scan, MRI, PET, angiography, cardiac catheterization procedures, and mammography.

Employment opportunities are many. Positions are available in health screening clinics with patients who are healthy; in acute care settings with patients who are critically ill; and in treatment centers where radiation treatments are administered to patients who have been diagnosed with malignant diseases. In acute care settings, X rays are taken in all departments of the hospital including emergency room, nursing units, cardiac catheterization lab, and surgery. Other positions are located in physician offices, clinics, industry, military,

FIGURE 15-2. Many responsibilities fall on the radiologist.

veterans administration, education, freestanding emergency centers, and in mobile vans.

Work hours vary according to the work site. Radiology departments are open twenty-four hours a day in acute care facilities. Positions are available there on day, evening, and night shifts. Workers are in such demand that a choice of full-time, part-time, flextime, or independent agency placement is possible for qualified radiographers. Office, clinic, and mobile unit positions are available during day shift on weekdays.

Job satisfaction comes from obtaining quality images and from establishing good patient rapport in a short time, Figure 15-3. In most settings, radiographers render a complete service at one meeting with a patient. They take one X ray or perform one test and do not meet with the patient again. However, radiation therapy technologists do have the opportunity to develop relationships with patients and their family members because treatments are given over time. Rewards come from the friendships that evolve as technologists and patients work together to contain the malignancy. Professionals and patients are partners in the fight for survival and share in the hope that life will be spared and health will return. Job satisfaction also comes from the mutual respect of peers.

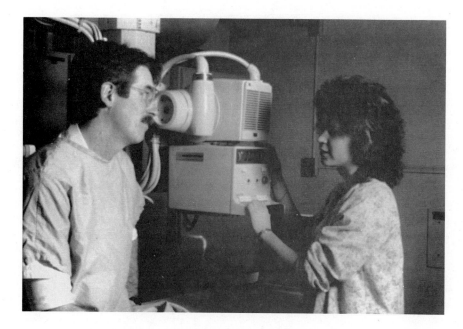

FIGURE 15-3. *Good rapport with the patient is important.*

Career advancement comes from moving into a supervisory or staff development position in a large department, by changing specialties, by learning new techniques (CT scanning, MRI), or by changing facilities. Radiology is a rapidly expanding career because of the explosion of knowledge in visualization of internal body structures, advancing techniques, and the development of new equipment. Career opportunities will continue to expand for those who keep up with new procedures. The **job market** is excellent.

Desirable characteristics of workers in the radiology department include a warm, compassionate manner, pleasant personality, ability to work with others, accurate work habits, patience, an interest in science and in computer-assisted medical technology. The ability to follow instructions, painstakingly complete procedures, work in emergency situations, and maintain safety standards are essential attributes. Physical strength to lift equipment and patients, manual dexterity to manipulate instruments, and audio, visual, and verbal skills to observe and communicate with patients are necessary assets.

The *radiologist* is a physician with a specialty in interpreting X rays and other diagnostic tests, Figure 15-4. This specialty is achieved by completing years of study and practice after medical school in the

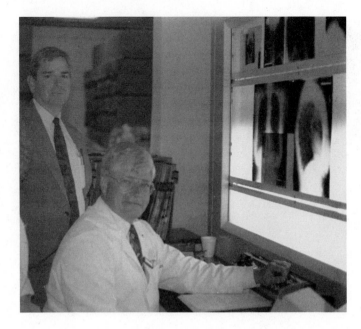

FIGURE 15-4. The radiologist's specialty is interpreting X rays.

field of radiology and passing specific exams. A radiologist may specialize by working exclusively in an area of diagnosis, treatment, or nuclear medicine. Responsibility and liability are great because patients' medical diagnoses and treatment are based on the interpretation of tests by this professional. The radiologist studies the results of each test, comes to diagnostic conclusions, and sends a report to the ordering physician. Also, the radiologist serves as a resource to the department by assisting with the development of policies and procedures that will improve patient care. Responsibilities also include continuing education, learning new techniques, and updating diagnostic equipment. The radiologist is either employed by the facility or works in private practice.

Radiographers or *radiologic technologists* use X rays to produce body images on a film or video monitor as an aid to physicians in diagnosis, Figure 15-5. This technologist has completed the basic educational program that serves as a basis for specializing in this expanding field. Responsibilities include patient identification and instruction, positioning the part to be studied, protection of parts not to be x-rayed, manipulation of equipment, positioning the film, adjustment of the exposure, taking the X ray, processing the film, and inspection of the film for quality. The radiographer also cali-

FIGURE 15-5. *A video monitor aids in diagnosis.*

brates, runs daily maintenance checks, cleans, and disinfects the equipment. Additional responsibilities including filing films, maintaining reports, and copying and sending radiographs according to policy.

Nuclear medicine technologists work with radioactive compounds that are absorbed by particular body tissues to diagnose and treat certain diseases. In a lung scan, a radioactive solution is injected into the blood and is absorbed by the lungs. Then an uptake of the radioactive material is recorded on a special film by a scanner and used to diagnose lung disease.

The Nuclear Regulatory Commission has developed strict guidelines on the use of radioactive materials to guard the environment and protect workers and patients. Though only tiny amounts of radioactive materials are used for each test, technicians are careful with technique and wear protective gear. The storage, handling, transportation, use, and disposal of these materials are strictly mandated to minimize risks associated with radiation. Because of risk to the fetus, special care is taken if a female patient is pregnant.

The *sonographer* works with sound waves (ultrasound) and a computer to create images of soft tissues, vessels, or organs on film or videotape and monitor, Figure 15-6. Ultrasound is a noninvasive technique used to identify and diagnose various conditions. It is a safe procedure that uses no X rays or radioactive materials. A

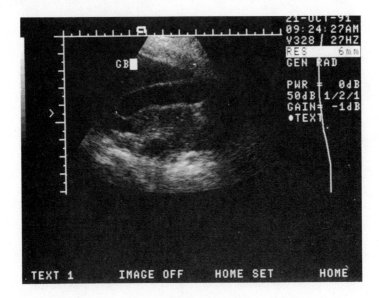

FIGURE 15-6. A sonogram.

physician reviews the images and reports to the patient's doctor. Sonographers specialize in cardiac, vascular, or abdominal areas. The abdominal specialty includes obstetrics, gynecology, and general conditions in the abdominal cavity. In obstetrics, a baby's abnormalities can usually be detected before birth. Depending on the position and age of the developing infant, the child's gender can also be determined.

The *radiation therapy technologist* works with patients who were diagnosed with cancer or other malignant diseases. Administration of radiation involves careful patient preparation, the operation of complex machines, careful patient positioning, marking specific zones for treatment, and creation of individualized masks and blocks to ensure exactness of radiated area. Responsibilities include patient assessment, education, comfort, reassurance, and emotional support. Duties include documenting physical symptoms, procedure tolerance, and treatment administration. The technologist also therapeutically interacts with the patient's family members.

► EDUCATION AND CREDENTIALS

CAREER NAME	YEARS OF EDUCATION AFTER HIGH SCHOOL	DEGREE OR DIPLOMA	TESTED BY: LICENSED BY:
Radiologist M.D. or O.D.	13 years: 4 yrs. college 4 yrs. medical school 4 yrs. radiology internship 1 yr. fellowship	M.D. O.D.	National boards exam by American College of Radiology; licensed by the state based on above exam; some states require an additional test to be licensed
Radiographer (Radiologic Technologist) RT	2 years: (8 quarters)	A.A.S.D. in radiography	National exam ARRT; National registry exam; licensed by the state; some states require tests every year to renew state license. Basic life support-CPR (recommended)
Nuclear Medicine Technologist RT and CNMT	3 years: 2 years plus 1 year nuclear medicine course	A.A.S.D. in radiography Certificate	Same as radiographer plus National exam by NMTCB; some states have an additional test in nuclear medicine
Sonographer RT and RDMS	3 years: 2 years plus 1 year	A.A.S.D. in radiography or allied health Certificate	Same as radiographer
Computed Tomography Technologist (CT) RT	2½ years: 2 years college plus 6 month OJT or course at manufacturer	A.A.S.D. in radiography	Same as radiographer
Magnetic Resonance Imager (MRI) Technologist RT	2½ years: 2 years college plus 6 months OJT or course at manufacturer	A.A.S.D. in· radiography	Same as radiographer

CAREER NAME	YEARS OF EDUCATION AFTER HIGH SCHOOL	DEGREE OR DIPLOMA	TESTED BY: LICENSED BY:
Positron Emission Tomography Technologist (PET) RT	2½ years: 2 years college plus 6 months OJT or course at manufacturer	A.A.S.D. in radiography	Same as radiographer
Radiation Therapy Technologist RT	3 years: 2 years plus 1 year course in radiation therapy	A.A.S.D. in radiography Certificate	Same as radiographer

Key to Abbreviations:
  A.A.S.D.: Associate of Applied Science Degree
  ARRT: American Registry of Radiological Technologists
  CNMT: Certified Nuclear Medicine Technologist
  CPR: Cardiopulmonary Resuscitation
  CT, CAT: Computer Assisted Tomography
  M.D.: Medical Doctor
  MRI: Magnetic Resonance Imaging
  NMTCB: Nuclear Medicine Technology Certification Board
  O.D.: Osteopathic Doctor
  PET: Positron Emission Tomography
  RDMS: Registered Diagnostic Medical Sonographer
  RT: Radiation Therapist

● ● ● ●

▶ JOB AVAILABILITY

Job availability is excellent for all radiology positions. The U.S. Bureau of Labor statistics estimate a 70 percent increase in job openings for radiographers and 53 percent for nuclear medicine technologists to the year 2005.

▶ SKILLS

Skills learned by radiographers relate to **imaging techniques** and **treatment techniques.** After completing the basic educational program and becoming licensed, radiographers often specialize in certain techniques that may require additional education.

Imaging Techniques

Imaging techniques are procedures that allow visualization of the interior of the body. This is done through four techniques: **X ray, ultrasound, magnetic resonance imaging,** and **nuclear scans.**

X ray involves the use of radiation that penetrates the skin, muscle, organs, and bones, Figure 15-7. As X rays pass through the body, a **picture** is taken of the **inside of the body** on a special kind of film, like a photograph. The film is developed, evaluated by a physician, and stored as a permanent record. It shows the condition of the anatomical part at the time of the X ray. The picture is called a radiograph.

This technique is used to diagnose a broken bone or the presence of stones in the gallbladder or kidney. Sometimes a liquid contrast medium is needed to visualize soft tissue organs. The contrast medium can be seen on the X-ray picture as it defines the structure. The contrast medium of a barium solution is swallowed to visualize the stomach; an iodinized solution is injected to visualize kidneys or blood vessels.

X-radiation is the ray that allows the inside of the body to be seen on X-ray film. Because this ray is potentially harmful to the body, care is taken to use only enough to visualize the affected part. Other areas

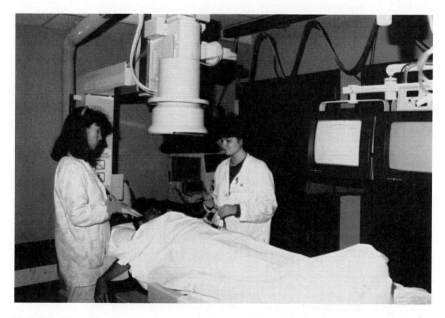

FIGURE 15-7. The X ray penetrates the body and leaves the body's imprint on the X-ray plate under the patient.

of the patient's body are protected from rays by a shield made of lead. X-radiation cannot penetrate lead. The technician also needs to be protected from rays. This is done by wearing a lead apron, leaving the room, or standing behind a lead shield when the X ray is taken. The lead apron used in the radiology department is the same type placed over a patient in a dentist's office when teeth are x-rayed.

Fluoroscopy is a technique that produces **X-ray like images in motion** on a television monitor, Figure 15-8. When the area that best shows the internal problem is seen, an X ray is taken.

The *computerized axial tomography scanncer (CAT scan),* also called *computed tomography (CT scan)* combines advanced X-ray scanning with a high-speed computer to visualize cross-sectional views of the body. Each cross section can be compared to a slice (axial) of the body. Cross sections are pictured from the top of the body downward. The X-ray beam rapidly enters the body while the computer transfers the information about tissue density into numerical or pictorial displays. This type of X ray is at least one hundred times more sensitive than conventional X-ray procedures due to computer enhancement. It is used to diagnose several types of diseases and conditions, including tumors and cancer. It directly pictures organs and surrounding tissues. Sometimes a contrast

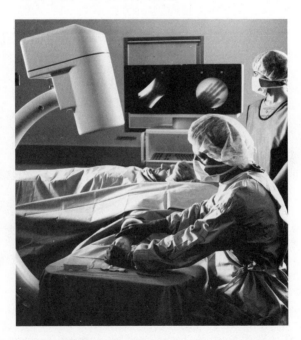

FIGURE 15-8. *The fluoroscope—X rays in motion.*

medium is administered to "light up" certain structures so they are not confused with other body parts. An oral contrast medium allows identification of the bowel; an intravenous contrast enhances kidneys. Use of the CAT scan technique often eliminates the need for risky exploratory surgery. The average exam time is about fifteen minutes.

Standard angiography is a diagnostic procedure that studies the condition of the arteries and veins. A catheter is maneuvered through blood vessels while a contrast medium is intermittently injected into the bloodstream. The contrast medium illuminates blood vessels to produce images of the vessels onto X-ray film and a television monitor. The picture continuously changes as the heart pumps. Throughout the injection of the contrast medium, films are taken and developed. After viewing these films, the physician decides if the vessels are satisfactorily visualized or if more contrast medium and more films are needed before the standard angiography is completed.

Digital subtraction angiography (DSA) uses the same basic technique as standard angiography, except the pictures of veins and arteries are stored in the computer. The pictures can then be recalled to identify where blood vessel problems are located rather than waiting for films to be developed. Advantages of the DSA test include the production of **sustained pictures,** using **less contrast medium** than with standard angiography. Newer equipment allows structures to be visualized from many different angles without changing the patient's position. In addition, the computer can store up to twenty-eight thousand images that remain available for review either one at a time or in a motion picture format.

Other diagnostic techniques that visualize the inside of the body without the use of radiation are ultrasound and magnetic resonance imagers. These techniques include the use of computers. Computer-enhanced equipment rapidly produces clear, sharp images of all body parts with no radiation exposure to the patient, Figure 15-9A. These tests are called noninvasive because they are done without performing surgery. Organs such as the brain and heart can be systematically examined and studied by the computer as it visualizes, organizes, and evaluates millions of messages during each test. Imaging techniques will continue to evolve and change as equipment becomes more sophisticated.

Ultrasound uses high-frequency sound waves with a computer to visualize the inside of the body. This procedure is done on the adrenal glands, heart, aorta, gallbladder, kidneys, liver, uterus,

FIGURE 15-9A. X ray in progress.

pancreas, pelvis, spleen, and blood vessels. When it is done on a pregnant uterus, the baby is visualized. The technologist is called a sonographer.

The **magnetic resonance imager (MRI)** utilizes magnetic fields with a computer to show inner body structures, Figure 15-9B. No radiation is involved. The patient is placed in a high-magnetic field. In the body, atoms in each cell spin with radio frequency to create energy. This energy images on film. In this way, the proton structure of every cell is evaluated by the computer. Because of the clarity and high quality of its imagining capabilities, MRI is especially useful in the evaluation and diagnosis of aneurysms, congenital cardiac abnormalities, brain and spine diseases, and orthopedic conditions. It is also useful in the assessment and evaluation of the liver, pancreas, uterus, and kidneys.

Magnetic resonance angiography (MRA) provides information about blood flow and images the anatomy inside blood vessels, such as the carotid artery, without injection of a contrast medium. MRA is used to determine vascular pathology and flow abnormalities.

Positron emission tomography (PET) is a nuclear imaging technique used to detect receptor abnormalities of the brain and nerves. It also validates drug effects and drug metabolism. Specially tagged chemicals that cross the blood-brain barrier are administered so that

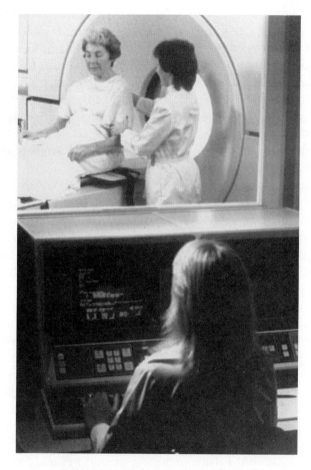

FIGURE 15-9B. Ready to have an MRI.

the brain can be imaged and studied to determine nerve function and effects of certain drugs on those nerves. PET is used to study neuropsychiatric disorders, cancer, and coronary artery diseases. It can also be used to determine the effectiveness of chemotherapy by following the metabolic response of the tumor. In the future, it may also be used to identify brain, lung, and breast cancers. PET is used in conjunction with mammography when breast cancer treatment is being evaluated.

Single photon emission computed tomography (SPECT) is another nuclear imaging technique that can be used in brain studies after strokes, in Alzheimer's patients, and after drug use. SPECT detects abnormalities in brain metabolism and blood flow with the use of radioactive glucose and brain scanning. Following strokes, the effect of speech and other therapies can be evaluated. In Alzheimer's patients, the brain's reaction to specific thinking tasks can be evaluated. After use of cocaine, crack, and marijuana, SPECT can detect long-term and probably irreversible changes in brain function.

Cardiac catheterization is a diagnostic procedure that is done by passing a catheter through a major vessel of the body into the heart. This test can determine heart function and circulation to the heart muscle. Also, a contrast medium can be inserted through the catheter into the coronary vessels and **angiography** and **angioplasty** can be done in the same procedure.

Angiography may show that a coronary artery in the heart is either partially or completely obstructing circulation. That patient is experiencing a heart attack. A repair procedure called *angioplasty* may be done. Angioplasty is a procedure that enlarges the lumen (inside) of the blood vessel and restores circulation to that area of the heart muscle. The procedure is done while visualizing the coronary arteries. The patient is awake throughout the procedure.

To do the angioplasty, a tiny catheter is passed into a vessel in the groin and threaded through the major vessels and into the coronary artery until the blockage is reached. A balloon catheter is inserted and inflated against the blockage. The inflated balloon pushes the arterial wall outward and reopens the clogged vessel so blood can again flow through. (If the artery is totally blocked, a hole can be made through the blockage so the balloon can be positioned and inflated.) Other treatments that can be done during this procedure include removing pieces of the blockage and placing supporting meshwork to prevent future reclosing of that vessel. Angioplasty is done to reestablish circulation in the heart muscle to decrease angina (pain), to minimize damage from an existing heart attack, and to provide improved circulation to the heart muscle.

Mammogram is a diagnostic X ray of the breasts. Images are produced on sensitive film for early detection of any cancer, about two years before a lump is felt. With early detection, over 90 percent of breast cancers can be successfully treated. *Needle localization mammography* is the insertion of a sterile needle into the site of the cell changes immediately before the surgical biopsy. That needle is left in place until the biopsy is completed to identify the exact spot to be excised because the lump is not palpable.

Nuclear scans use radioactive materials to help diagnose and treat diseases and disorders. Scans are performed to study the structure and test the function of certain organs and to determine the extent of some conditions. Radioactive isotopes are administered by inhalation, swallowing, or injection, depending on the part to be studied. This radiopharmaceutical gives off gamma rays. Though these rays are invisible, a gamma camera records them as bursts of light. These bursts are translated by the computer into images. Scans are done on the brain, thyroid gland, lungs, liver and gallbladder, bone, and cardiac muscle and vessels. A commonly used material is radioactive thallium. It is given to facilitate blood flow studies during and after a stress test. The heart and coronary vessels are imaged while the patient exercises on the threadmill and again a few hours later. This test is done to determine blood flow to the myocardium and to detect a recent heart attack.

Treatment Techniques

Radiation treatment consists of the use of a radioactive agent to control the growth and prevent the spread of malignant cells. There are several agents that are available for this increasingly successful treatment. Routes of administration vary according to the agent and the area to be treated. Some radioactive agents, such as **cobalt,** are encased in a machine external to the body and the rays fired into the affected spot. Other agents are taken into the body by mouth, by vein, or by direct injection into the body part. Treatments may be scheduled as a one-time procedure or repeatedly during an established time period.

Radioactive implants can be used to shrink or destroy some types of tumors. In this case, the capsule is placed inside the body, adjacent to the tissue to be destroyed. The patient is hospitalized. In a few days, the capsule is removed and the patient is discharged from the hospital.

16 Respiratory Therapy Department

▼
OBJECTIVES

After completing this chapter, you will be able to
- Explain department goals
- Define the major breathing problems
- Describe each career in this department
- Identify required education and credentials for each career
- Describe the skills performed in this department

▼
TERMS

Diagnostic tests:
  Vital capacity
  Pulmonary function test
  Bronchoscopy
  Blood gases
  Breath sounds

Problems:
  Dyspnea
  Emphysema
  Pneumonia

Asthma
Carcinoma

Treatments:
  Bronchopulmonary treatment
  Metered-dose inhaler
  Cardiopulmonary resuscitation
  Endotracheal tube
  Tracheostomy

▶ INTRODUCTION

Tests and treatments of patients with heart and lung problems are coordinated by the cardiopulmonary department. Respiratory therapy and perfusion sections are parts of that department. Both sections are concerned with the exchange of gases in the life-sustaining process of breathing and with the circulation of oxygenated blood throughout the body, Figure 16-1.

The respiratory therapy section provides lifesaving and therapeutic procedures to acutely ill and chronically ill patients of all ages. Diagnostic tests and treatments are performed in the department for outpatients and on nursing units throughout the facility for hospitalized patients. Tests and procedures are ordered by physicians and results are reported to them.

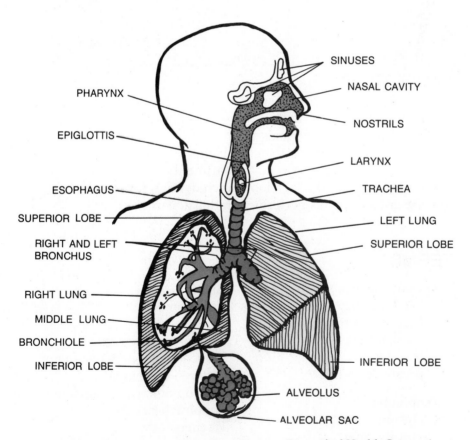

FIGURE 16-1. The respiratory system (From Simmers, Diversified Health Occupations, *2d ed. Copyright 1988 by Delmar Publishers Inc.)*

The perfusion section is responsible for providing cardiac and pulmonary support with the heart-lung machine. In some types of heart surgery, heartbeats are stopped so that a delicate repair or a transplant can be done. But the need for the delivery of oxygen to all tissues continues, Figure 16-2. Blood must be pumped, oxygen added to blood cells, and carbon dioxide removed if the patient is to survive without tissue damage. While the heart is not pumping, a machine takes over the functions of the heart and lungs. The perfusion section serves patients of all ages, but more adults than children.

Breathing is the act of inhaling oxygen and exhaling carbon dioxide. This function is essential to life, but there is an increasing number of people who have problems with this process, Figure 16-3. Respiratory problems can be caused by smoking, air pollution, allergies, chronic illness, or poor nutritional status and health practices. Respiratory illnesses such as asthma, chronic bronchitis, emphysema, and lung cancer can develop and seriously affect the breathing process.

When breathing is adversely affected, oxygen may need to be administered, Figure 16-4. Certain medications and moisture may

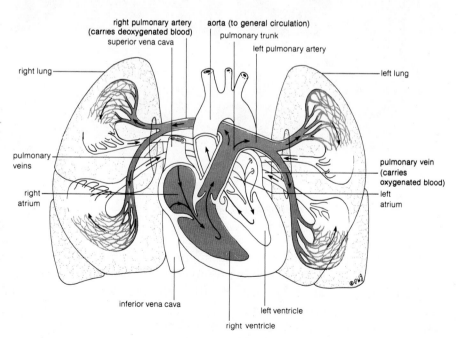

FIGURE 16-2. *Pulmonary circulations (From Fong, Ferris, and Skelly,* Body Structures and Functions. *Copyright 1989 by Delmar Publishers Inc.)*

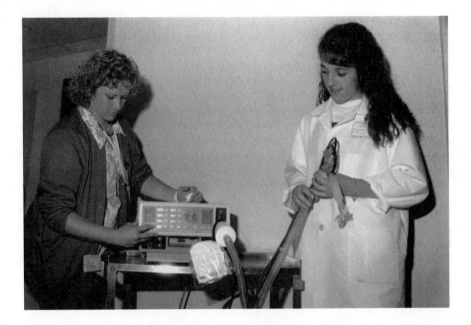

FIGURE 16-3. *Breathing is essential to life.*

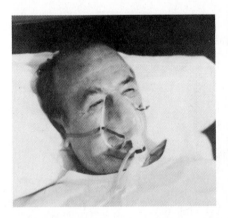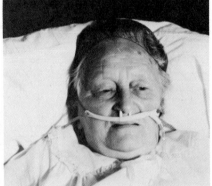

FIGURE 16-4. *Oxygen administration by mask (left) and cannula (right).*

need to be inhaled to ease the breathing process. Sometimes, breathing is so seriously impaired that patients cannot move air in and out without mechanical assistance. At that time, an endotracheal or tracheostomy tube may be inserted to provide an artificial airway. Then, manual or mechanical ventilations can be used as a temporary substitute for the natural breathing process until the patient's condition improves and natural breathing resumes.

▶ GOALS

The goals of the respiratory therapy department are to provide **pulmonary assessment,** perform **diagnostic tests,** administer **treatments,** and provide **artificial respirations** when needed. Goals also include the development of **health education** and **rehabilitation programs.**

The goal of the perfusion section of the department is to **support the vital functions** of blood circulation and gas exchange when the heart is not pumping.

▶ CAREER HIERARCHY

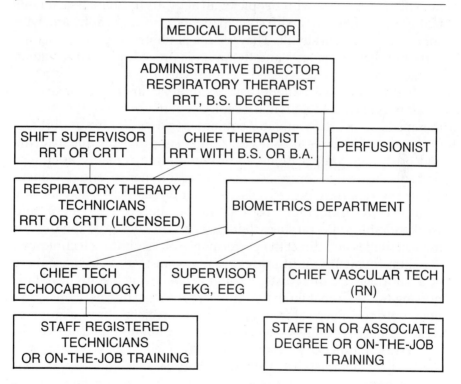

▶ CAREER DESCRIPTIONS

Respiratory Therapy is the career within the cardiopulmonary department that participates in the assessment, diagnosis, treatment, management, and rehabilitation of people with breathing problems. Some procedures are done routinely to ease breathing and some are done as emergency measures to save lives. Respiratory Therapy also participates in health education programs for the maintenance and prevention of breathing conditions.

Pulmonologists are physicians who specialize in breathing problems. These physicians are either employed by an institution as the medical director of the respiratory therapy department or are in private practice and serve as a resource to the department. They interpret the pulmonary function tests and prescribe medications and treatments to improve respiratory status. They work with department members to develop policies and procedures that result in effective patient care.

Respiratory therapists work under the supervision of a pulmonologist. They work with people of all ages, from premature infants to the aged. They work with some patients who are healthy and with some who are critically ill. They assess patients' respiratory status, carry out diagnostic tests and therapetuic procedures, participate in pulmonary rehabilitation, and perform cardiopulmonary resuscitation (CPR). They visit patients before surgery to instruct them in deep breathing and postoperative respiratory treatments. Respiratory therapists adjust the ventilator equipment necessary to support life. Other responsibilities include education to improve the quality of life and postpone complications and deterioration. Quality assurance procedures, quality control, equipment maintenance, and documentation and reporting procedures are other duties. Tasks may include doing electrocardiographs (EKGs) during the evening, night, and weekend shifts. Respiratory therapists are in charge of the department activities and direct the performance of respiratory technicians.

Employment opportunities are many and varied because there is a shortage of therapists. Positions are available in hospitals, nursing homes, rehabilitation facilities, physician offices, clinics, and home settings. Respiratory therapists can specialize by age group or facility. Some specialties are neonatal, rehabilitation, or acute care.

Work hours vary according to the facility and type of job. Respiratory therapists are needed in acute care facilities twenty-four hours a day, every day of the year. Full-time and part-time positions are available and flextime is often an option. Work in offices, clinics, and home care is usually during the day, with some Saturday and evenings hours.

Career advancement comes from promotion within the department to a supervisory position. With additional education, section head or department director positions may be an option. Career promotion can come from developing a clinical specialty or by changing to a position in education, research, or pharmaceutical sales. Respiratory therapy is a good basis for other careers within health care, such as perfusionist or physician assistant.

Desired characteristics include a strong desire to help people who are struggling to breathe. Patience, sympathy, empathy, and ability to work in a stressful environment are useful attributes. Physical endurance and tolerance for working with respiratory secretions are other characteristics that are helpful. Therapists constantly move from patient to patient administering treatments. They often participate in resuscitation measures.

Job satisfaction comes from helping people who are in physical crisis, knowing that they might die if the therapist's assistance was not available. A sense of pride is generated by the performance of lifesaving measures and being valued members of the health care team. Therapists know that patients and other professionals depend on them for lifesaving and life-sustaining procedures. In addition, therapists work with many of the same patients over time because of repeated hospitalizations for chronic lung disease. Feelings of job satisfaction come from helping these patients accept their conditions and showing them how to live with their disease. Therapists recognize that these patients depend on their therapeutic care, good advice, and calming influence.

Respiratory technicians work under the direction of respiratory therapists and report to them. Technicians perform most of the procedures that the therapists do, depending on training, job performance, and amount of experience. Technicians are responsible for cleaning equipment, patient billing, equipment purchasing, and stocking the department.

Perfusionists, extracorporal circulation technologists, are in the section of the cardiopulmonary department that is responsible for the support of respiration and circulation by operating the heart-lung machine. They monitor blood gases and electrolytes during heart surgery. Perfusionists interact with patients, surgeons, anesthesiologists, and nurses. Responsibilities include preoperative patient assessment, the setup and management of the heart lung-machine during the repair or replacement of the heart, and monitoring oxygen, carbon dioxide levels, and other substances in the blood. Other duties entail monitoring vital signs; administering blood, anesthetic agents, and other drugs; and inducing hypothermia (lowering body temperature) by lowering the temperature of the blood. At the end of surgery, the technologist is responsible for weaning the patient from the machine when the heart resumes pumping. The technologist specializes in adult or pediatric perfusion.

Employment opportunities exist in hospitals where heart surgery is performed and in university research centers. The number of positions needed in the future will increase as more hospitals develop heart surgery teams. A limited number of perfusionists are trained each year in the twenty existing schools in the United States.

Working hours are daytime hours, Monday through Friday, for scheduled surgeries. Emergencies sometimes occur that require surgery during evening, night, or weekend hours. So perfusionists are on call during those hours. Full-time, part-time, and "on call" positions are available.

Career advancement is usually lateral. Perfusionists can change institutions but the work remains the same. In a large facility where many perfusionists are employed, supervisory and management positions may be available. With additional education, teaching positions may be an option.

Desired characteristics include accuracy in carrying out procedures, conscientious monitoring, responsibility, good communication skills, manual dexterity, expert medical aseptic technique, patience, and the ability to function in stressful situations. Other attributes include understanding chemistry and biological sciences.

Job satisfaction comes from competent performance. Perfusionists know that patients' lives are dependent on their technical ability to keep oxygenated blood flowing throughout the body and brain while the heart is not functioning. Respect from fellow professionals, particularly surgeons and anesthesiologists, is also gratifying. Financial compensation is another source of satisfaction. The perfusionist is well paid—most heart surgery cannot be performed without this professional.

Safety is a concern in the cardiopulmonary department. Both respiratory therapists and perfusionists are considered to be in high-risk careers because they consistently work with body substances, specifically sputum and blood.

► EDUCATION AND CREDENTIALS

CAREER NAME	YEARS OF EDUCATION AFTER HIGH SCHOOL	DEGREE OR DIPLOMA	TESTED BY: REGISTERED BY:
Pulmonologist (M.D. or D.O.)	13 years: 4 yrs. college 4 yrs. medical school 3 yrs. internal medicine internship & residency 2 yrs. pulmonary medicine residency	M.D. or D.O.	ABIM certified in internal medicine; exam in pulmonary disease; licensed by the state
Registered Respiratory Therapist (RRT)	2 years (7 quarters)	A.A.S.D. in respiratory therapy	Entry-level exam by NBRC and registry exam (written & simulation) and state license; Advanced Cardiac Life Support (recommended); basic CPR (required)
Certified Respiratory Therapy Technician (CRTT)	1 year (12 months)	Diploma from vocational, technician school, community college, hospital program, job experience	Entry-level exam by NBRC and state license and Basic Life Support (required)
Perfusionist; Extracorporeal Circulation Technologist	4 years 5 years: 4 years 1 year 4 years: 2 years 2 years	Bachelor of Science in circulatory technology or Bachelor of Science plus perfusion program or college courses plus perfusion program	National license; Testing body is American Board of Cardiovascular Perfusionists (ABCP)

Key to Abbreviations:
A.A.S.D.: Associate of Applied Science Degree

ABCP: American Board of Cardiovascular Perfusionists
ABIM: American Board of Internal Medicine
CRTT: Certified Respiratory Therapy Technician
D.O.: Doctor of Osteopathy
M.D.: Medical Doctor
NBRC: National Board for Respiratory Care
RRT: Registered Respiratory Therapist

●　　　●　　　●　　　●

▶ JOB AVAILABILITY

Job availability is excellent for positions in respiratory therapy. The U.S. Bureau of Labor statistics estimate additional positions for respiratory therapists will be 52 percent to the year 2005.

Perfusionist programs are usually located in major medical centers or in a hospital associated with a medical school, university, or research center. Positions for perfusionists are increasingly available. There are a limited number of graduates each year because there are only twenty schools in the United States.

▶ SKILLS

Skills performed by respiratory therapists and technicians relate to **diagnostic tests** and **treatments** of the pulmonary system. In some facilities, respiratory therapists also do **electrocardiographs.**

Respiratory therapists work with sophisticated equipment with newborn, pediatric, and adult patients in intensive care units, on nursing units, and in patient homes. They administer medications and treatments, provide resuscitation procedures to all ages, and instruct in preventive and rehabilitation measures.

Oxygen therapy is the administration of a specific percentage of oxygen through a gauge from a tank or wall mount. A humidifier is attached to the gauge to moisturize the gas, Figure 16-5. Disposable tubing delivers oxygen from the source to the patient through a nasal cannula, mask, endotracheal tube, tracheostomy tube, tent, or ventilator.

An *aerosol treatment* is a procedure that delivers medication directly into the patient's respiratory tree by the inhalation of tiny droplets. The liquid medication is converted into a mist and topically delivered through the act of inhaling. Aerosol treatments ease the

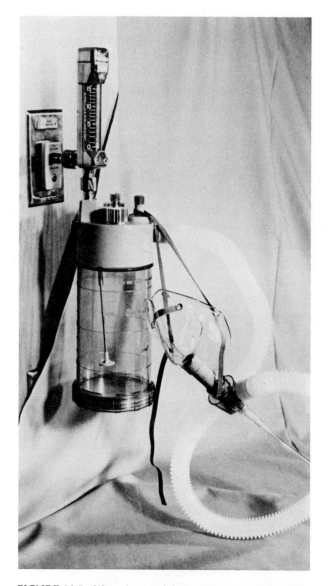

FIGURE 16-5. *Water is passed through the oxygen to moisten it for the patient's use. (From Simmers,* Diversified Health Occupations, *2d ed. Copyright 1988 by Delmar Publishers, Inc.)*

breathing process by relaxing and dilating the bronchi so that air can pass with greater ease.

Incentive spirometer is a device used to encourage deep breathing. Respiratory therapists instruct patients in the use of this instrument before surgery, then follow up with regular therapy sessions postoperatively to prevent pneumonia.

Metered-dose inhalators are hand-held medicated atomizers used to dilate breathing passages and ease respirations. These inhalators are prescribed for patients with constrictive lung disease. Respiratory therapists teach patients the correct technique of administration.

Intermittent positive pressure breathing is a procedure that forces a measured amount of air into the lungs during the inhale cycle, Figure 16-6. This procedure is ordered for a short period of time (ten minutes) to increase the amount of air exchanged. A bronchodilator medication may be ordered to be given topically in aerosol form with this procedure.

Cardiopulmonary resuscitation (CPR) is the process of reviving a person by administering breaths manually and by cardiac compres-

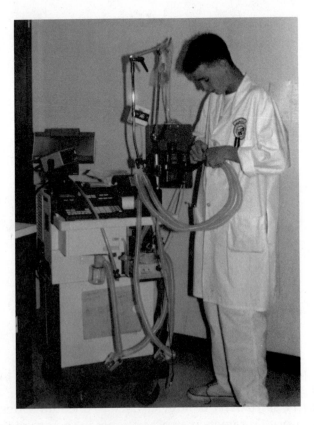

FIGURE 16-6. *Assembling a ventilator.*

sions. It is the treatment prescribed for cardiac and respiratory arrest. Respiratory therapists administer both artificial respirations and cardiac compressions.

Artificial respiration is manually breathing for a patient by forcing air into the lungs when breath is not spontaneous. Artificial respiration can be done mouth to mouth or with a bag/mask apparatus. Whatever the method, oxygen needs to be given (and circulated) within four to five minutes to avoid brain damage. If resuscitation efforts need to continue for an extended period of time, a ventilator may be used to continue mechanical respirations.

Cardiac compressions consist of depressing the lower third of the sternum one and one-half inches in an adult patient, sixty times a minute, with the heel of the hand. This action forces the blood out of the heart, simulating the natural heartbeat. The heart refills between each compression.

Bronchopulmonary treatment is the process of helping the patient clear the airway passages to improve breathing. The procedure involves **chest percussion** (tapping) and **postural drainage.** Chest percussion is the firm but gentle clapping on the chest to loosen secretions that clog airways. Once loosened, they can be coughed out of the lungs and bronchi. Postural drainage is the positioning of a patient so that gravity can help with the removal of those secretions that have been loosened by an aerosol treatment and the precussion procedure.

Arterial blood gas is a test done on blood from an artery to determine the oxygen and carbon dioxide levels. This test determines the effectiveness of natural breathing and mechanical ventilations. Based on these test results, physicians will decide the amount of oxygen and medication to be administered.

Vital capacity is a test to measure the amount of air that passes in and out of the lungs when a patient breathes. The test consists of exhaling completely, inhaling deeply, then exhaling all breath into a machine that measures the amount of air exhaled. The total volume of exhaled air is called vital capacity.

A *pulmonary function test* is a series of tests that measure and record the breathing ability of a patient. The first test is done without medication. The second test is done after inhaling medication to dilate the bronchi. The physician compares test results to determine if the bronchodilator medication improved the breathing process. A pulmonary function test helps the physician identify the nature of respiratory problems so that appropriate treatment can be prescribed.

Extracorporeal circulation is the pumping of blood out of the body, through the heart-lung machine, and back into the body, bypassing the human heart and lungs. The word extracorporeal means "outside the body." While the heart is not functioning, blood is pumped by the machine. This machine can monitor the oxygen, carbon dioxide, and electrolyte levels and can deliver anesthetic agents.

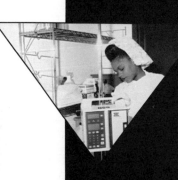

17
Support Departments: Admitting, Business, and Central Service

---

OBJECTIVES

After completing this chapter, you will be able to
- Explain department goals
- Relate how the different support departments affect health care
- Describe each career in these departments
- Identify required education for each career
- Describe the skills performed in these departments

TERMS

Admitting:
  Admission
  Transfer
  Discharge

Business:
  Charges
  Collection
  Insurance claim
  Medicare
  Medicaid

Central Supply:
  Clean
  Dirty
  Sterile
  Requisition

Storeroom:
  Automatic stocking
  Par level
  Exchange carts

▶ INTRODUCTION

Support departments are essential to the existence of a health care facility. In a hospital setting, Admitting, Business, and Central Service are a few of those support departments. Others include Data Processing, Housekeeping, and Maintenance.

The **admitting department** is the "front door" of the hospital. Workers greet patients, conduct confidential interviews, and direct patients to their proper destinations. They make registration as easy and efficient as possible.

Two **business departments** are **Patient Accounting and Credit and Collection.** These divisions take care of billing and collecting money to pay for staff salaries, supplies and to ensure financial solvency.

Materiel service departments order, prepare, stock, and deliver supplies needed by workers at the facility. Divisions include central service, linen room, print shop, purchasing, and storeroom, Figure 17-1.

▶ GOALS

Support departments exist to facilitate quality patient care.

The goal of the **admitting department** is the smooth expeditious processing of patients' entry into the hospital for diagnostic tests, patient care, same day surgery, and outpatient treatments.

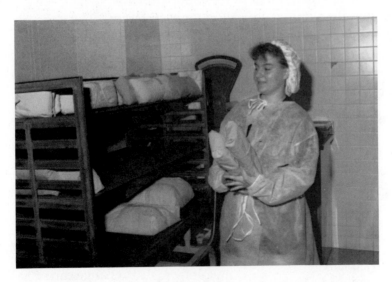

FIGURE 17-1. One of the many medical services departments.

The goals of the **business department** include issuing precise bills and arranging for payment of hospital bills.

The goals of **materiel service** include developing effective methods to order, stock, process, dispense, inventory, replace, and charge items used by facility workers.

▶ CAREER HIERARCHY

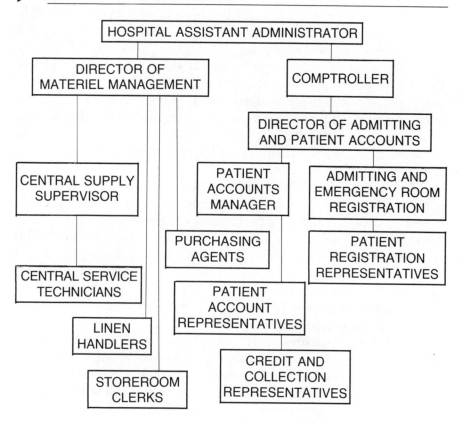

▶ CAREER DESCRIPTIONS

Support departments help health care workers do their jobs. Workers interact with staff in other hospital departments; only admitting and collection clerks interact with patients.

Employment opportunities are found in hospitals, large nursing homes, and clinics. In most facilities, workers are trained on the job. Once trained, they usually remain, so job availability is limited.

Work hours vary according to department and facility. Admitting departments are usually open five days a week on day shift, with some evening and weekend hours. Business offices are usually open during the day shift. Central service departments are usually open seven days a week during day and evening shifts. Some large facilities provide twenty-four-hour central service coverage.

Career advancement includes a coordinator position within the department or a lateral move within the facility. To move up the career ladder, education beyond the high school diploma or additional job training is often necessary.

Desired personal characteristics include good verbal skills, a courteous manner, good organizational skills, and ability to work under pressure. Communication needs to be calm, clear, pleasant, and positive—even in stressful situations. Ability to accept responsibility and work independently are other desirable traits. Experience in math skills and aptitude for detail tasks are helpful in business departments. Creative planning is important in credit and collections.

Job satisfaction in the support departments comes from the good feeling of doing a job well and from pride in service. It comes from knowing that adequate performance makes it possible for those who give direct patient care to do their jobs better, from perfecting job skills, and from taking pride in achieving a standard of excellence. It comes from making a difference in the lives of patients and fellow workers. Workers in the admitting and credit and collection departments gain satisfaction from making the admission process and payment process as smooth as possible.

Admitting department workers are *patient registration representatives.* They do a variety of tasks to ensure prompt, thorough service as receptionists, preregistration scheduling clerks, precertification agents, and bed allocation clerks. They interact with patients, physicians, staff nurses, and insurance clerks to process patient admissions, an occurrence that must be ordered by a physician. Admissions are classified as direct, emergency, or conversion.

A direct admission occurs when a patient comes to the hospital from home, a nursing home, or a physician's office. In this case, the physician calls the admitting department to request a bed. An emergency admission occurs when a patient was seen by the emergency room physician and is too sick to go home. A conversion admission occurs when a patient was scheduled for same day surgery but had a more extensive operation or has become too unstable to go home.

Interaction with physicians is an important facet of patient registration representatives. Physicians want patients admitted and served promptly and will direct their patients to those hospitals giving courteous and expedient service. They also need to be kept informed as to their patients' room assignments and changes.

Receptionists greet patients when they come to the facility, interview patients for personal data, enter health insurance information into the computer, and direct patients to appropriate locations, Figure 17-2. They confirm that patients' physicians are active and in good standing on the medical staff and have admitting privileges. Receptionists work in the admitting department and in the emergency room where, in addition to other duties, they help identify unnamed patients and locate relatives. They prepare patient identification bracelets and imprinter plates for chart form identification.

Preregistration scheduling clerks register outpatients and arrange for their diagnostic tests. They confer with patients on the telephone about date, time, and test instructions. Though some departments schedule tests directly with patients, most outpatient tests are arranged through this central scheduling service. Preregistration clerks also schedule diagnostic tests before planned admissions and elective surgeries.

Precertification agents call insurance companies to ensure coverage for patients' charges. Insurance companies may refuse to pay

FIGURE 17-2. A receptionist station.

the cost of hospitalization, surgery, diagnostic tests, and physicians' bills unless they approved the procedures **before** patients were treated.

Bed allocation clerks assign newly admitted patients to nursing units and rooms. There are many factors to consider when doing this complex task, including acuity level, age, gender, and presence of infection. Most hospital rooms are double, i.e., two patients to a room. Patients may be very sick, dying, and confused and calling out. Bed allocation clerks may not know the mental and physical status of new patients or potential roommates on the nursing units. Another consideration is diagnosis. If the facility has specialty units, patients should be assigned accordingly. For example, those with cancer should be assigned to the oncology unit.

Bed allocation clerks handle all bed assignments for inpatient transfers as well. When patients become stable, they are moved out of intensive care to the step-down unit. Often, other patients may need to be moved off the step-down unit to make that possible. When most hospital beds are full, it is hard to assign and relocate patients. Sometimes the nurses and nursing supervisor become involved, particularly if a critical change has occurred in a hospitalized patient, necessitating immediate transfer to the intensive care unit.

Business departments are essential to the existence of a facility. Without efficient functioning of the departments of patient accounts, credit and collection, and purchasing, the facility could go into bankruptcy and close.

Patient account representatives are responsible for billing. Charges are entered into the computer by workers in each department and the final bill is compiled by the computer, Figure 17-3. Approximately seven days after discharge or treatment, patient account representatives send computer-generated bills to insurance companies or patients. They post payments in patients' computer files, and send a computer-generated follow-up letter if payments are not received in a reasonable time. They check the percentage of payment against the insurance company's policy or contract with the hospital to be sure that each payment is correct. If bills become delinquent, accounts are assigned to the credit and collection department.

Patient accounts representatives correspond with attorneys, cash balance all payments to patient accounts, and develop form letters and flow charts. Each day, patient charges are downloaded from the mainframe so representatives can send a bill to the proper company or person. Tasks also include checking microfiche to see

FIGURE 17-3. Patient account representatives are responsible for billing.

that daily reports and billing are accurately recorded. In a paperless department, records are kept on microfiche, not on paper.

Credit and collection representatives also work to keep the facility financially solvent. They follow up on bills that are rejected by insurance companies and document the amounts to be paid by patients. If insurance carriers pay only a portion of the medical bills, patients may be responsible for the remaining part.

Representatives work with patients who come to the hospital for an explanation of charges and to devise a payment plan. Others develop payment plans by telephone. Workers need to be particularly aware of the stresses associated with illness and the recovery period. They need to be careful about how they approach the issue of indebtedness and be sensitive when developing a payment schedule.

Materiel service workers perform tasks in Purchasing, Central Service, the linen room, and the storeroom. Central Service is the focus here.

Purchasing agents order hospital equipment and supplies requested by members of other departments of the hospital. Agents work with staff to operate an efficient system to inventory, order, receive, store, and pay for necessary items.

Purchasing agents assign a number to each order submitted to companies, ascertain a delivery date, monitor actual delivery, and affirm product satisfaction. They may be responsible for presenting new product information and coordinating new product evaluations before establishing the new product as standard equipment in the facility.

Purchasing agents coordinate presentations by hospital supply sales representatives who are often available to show new equipment. These agents may contact supply companies when searching for a product.

Central Service clerks provide reusable supplies and machines for patient care. Workers are responsible for decontaminating, cleaning, sterilizing, and assembling small equipment, e.g., treatment trays for biopsies, and large equipment, e.g., suction machines and IV pumps. They clean and replenish emergency carts used in cardiac arrests, and disinfect and refurbish resusci-manikins used to teach CPR. They package equipment according to protocol and operate the steam autoclave, gas sterilizer, and aerator. They keep records on preventive maintenance procedures done on major equipment.

Linen room workers furnish linens for patient care, treatments, and surgery, Figure 17-4. Workers deliver clean or sterile linens to patient care units, surgery, and other departments, and collect soiled linen in a manner compatible with infection control standards. Workers in this department fold and package linens to be sterilized

FIGURE 17-4. *Linen room workers furnish patient linens.*

and used to cover patients in the operating room (if disposable drapes are not used). Workers either launder soiled linen or deliver it to a designated location to be picked up for processing by a commercial laundry. Workers wear protective coverings, such as gloves, when handling soiled linen. In some facilities, the linen room or laundry is part of the housekeeping department.

Storeroom workers maintain a stock of paper materiels and commercially packaged supplies for the facility. They distribute sterile disposable treatment kits, dressings, intravenous fluids and tubing, bath and other personal hygiene items, secretarial supplies, medical record forms, and other items by requisition. In many facilities, storeroom workers automatically stock specific items in designated departments. They also fill individual orders, follow protocol for supply charges, and deliver materiels as requested. Special instruments for surgery may be ordered directly by that department.

▶ EDUCATION AND CREDENTIALS

CAREER NAME	YEARS OF EDUCATION AFTER HIGH SCHOOL	DEGREE OR DIPLOMA	TESTED BY: REGISTERED BY:
Patient Registration Representative	On-the-job training; medical terminology and computer knowledge (helpful)	—	—
Patient Account Representative	On-the-job training; medical terminology and math skills and a typing course (helpful)	—	—
Credit and Collection Representative	On-the-job training; business course (helpful)	—	—
Central Service Technician	2 years or On-the-job training	A.A.S.D. in sterile processing and distribution technology	—

CAREER NAME	YEARS OF EDUCATION AFTER HIGH SCHOOL	DEGREE OR DIPLOMA	TESTED BY: REGISTERED BY:
Purchasing Agent	4 years	B.S. in business	—

Key to Abbreviations:
    A.A.S.D.: Associate of Applied Science Degree
    B.S.: Bachelor of Science degree

●   ●   ●   ●

▶ JOB AVAILABILITY

The U.S. Department of Labor projects an increase in the number of positions of 68 percent for medical secretaries, 47 percent for receptionists and information clerks, and 39 percent for interviewing clerks.

▶ SKILLS

Tasks done in support departments vary according to the facility. Some workers are trained to do more than one job within a department in case of illness, absence, or a heavy work load.

In the **admitting department,** the skill of *communication* is utilized with patients, physicians, nurses, and insurance company clerks. Interviewing incoming patients, providing clear directions, and keeping physicians informed about the room assignment are necessary tasks. Documenting insurance approval is also required.

Tactful investigative skills are used to confirm that patients' physicians are active and in good standing on the medical staff and have admitting privileges. These skills also needed to help identify unnamed patients and locate relatives.

Organizational skills are used to register outpatients and arrange for their diagnostic tests.

Negotiation skills are helpful with bed allocation. If one site is not available or acceptable, another plan must be worked out.

In the **purchasing department,** *accuracy* is essential. Accurate *ordering* and *documentation* of requisitions and potential and real **receiving** dates are tasks to be done. **Research** on price comparison, quality review, and coordination of product evaluation are facets of the *organizational skills* needed in this department.

In **patient accounting,** *accuracy in* **math** and **detail tasks** is necessary. **Computer entry** and **data retrieval** are skills used as departments become "paperless," i.e., workers interact with computer terminals; no hard copy is printed and no paper files are used. *Organizational skills* and accuracy in **gleaning** and **collating information** from face sheets of medical records are other talents utilized.

In the **credit and collection department,** telephone courtesy, and the ability to give clear explanations are necessary *communication skills. Imagination* and *creativity* are helpful when developing payment plans.

In **central service, following** *detail routine tasks* and *following established practices* are skills needed to ensure cleanliness, safety, and completeness of issued equipment.

In the **storeroom,** organizational skills, careful rotation of items, and attention to expiration dates ensure the stocking of equipment that is safe and usable for the staff. A *spirit of service* and *accuracy* in ordering and receiving supplies are valued assets.

18
Surgery
Department

▼

OBJECTIVES

After completing this chapter, you will be able to
- Explain department goals
- Identify the difference between emergency and nonemergency situations
- Describe each career in this department
- Identify required education and credentials for each career
- Describe the skills performed in this department

▼

TERMS

Abbreviations:
  OR
  RR
  I&O surgery

Prefixes:
  pre-
  post-
  peri-
  sub-
  hyper-
  hypo-

Suffixes:
  -itis
  -ectomy
  -otomy
  -ostomy
  -orraphy
  -plasty

Techniques:
  Sterile
  Scrub
  Laser

▶ INTRODUCTION

The Department of Surgery is pictured as the land of mystery and miracles. It is. Wonderful things happen there because of the education, training, teamwork, and dedication of the surgical team.

Even members of the surgical team are sometimes impressed by activities in the operating room. They see how vital organs are cut, sewn, restructured, and replaced so that the body can function and patients continue to live.

During minor surgical procedures, e.g., removal of a skin mole or cataract, patients may remain awake. During major surgical procedures, e.g., stomach removal, hip replacement, or heart surgery, patients are anesthetized into an unconscious, unfeeling state.

Surgical procedures may be done in emergency and nonemergency situations. Repairing major blood vessels after a gun shot wound or automobile accident is classified as an emergency procedure because the patient's life depends on immediate action. Removing cysts or cataracts is classified as a nonemergency or elective procedure because it relieves a patient's discomfort and improves the quality of life, but these conditions are not life-threatening.

▶ GOALS

The goals of the department of surgery include the successful performance of necessary operative procedures, administration of medication and anesthetics, and the monitoring and support of patients' vital functions to sustain life.

Goals in same-day surgery, preoperative holding area, and recovery room include preparing patients for designated procedures and monitoring their conditions afterward until their condition is stable and their mental status clear.

▶ PATIENT CARE FLOW CHART

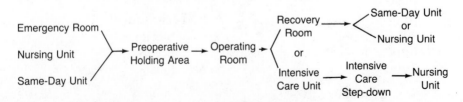

► CAREER HIERARCHY

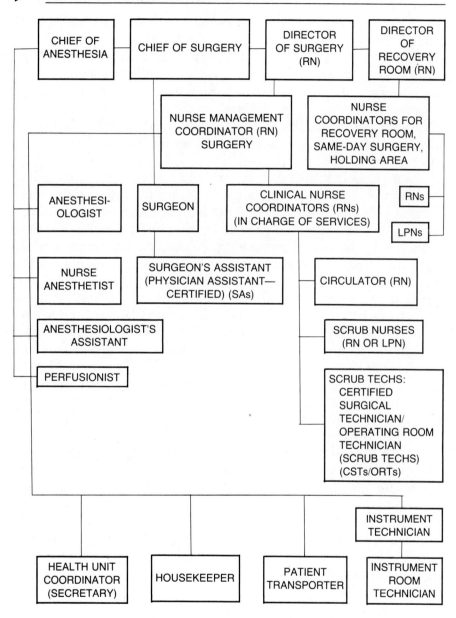

▶ CAREER DESCRIPTIONS

There are many careers associated with the care of patients before, during, and after surgery. The department of surgery includes the same-day surgery unit, preoperative holding area, operating rooms, and recovery room. Specialties within surgery include neurosurgery; thoracic/open heart surgery; abdominal surgery; vascular surgery; gynecology; urology; orthopedic surgery; plastic surgery; eye, ear, nose, throat, and maxillofacial surgery. Except for physicians, most workers in a hospital setting are employed by the institution.

Nurses in the same day surgery unit and preoperative holding area discuss procedures with patients, administer preoperative medications, and begin intravenous fluids. Anesthesiologists and surgeons may meet with their patients there. The staff in the operating room greet patients and prepare for the surgery. The circulator does a preoperative assessment that includes checking patients' understanding of the operative procedure, reviewing lab results and physical and mental status, and making sure that permissions are signed. Once the surgeons, surgeon's assistants, nurses, and technicians have scrubbed and dress in sterile gown and gloves, they cannot touch anything that is not sterile. They depend on the circulator to obtain items and position patients.

In the recovery room, staff nurses monitor patients' conditions and help them awaken from anesthesia. In some hospitals, recovery room nurses meet hospitalized patients and establish a relationship the day before surgery is scheduled.

Employment opportunities include hospitals, freestanding surgical clinics, and surgeons' and oral surgeons' offices. Other options are health maintenance organizations, research centers, veterans administration, the military, and civic organizations and private industry.

Work hours. In a hospital setting, surgery is usually scheduled Monday through Saturday on day and evening shifts, with on-call duties during the night and on Sunday. If an emergency arises, on-call staff come to the hospital. Freestanding surgical clinics are open Monday through Friday during the day. Generally, clinics perform less complicated types of surgery than hospitals do because of the limited resources available to cope with emergencies.

Job satisfaction comes from having special knowledge and skills that contribute to improving the patients' quality of life and, in some cases, saving lives. It comes from making good decisions in stressful situations, functioning in emergencies, associating with technically talented professionals, and enjoying the respect of colleagues and the admiration of other health care staff. Though surgery is sometimes stressful, it is always a prestigious place to work.

Career advancement may depend on returning to school for further education or more on-the-job training. Nursing assistants may become surgical technicians; practical nurses and surgical technicians may become registered nurses or surgeon's assistants; registered nurses may become specialty coordinators or directors of surgery. Surgeons may work in private practice, in health maintenance organizations, government or industry, or as advisors to institutions, chief of surgery, or chief of a specialty. Some of these may be lateral moves rather than career advancements.

The **job market** is good, particularly for surgeons, surgeon's assistants, surgical technicians, and registered nurses.

Desired characteristics include an aptitude for detail tasks, working under stressful conditions, and reacting constructively in emergency situations. Good vision, manual dexterity, good hand-eye coordination, self-confidence, a sense of humor, and team spirit are other helpful traits. The stamina to stand in one place for many hours is necessary.

Anesthesiologists are physicians who administer agents that induce muscle relaxation, drowsiness, and loss of consciousness. Anesthetic agents are administered by intravenous, inhalation, or spinal routes to ensure freedom from pain during surgery or delivery of a baby. Anesthesiologists meet with patients before surgery, review their medical records, then choose anesthetic agents. When unconsciousness has been induced, an airway is established by inserting an endotracheal tube to facilitate gas exchange and to administer anesthesia. Throughout surgery, anesthesiologists monitor vital signs, state of hydration, level of consciousness, skin color, and pupil reaction. They look for symptoms of shock, respiratory distress, arrhythmias, and other adverse conditions.

Job responsibilities include administration of anesthesia, oxygen, intravenous fluids and blood transfusions, and constant observation of the patient's physiological condition as the body reacts to the stress of surgery. Heart function, vital signs, and blood oxygen levels are monitored, recorded, and reported to the surgeons. While surgeons concentrate on the technical aspects of the operation, anesthesiologists are responsible for the patient's overall condition. The first responsibility of the surgical team is the patient's survival.

Nurse anesthetists and *anesthesiologist assistants* work under the direction of anesthesiologists and perform the same tasks. They administer anesthesia by spinal, intravenous, and inhalation methods, and give intravenous fluid, blood transfusions, and oxygen. They monitor and record patients' conditions, record anesthesia and medications, and report to the anesthesiologist and to the surgeon. Questions that arise are addressed to the supervising (physician) anesthesiologist.

Surgeons are physicians who have completed extra studies in general surgery or a specialty, such as neurosurgery, orthopedic surgery or plastic surgery. The number of years to become board certified depends on the specialty. Neurosurgery is the longest program of study, requiring seven years after medical school.

Surgeons usually specialize in a particular area. Family physicians refer patients to them when operations are needed, Figure 18-1. Surgeons meet with their new patients, examine them, review diagnostic tests, and explain procedures to be done.

Surgeons study every nerve, muscle, and blood vessel of each organ and section of the human body. The procedure of surgery includes making an incision and tieing off or cauterizing blood vessels to stop bleeding and ensure a clear visual field. Then the

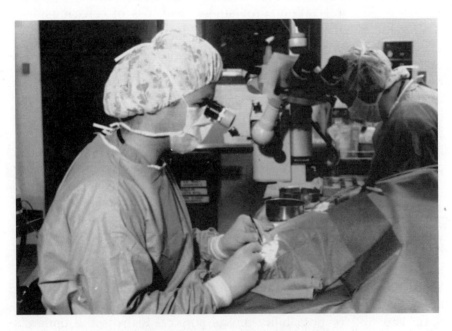

FIGURE 18-1. *Surgeons generally specialize.*

problem part is located, cut, or stapled and sewn until that part is repaired, removed, replaced, or revascularized. When this is done, the incision is sewn or stapled closed.

The surgeon is the head of the surgical team. Surgeons depend on others for help, but they make the decisions about procedures and techniques, designate tasks, and decide equipment to be utilized.

Surgeon's assistants are physician assistants who specialize in surgery. They work in the operating room as a first or second assistant to the surgeon, doing tasks that would otherwise be done by a resident physician. They are also trained to work with patients before and after surgery.

Surgeon's assistants may be responsible to meet with patients before surgery, obtain medical histories, assess physical conditions, request laboratory and diagnostic tests for pre- and postoperative assessments, perform therapeutic procedures, explain the operative and postoperative course, and answer questions. During surgery, they work under the direction of the surgeon and function as the first and second assistants. This role includes tieing off blood vessels and retracting the incisional opening to enlarge the visual field inside the patient. They sew, handle special instruments, irrigate, and hold organs and parts for the surgeon. Some may sew together layers of tissue to close the incision and finish with skin sutures, staples, or clips. After surgery, surgeon's assistants visit patients to remove sutures or staples.

Surgeon's assistants have some of the same technical skills as the surgeons. The difference is in the depth of education, technical skill, and responsibility to patients. Surgeons have had more in-depth education of anatomy and physiology, more practice in surgical techniques, and actually perform the operation. Surgeons are responsible to patients for the surgical diagnosis, professional decisions, and the technical quality of the operation.

Certified surgical technicians, operating room technicians, and *scrub nurses* prepare the room, assist with positioning patients, and prepare and drape the operative site. They pass instruments, drains, sponges, and dressings to surgeons and surgeon's assistants. They need to learn the name and function of each instrument, anticipate when each instrument will be needed, and pass that instrument when appropriate without being asked. They set up instrument tables, prepare sutures, count sponges before use, pass and retrieve sponges, and maintain the sterile field during the procedure.

It takes time to learn the many instruments for each surgical service. Different instruments are needed to remove a cataract than to perform open heart surgery or replace a hip joint. But when staff members are on call, they work on any case that presents an emergency.

Surgeons expect that scrub technicians or nurses will place (not slap) correct instruments into their extended palms. Ideally, the surgeon's eyes never leave the operative site, never look at the instruments. Placing incorrect instruments into the surgeon's palm interrupts thought processes and breaks concentration.

Circulators are registered nurses who meet the needs of the scrub team that is dressed in sterile attire. Members of the scrub team cannot obtain extra supplies and sutures from storage cupboards, position X rays on the lighted viewer, or use the telephone without contaminating their whole outfit. Circulators prepare the rooms, assist in the transfer and positioning of patients, open sterile supplies, obtain additional supplies and special instruments, and call for additional support when needed. Other responsibilities include administering intravenous medications, ordering blood components, sending specimens to the lab, calling the pathology department for biopsy results, obtaining X rays, and counting used sponges, needles, instruments, and sharps to be sure all are accounted for before incision closure takes place. They complete some forms that document the procedure and assist anesthesiologists who cannot leave unconscious patients.

Perfusionists operate the heart-lung machine that is used during open heart surgery when the heart is not beating. In this procedure, the patient's blood is passed through this machine in special tubing. Since this machine temporarily replaces the heart and lungs, it pumps blood, adds oxygen, and removes carbon dioxide. (See "Respiratory Therapy Department," chapter 16 for more information.)

Surgery transporters bring patients from same-day surgery, hospital rooms, and the emergency department to the preoperative holding area. To ensure proper identification of each patient, the name and hospital number on the transport card are compared with the name and number on the chart and on the patient's identification wrist bracelet. This procedure eliminates the chance of transporting the wrong patient to surgery.

Instrument room technicians clean, wrap, and sterilize instruments and stock operating rooms. They inspect instruments for wear and replace worn parts or the whole instrument. After cleaning, instruments are packaged and readied for sterilization. Technicians have been trained in the proper use of the steam autoclave and gas sterilizer. These procedures are crucial to the process of killing organisms, creating a sterile field in the operating room, and preventing infection that would result if unsterile instruments were used.

Health unit coordinators (secretaries) are an integral part of the surgical department. Telephone management is a central task in this role. Coordinators call to inform nurses when to administer preoperative medication. They call for patients to be transported to the holding area, then to the operating room. They call the visitors' waiting room to tell the visiting room coordinator to inform family members when patients have gone to the recovery room and when surgeons will meet with them.

In some facilities, there is a scheduling secretary/coordinator in the operating room. This is a complex procedure that requires knowing what surgeons operate on what days, how long each procedure lasts, and what rooms are to be scheduled for what specialty cases. If an emergency arises, cases may have to be shifted to a different time or day, depending on other procedures, patients' conditions, and surgeon and staff availability.

RNs and LPNs in same-day surgery assess and instruct patients for the impending procedure, answer their questions, inform patients and family members about scheduling details, affix patient identification bracelets and transport patients to the holding area.

RNs in the preoperative holding area start intravenous fluids, check patient understanding, give preoperative medications, facilitate the patient's meeting with the anesthesiologist, and transport to the operating room.

RNs and LPNs in the recovery room monitor patients' vital signs, monitor the cardiovascular and respiratory status, check dressings, connect drains and tubes, and apply ice bags and traction as needed. They carry out physician's orders and remain with patients until stability is assured.

▶ EDUCATION AND CREDENTIALS

CAREER NAME	YEARS OF EDUCATION AFTER HIGH SCHOOL	DEGREE OR DIPLOMA	TESTED BY: CREDENTIALED BY:
Anesthesiologist (M.D. or D.O.)	12 years: 4 years college 4 years medical school 1 yr. internship 3 yrs. residency in anesthesia	M.D. or D.O.	Board exams by ASA and licensed by the state

CAREER NAME	YEARS OF EDUCATION AFTER HIGH SCHOOL	DEGREE OR DIPLOMA	TESTED BY: CREDENTIALED BY:
Nurse Anesthetist (CRNA)	7–8 years: 4 years B.S.N. degree plus 1 year critical care plus 2–3 years anesthesia program	B.S.N. degree plus M.S.N. in anesthesia	Exam for certification by AANA Council of Certification and licensed by the state
Anesthesiologist's Assistant (AA)	6–7 years: 4 years B.S. degree plus 2–3 years anesthesia program	B.S. in health science plus M.S. in anesthesia	Exam for certification by AAAE and AAAA
Surgeon (M.D. or D.O.)	11–16 years: 4 yrs. college 4 yrs. medical school 1 yr. internship Number of years residency varies with specialty (2 for general surgeon; 7 for neuro-surgeon)	M.D. or D.O.	Certified by ACS plus board exams given by the specialist medical organization and licensed by the state
Surgeon's Assistant (SA)	5–7 years: 3–5 yrs. before program, applicant must have 1 year health care experience and A.A.S.D. in health field or a baccalaureate degree in a related field. plus 2 yrs. SA program or	A.A.S.D. in SA	Certification exam by NCCPA

CAREER NAME	YEARS OF EDUCATION AFTER HIGH SCHOOL	DEGREE OR DIPLOMA	TESTED BY: CREDENTIALED BY:
	4 years: (with previous experience in a health career) 2 years college 2 years A.A.S.D. in SA program	A.A.S.D. in SA	Certification exam by NCCPA
Scrub Techs: Certified Surgical Technician (CST) or Operating Room Technician (ORT)	1 year: 9–12 months in hospital or school program or On-the-job training	Certificate	Certification through AST to become a CST (optional)
Scrub Nurse (RN or LPN)	1, 2, 3, or 4 years: nursing program	2 year: A.A.S.D. in nursing 3 year: diploma from hospital school 4 year: B.S.N. from college or university	State Board exam; and licensed by the state
Circulator (RN* or ORT with an RN present)	2, 3, or 4 years: nursing program	(See above for nursing programs)	Same as for RN or ORT
*JCAH and AORN require that an RN be the circulator in the operating room.			
Perfusionist	(See perfusionist in "Respiratory Therapy Department," Chapter 16.)		
Surgical Transporter	On-the-job training or HOE program		
Instrument Room Technician	On-the-job training		

CAREER NAME	YEARS OF EDUCATION AFTER HIGH SCHOOL	DEGREE OR DIPLOMA	TESTED BY: CREDENTIALED BY:
Health Unit Coordinator (Secretary)	(See "Nursing Department," Chapter 11.)		
Recovery Room Nurse RN, CPAN	2, 3, 4 years: nursing program plus workshops, continuing education courses, or on-the-job training	2 years: A.A.S.D. in nursing 3 years: diploma from hospital school 4 years: B.S.N. from college or university	Certification from ASPAN

Key to Abbreviations:
AA: Anesthesiologist's Assistant
AAAA: American Academy of Anesthesiologists' Assistants
AANA: American Association of Nurse Anesthetists
A.A.S.D.: Associate of Applied Science Degree
AAAE: Association for Anesthesiologists' Assistants Education
ACS: American College of Surgeons
ASPAN: American Society of Post Anesthesia Nurses
AST: Association of Surgical Technicians
ASA: American Society of Anesthesiologists
AORN: Association of Operating Room Nurses
B.S.N.: Bachelor of Science in Nursing
CRNA: Certified Registered Nurse Anesthetist
CST: Certified Surgical Technician
D.O.: Doctor of Osteopathy
HOE: Health Occupation Education Program
JCAH: Joint Commission on Accreditation of Hospitals
M.S.: Master of Science
NA: Nurse Anesthetist
NCCPA: National Commission on Certification of Physician's Assistants
ORT: Operating Room Technician
RN: Registered Nurse
SA: Surgeon's Assistant

● ● ● ●

▶ JOB AVAILABILITY

Job availability is excellent for positions in surgery. The U.S. Bureau of Labor statistics estimate additional job openings to the year 2005 to be 34 percent for nurse anesthetists and anesthesiologist's assistants, 55 percent for surgical technologists, 44 percent for registered nurses, and 42 percent for licensed practical nurses.

▶ SKILLS

Staff in the department of surgery develop special skills according to their education, position, and work site. Tasks required in same-day surgery are not the same as those required in the operating room. Every staff member does not perform every skill.

Airway management is an important responsibility of those who administer anesthetic agents. To manage an airway safely in an unconscious patient, an endotracheal tube may be inserted to facilitate gas exchange and administer anesthetic agents.

Intubation is the procedure of inserting a laryngoscope and an endotracheal tube into a patient's windpipe through the mouth or nose to maintain the airway. This tube is connected to the anesthesia machine and ventilator. It remains in place until the operation has been completed and the patient can breathe without mechanical assistance. The procedure is done by anesthesiologists, their assistants, or nurse anesthetists.

Insertion of intravenous and arterial lines is another skill performed by anesthesia team members, Figure 18-2A and B. Central venous pressure monitoring and insertion of special catheters are other procedures done. Health history, type of surgical procedure, and anticipated length of unconsciousness are all factors considered before deciding what lines are necessary.

Surgical scrub is the procedure of washing hands and forearms to the elbow for ten minutes with antibacterial soap, a scrub brush, and a nail file or orange sticks. This procedure is done by every staff member who will dress in sterile attire for the operation. Anyone performing surgery or passing sterile instruments will scrub. Though the skin is never sterile, scrubbing decreases the number of bacteria present on the skin of the hands and forearms.

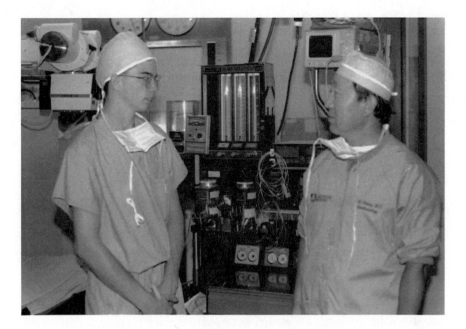

FIGURE 18-2A. Anesthesia is an important responsibility.

Sterile technique is a skill learned by all professional staff members who work in surgery. "Sterile" indicates the absence of bacteria. Introduction of bacteria into a patient's incision can cause a serious infection, debilitation, and sometimes death. Only instruments that have been steam or gas sterilized or purchased in a prepackaged sterile container are used in the operating room, Figure 18-3. Staff wear masks to avoid breathing into the incision or on the sterile field, which is made up of instrument tables and drapes that cover the patient.

Principles of sterile technique need to be strictly followed in the operating room. If something becomes contaminated, it is not used. If a fly landed on a sterile table that contained 150 instruments, the entire table is considered contaminated and would be removed from use. Another set of instruments would be obtained and readied for use as quickly as possible.

Passing instruments is the technique of handing the right instrument to the right surgeon at the right time, Figure 18-4. It also includes wiping used instruments with a sterile sponge and returning them to the sterile field. Instruments are passed back and forth from incision site to table during an operation.

The skill of passing instruments depends on learning the names and functions of more than one hundred instruments. Because each

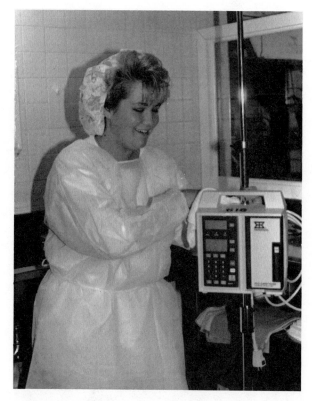

FIGURE 18-2B. IV pumps control fluid administration.

specialty has its own instruments, the name and function of each are different, though there are similarities. About twelve instruments are commonly used in each specialty. During the training program and orientation period, there is time to learn each instrument.

The goal of the person passing the instruments is to know the technique of the surgical procedure well enough so that the next instrument to be used is anticipated, selected, and pressed into the extended hand of the surgeon without it being requested. The surgeon expects the correct instrument to be passed without looking away from the operative site, without looking at the instrument, and without asking for it.

Surgical technique is the procedure of cutting into, dissecting, repairing, removing, and closing, i.e., the step-by-step process of performing the operation. It is the surgeon's method of getting the job done with the least amount of trauma to the patient, in the least amount of time. Surgical technique is important to the patient. After the surgery, it may matter to the patient where the surgeon placed

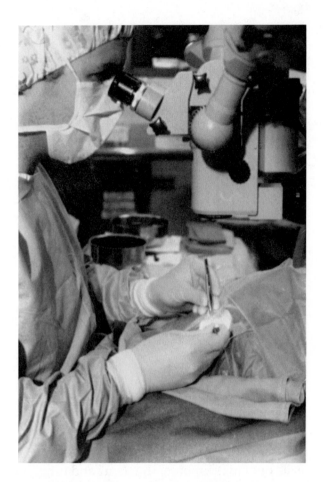

FIGURE 18-3. Surgeons generally specialize.

the incision; how the organs were cut, stapled, and stitched; how the laser was used; how blood vessels were tied or cauterized; how much tissue was removed; how gently were the surrounding organs and tissues handled; and how much time it took.

Positioning the patient is an important skill carried out for and by several of the operating room team members. The surgeon directs positioning for the best view of the operative field. The anesthesiologist is concerned about lung expansion and the maintenance of an open airway. The circulator protects the patient from pressure points and overextension of joints and muscles. The patient needs to be positioned on the surgical table with the least amount of trauma to the body. Pressure points need to be padded and cushioned, and

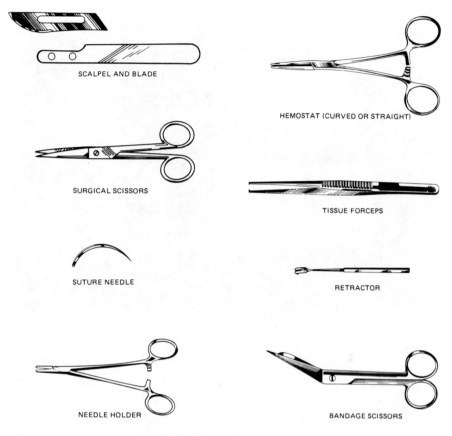

FIGURE 18-4. The right instrument at the right time.

safety cuffs and straps need to be carefully placed to avoid tissue damage and restriction of circulation. Special techniques need to be used to move an unconscious patient to avoid skin, muscle, and joint damage.

Monitoring is an important skill performed by everyone in the operating room and in the recovery room, Figure 18-5. Each team member has a responsibility for certain aspects of the monitoring process, but the patient's over all physical status is the primary consideration of the entire surgical team. Anesthesia team members monitor pulmonary and cardiac status through electrocardiograph, arterial blood gases, and vital signs. Surgeons monitor the procedure and progress of the operation to ensure the best technique and accomplish the operative goal. Scrub nurses or technicians monitor the surgical procedure to pass the correct instruments to the sur-

FIGURE 18-5. *Surgical monitoring is vital.*

geons. Circulators monitor the needs of the team and perform unsterile tasks for sterile-suited team members. Recovery room nurses monitor the patient's vital processes, check to see that all systems and all equipment are working properly, and observe the patient's return to consciousness and a physically stable state. Though team members carry out their independent roles, they are interdependent and work together to make the operative experience successful for the patient.

Appendixes

A
Body Systems

▶ CARDIOVASCULAR

The cardiovascular system consists of the heart and blood vessels. **Arteries** come off the heart and carry oxygenated blood through the **arterioles** to the **capillaries** where oxygen is delivered to the cells and carbon dioxide removed. The blood then passes through the **venules** and then **veins** that return the blood to the **heart.** The pulmonary artery comes off the heart and carries blood to the lungs; it is the only artery that carries nonoxygenated (venous) blood.

The heart is a pump that forces blood through blood vessels throughout the body. An electrical stimulus initiated within the heart muscle triggers heartbeats, keeps heartbeats strong/effective, and maintains regular rhythm.

The heart is a four-chambered, hollow muscular organ with valves that prevent back flow of blood. It is important that the heart muscle get enough oxygen to pump effectively and remain disease free. When circulation to the heart muscle becomes obstructed from arteriosclerosis or a blood clot, a heart attack follows. When other conditions cause the heart to work harder than usual, it tires and begins to fail as a pump.

Blood flows through the right side of the heart, to the lungs, to the left side of the heart, and out to the body. It takes about one minute for a blood cell to make the complete trip through the body—from the heart, through the lungs, to the heart, through the body to the farthest cell, and back to the heart. There is a total of about sixty thousand miles of blood vessels in an adult body.

Blood flows through the cardiopulmonary system as follows (Figure A-1): vena cava—right atrium—through the tricuspid valve—to the right ventricle—through the pulmonary valve—to the pulmonary artery—to the lungs—to the pulmonary vein—to the left atrium—through the tricuspid or mitral valve—to the left ventricle—through the aortic valve—to the aorta—out to the body.

The coronary arteries carry blood from the aorta to the heart muscle. These coronary arteries bring a large concentration of oxygen to the heart muscle so that the heart will continue to pump effectively. Diagnostic tests to determine partially or totally clogged vessels and abnormal heart rhythms can prevent severe symptoms and life-threatening illnesses.

Cardiac and vascular problems are increasing in the United States. Several factors are blamed. Among those factors are high-fat diets, overweight, lack of sensible exercise, smoking, gender, and heredity. Some of these factors can be changed with education and determination.

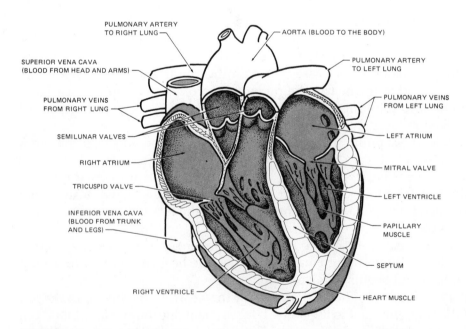

FIGURE A-1. Internal heart structures (From Keir, Wise, and Krebs-Shannon, Medical Assisting, 3rd ed., copyright 1992).

▶ GASTROINTESTINAL

The gastrointestinal system is made up of the alimentary canal, consisting of the main organs of digestion and the accessory organs of digestion. The function of this system is to take in food, prepare it for digestion, break it down into elements that can be used by the body, absorb those elements, reabsorb liquid, and expel solid waste. This is a complex process that involves many steps and several organs.

Food passes through the alimentary canal as follows: mouth—pharynx—esophagus—stomach—small intestine, consisting of duodenum, jejunum, and ileum—large intestine, consisting of cecum, ascending colon, transverse colon, descending colon, sigmoid colon, and rectum—anus.

The accessory organs of digestion are attached to the main organs, but food does not actually pass into them. They contribute to the process by making digestive juices. These organs are (Figure A-2, page 256): salivary glands (three pairs; submaxillary, sublingual, parotid)—gallbladder—pancreas—liver.

▶ NERVOUS

The nervous system consists of the brain (Figure A-3, page 257), spinal cord, and nerves. The neuron is the basic cell that carries messages throughout the body from the brain, down the spinal cord, to the periphery, and back again. There are three types of neurons, each of which receives (via dendrite fibers) and transfers (via axon fibers) messages; motor, sensory, and interdendrites. Motor neurons carry impulses from the brain and spinal cord toward the destination. Sensory neurons carry impulses from the receptor fibers toward the brain and spinal cord. Interdendrites carry impulses from one neuron to another.

The nervous system is divided into three major parts: the central nervous system, the peripheral nervous system, and the autonomic nervous system. The central nervous system is made up of the brain and spinal cord. The peripheral nervous system consists of all the nerves from the brain and spinal cord to the body's surface. The autonomic nervous system contains all the nerves that carry messages to the vital organs of the body (heart, lungs, glands, eyes, bladder).

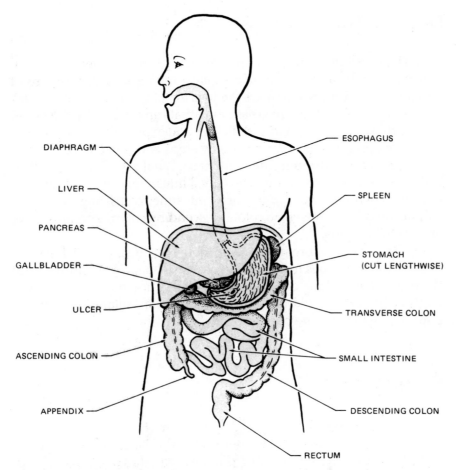

DIAPHRAGM

LIVER

PANCREAS

GALLBLADDER

ULCER

ASCENDING COLON

APPENDIX

ESOPHAGUS

SPLEEN

STOMACH
(CUT LENGTHWISE)

TRANSVERSE COLON

SMALL INTESTINE

DESCENDING COLON

RECTUM

FIGURE A-2. *The digestive system (From Keir, Wise, and Krebs-Shannon,* Medical Assisting, *3rd ed., copyright 1992).*

The brain is an essential organ of the body that contains centers vital to the process of life. The brain enables awareness and conscious and automatic movements. It controls and monitors all bodily functions including thinking, learning, memory, and speaking. If the brain does not function properly, life can be seriously disrupted. Unpleasant to life-threatening symptoms may develop. Double vision and seizures are symptoms that may indicate a neurological problem. Loss of consciousness or death can result from brain injury. The cause of problems resulting from brain disorders needs to be found and corrected, if possible. Medications may control some problems, while others may need surgery.

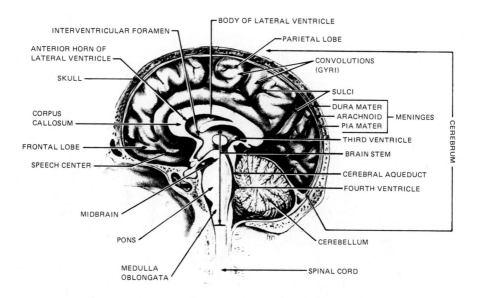

FIGURE A-3. Cross section of the brain (From Keir, Wise, and Krebs-Shannon, Medical Assisting, 3rd ed., copyright 1992).

▶ RESPIRATORY

The respiratory system is made up of passages and parts that draw air into the body, exchange oxygen for carbon dioxide, then blow the air out of the body. When air is drawn into the body, the process is called inhale. When air is blown out of the body, the process is called exhale. One inhale and one exhale make one breath, one respiration.

The respiratory tree looks like grapes on a stem. Air flows through the air passageways as follows (Figure A-4, page 258): nose—pharynx, consisting of the nasopharynx, oral pharynx, and laryngeal pharynx—past the epiglottis—through the larynx—trachea—bronchi—bronchioles—alveoli.

The actual gas exchange of oxygen and carbon dioxide takes place through thin membranes in the alveoli. The bronchioles and alveoli are held together by spongy elastic connective tissue. This combination of bronchioles, alveoli, and connective tissue makes up a lung. When air is drawn in through the mouth, air enters the oral pharynx and continues on the path to the alveoli in the lung.

The passage of air into the alveoli and the exchange of gases with the bloodstream are essential to life. If this exchange cannot take place because of obstruction or disease, the person will die. If the

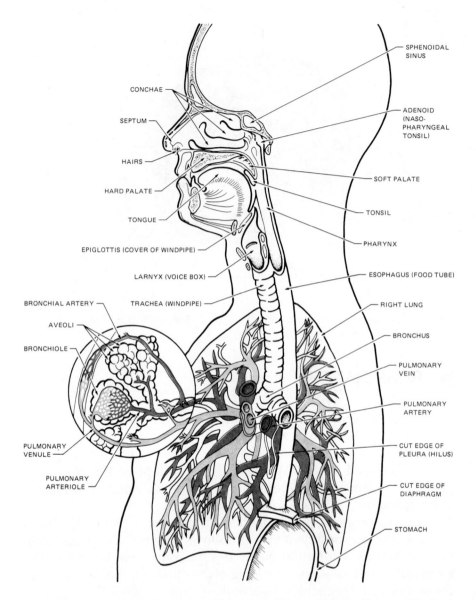

FIGURE A-4. The respiratory system (From Keir, Wise, and Krebs-Shannon, Medical Assisting, 3rd ed., copyright 1992).

process of breathing stops but the parts are capable of taking in air and exchanging it with the bloodstream, artificial respiration can maintain life, provided other parts of the body continue to function. Artificial respiration can be done manually by doing mouth-to-mouth breathing or mechanically by using a ventilator.

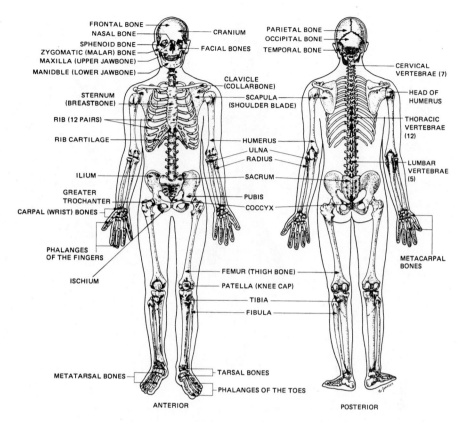

FIGURE A-5. *The skeleton (From Keir, Wise, and Krebs-Shannon,* Medical Assisting, *3rd ed., copyright 1992).*

▶ SKELETAL

The skeletal system is made up of long, short, flat, irregular, and sesamoid-shaped bones that consist of minerals, special cells, blood vessels, and nerves, Figure A-5. Bones provide support for soft tissues and protection for organs. They store calcium, make blood cells (in marrow), and enable body movements by providing structure for muscles. Calcium, phosphorus, and vitamin D are important to bone health and prevention of disease and fractures.

▶ URINARY

The urinary system cleanses the blood of waste elements and excessive fluid. It consists of the kidneys, ureters, urinary bladder,

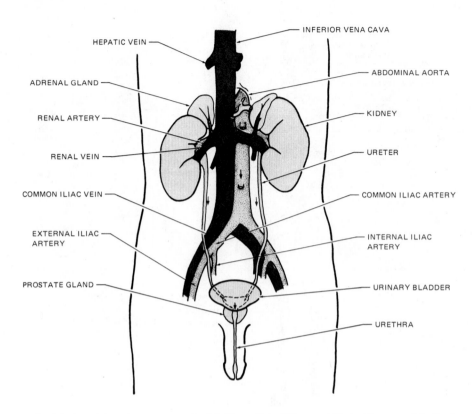

FIGURE A-6. The urinary system (male) (From Keir, Wise, and Krebs-Shannon, Medical Assisting, *3rd ed., copyright, 1992).*

and urethra, Figure A-6. The kidneys are complex structures consisting of nephrons that filter blood plasma from the renal artery as it passes by the nephrons and tiny tubules that select what is to be excreted and what is to be reabsorbed into the blood, Figure A-7. Elements and fluid not reabsorbed in the tubules and elements secreted directly from the blood into the tubules result in the formation of urine. After being formed in the kidney, urine drains down the ureter into the bladder. It is held there by a sphincter muscle at the urethra, which remains closed until the act of voiding or urination occurs. The urinary tract is a sterile environment. The introduction of bacteria can cause an infection.

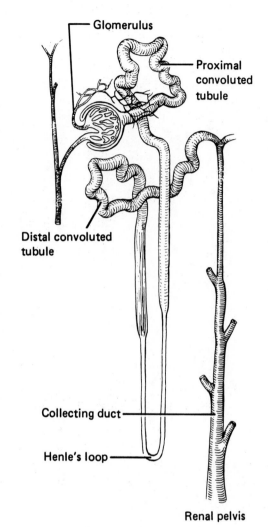

FIGURE A-7. Magnified view of nephron and tubule.

B
Mailing Addresses for Career Information (by Chapter)

Biometrics Department

American College of Cardiology
Heart House
9111 Old Georgetown Road
Bethesda, MD 20814

American Medical Association
Department of Allied Health Education and Accreditation
535 N. Dearborn Street
Chicago, IL 60610

American Society of Electroneurodiagnostic Technologists
6th at Quint
Carroll, IA 51401

American Institute of Ultrasound in Medicine
4405 East-West Hwy., Suite 504
Bethesda, MD 20814

American Society of Echocardiography
1100 Raleigh Blvd., PO Box 2598
Raleigh, NC 27602

National Alliance of Cardiovascular Technologists
5 W. Hargett St., Suite 1100
Raleigh, NC 27601

National Society for Cardiovascular Technology/National Society
for Pulmonary Technology
1133 Fifteenth St. NW, Ste. 620
Washington, DC 20005

Society of Diagnostic Medical Sonographers
12225 Greenville Ave., Suite 434
Dallas, TX 75243

Communication Disorders

American Speech-Language-Hearing Association
10801 Rockville Pike
Rockville, MD 20852

Dental

American Dental Association
211 East Chicago Avenue
Chicago, IL 60611

American Dental Hygienists Association
444 N. Michigan Avenue, Suite 3400
Chicago, IL 60611

American Dental Assistants Association
666 N. Lake Shore Drive, Suite 1130
Chicago, IL 60611

National Association of Dental Laboratories
3801 Mount Vernon Avenue
Alexandria, VA 22304

Dietary

American Dietetic Association
216 W. Jackson Blvd.
Chicago, IL 60606-6995

Emergency

American College of Emergency Physicians
PO Box 619911
Dallas, TX 75261-9911

National League for Nursing
10 Columbus Circle
New York, NY 10019

National Association of Emergency Medical Technicians
9140 Ward Parkway
Kansas City, MO 64114

National Registry of Emergency Medical Technicians
6610 Busch Blvd., Box 29233
Columbus, OH 43229

Medical Laboratory

American Society of Clinical Pathologists
2100 W. Harrison Street
Chicago, IL 60612

American Medical Technologists
710 Higgins Road
Park Ridge, IL 60068

American Society of Cytology
1015 Chestnut Street, Suite 1518
Philadelphia, PA 19107

American Society for Medical Technology
2021 L St., NW, #400
Washington, DC 20036

American Association of Blood Banks
1117 N 19th St., Suite 600
Arlington, VA 22209

American Society for Microbiology
1913 I St., NW
Washington, DC 20006

National Society for Histotechnology
5900 Princess Garden Pkwy, Suite 805
Lanham, MD 20706

Medical Office

American Medical Association
535 N. Dearborn St.
Chicago, IL 60610

American Academy of Family Physicians
8880 Ward Parkway
Kansas City, MO 64114-2797

American Academy of Pediatrics
141 NW Point Rd.—PO Box 927
Elk Grove Village, IL 60009-0927

American Academy of Physician Assistants
950 N. Washington St.
Alexandria, VA 22314

American College of Physicians
Independence Mall West
Sixth Street at Race
Philadelphia, PA 19106-1572

American College of Surgeons
55 E. Erie Street
Chicago, IL 60611

American College of Obstetricians and Gynecologists
1 East Wacker Drive
Chicago, IL 60601

American Osteopathic Association
212 East Ohio Street
Chicago, IL 60611

Association of Physician Assistant Programs
950 N. Washington St.
Alexandria, VA 22314

National League for Nursing
10 Columbus Circle
New York, NY 10019

American Association of Occupational Health Nurses
79 Madison Avenue
New York, NY 10016

American Association of Medical Assistants
20 N. Wacker Dr., Suite 1575
Chicago, IL 60606

Medical Records

American Medical Record Association
919 N. Michigan Ave., Suite 1400
Chicago, IL 60611

Mental Health

American Psychiatric Association
1700 18th Street, NW
Washington, DC 20015

American Psychological Association
1200 17th St., NW
Washington, DC 20036

National Association of School Psychologists
808 17th St., NW, Suite 200
Washington, DC 20006

National Association of Social Workers
7981 Eastern Ave.
Silver Spring, MD 20910

American Art Therapy Association
c/o Intermanagement
One Cedar Blvd.
Pittsburgh, PA 15228

Nursing

American Nurses Association
2420 Pershing Road
Kansas City, MO 64108

National League for Nursing
10 Columbus Circle
New York, NY 10019

National Association for Home Care
519 C Street, NE, Stanton Park
Washington, DC 20002

American Association of Critical Care Nurses
101 Columbia
Aliso Viejo, CA 92656

American Academy of Nurse Practitioners
179 Princeton Blvd.
Lowell, MA 01851

American Organization of Nurse Executives
840 N. Lake Shore Dr.
Chicago, IL 60611

National Association for Practical Nurse Education and Services
1400 Spring St., Suite 310
Silver Spring, MD 20910

National Federation of Licensed Practical Nurses
888 Seventh Avenue
New York, NY 10019

American College of Nurse-Midwives
1000 Vermont Ave., NW, Suite 1210
Washington, DC 20005

Maternity Center Association
48 East 92 Street
New York, NY 10028

Occupational Therapy

American Occupational Therapy Association
1383 Piccard Dr., Suite 300
Rockville, MD 20850

Pharmacy

American Association of Colleges of Pharmacy
1426 Prince Street
Alexandria, VA 22314-2815

American Pharmaceutical Association
2215 Constitution Ave., NW
Washington, DC 20037

Physical Therapy

American Physical Therapy Association
1111 N. Fairfax St.
Alexandria, VA 22314

Radiology

American College of Radiology
1891 Preston White Drive
Reston, VA 22091

American Society of Radiologic Technologists
15000 Central Ave.
Albuquerque, NM 87123

Society of Nuclear Medicine
136 Madison Ave., 8th Floor
New York, NY 10016

American Institute of Ultrasound in Medicine
4405 East-West Hwy., Suite 504
Bethesda, MD 20814

American Society of Echocardiography
1100 Raleigh Bldg., PO Box 2598
Raleigh, NC 27602

Society of Diagnostic Medical Sonographers
12225 Greenville Ave., Suite 434
Dallas, TX 75243

Respiratory Therapy

American Association for Respiratory Care
11030 Ables Lane
Dallas, TX 75229

American College of Chest Physicians
911 Busse Hwy.
Park Ridge, IL 60068

American Thoracic Society
1740 Broadway
New York, NY 10019

Support Departments

American Academy of Health Administration
PO Box 5518, 1–30 at Summerhill Road
Texarkana, TX 75503

American College of Hospital Administrators
840 N. Lake Shore Drive
Chicago, IL 60611

National Association of Health Care Access Managers
1101 Connecticut Avenue, Suite 700
Washington, DC 20036

Surgery

American College of Surgeons
55 East Erie Street
Chicago, IL 60611

American Society of Extracorporeal Technology
1980 Isaac Newton Square S
Reston, VA 22090

American Association of Nurse Anesthetists
111 Ease Wacker Drive, Suite 929
Chicago, IL 60601

American Academy of Anesthesiologists' Assistants
PO Box 33876
Decatur, GA 30033-0876

Association of Operating Room Nurses
10170 East Mississippi Avenue
Denver, CO 80231

Association of Surgical Technologists
8307 Shaffer Pkwy.
Littleton, CO 80127

Association of Operating Room Technicians
1100 W. Littleton Blvd., Suite 201
Littleton, CO 80120

C
Other Careers Associated with Health Care

Activity therapists work with patients to provide opportunities to increase socialization, dexterity, attention span, expression, and self-esteem through projects, creative play, games, excursions, and social interaction.

Athletic trainers are physical therapists who specialize in helping competitive sports men and women condition, providing first aid to injured parts, and carrying out treatment and rehabilitation plans prescribed by team or school physicians.

Biochemists study the function of human cells and the effects of chemicals on cell nutrition, reproduction, and growth.

Bioengineers design, develop the material, and construct artificial parts (joints), organs (heart), and electronic devices to improve the quality of patients' lives.

Building engineers maintain and repair the heavy machines that heat, cool, and provide electricity to the facility.

Chiropractors manipulate the spinal column and other parts of the body to relieve pain and discomfort.

Clinical engineers repair machines used to monitor patients or diagnose illnesses.

Dance therapists use movement and dance to diagnose and treat mental illness, physical disability, brain damage, or developmental handicaps.

Computer programmers develop systems to organize, store, and retrieve information specific to health data, health care, and the transfer of information.

Ecologists study the effects of the environment on health and relate those factors to human life.

Educational therapists teach academic subjects using methods that will increase self-esteem and motivate persons who are severely disabled physically, emotionally, or mentally, or who were drug addicted. They work primarily in rehabilitation facilities.

Epidemiologists study the factors that might affect health and cause disease on a given population.

Housekeepers perform procedures to ensure sanitary conditions and an attractive environment.

Forensic medicine relates to the study of pathology as it relates to human cells, tissue, the body, and the scene of death that may be associated with criminal behavior.

Geneticists study the effect of genes in the transmission of family traits and hereditary diseases.

Health economists act as advisors to administrators of health care agencies and develop management strategies and financial operating plans.

Health agency administrators plan, direct, and evaluate services offered, forecast future needs, and devise methods to provide and finance those new services.

Medical photographers photograph and videotape surgical procedures, set up cameras and video screens for operative procedures using scopes and microscopes, photograph patients before and after reconstructive surgery, and prepare slides for lectures.

Medical research scientists work in laboratories to test the effects of environmental elements, chemicals, drugs, artificial parts, and diagnostic instruments on living systems to improve the quality of human life.

Optometrists are doctors of optometry, not medical doctors. They test vision and determine abnormalities in structure or function of the eyeball. They prescribe glasses, contact lenses, or other treatments.

Ophthalmic technologists, technicians, and **assistants** work with patients during eye exams and fit glasses and contact lenses, depending on the amount of education and level of certification.

Opticians fit, adjust, and dispense glasses according to the opthalmologist's (M.D.) or optometrist's written prescription.

Patient representatives communicate with patients, interpret information, act as advocates in problem situations, and help to change the health care system to be more sensitive to patients' needs and perceptions.

Pharmacologists research the effects of chemicals on cells, tissues, and diseases and develop and refine medications for the treatment of illnesses.

Risk managers identify procedures, practices, and equipment that pose a hazard to staff or patients and make recommendations for change.

Veterinarians work with domestic, farm, food-producing, and research animals to maintain health, repair injuries, treat illnesses, and control diseases that spread to humans.

Veterinary science technicians assist veterinarians with the care, feeding, handling, treatment, and breeding of animals in clinics and research laboratories.

D
Abbreviations

ā: before
A/R pulse: apical/radial heart rate
AAA: aortic artery aneurysm
abd: abdominal
ABG: arterial blood gases
ac: before meals
ad lib: as much as desired
ADL: activities of daily living
AF: atrial fibrillation
AFB: acid fast bacillus
AIDS: Acquired Immune Deficiency Syndrome
A.M.: morning; after 12 midnight
amb: ambulate; walk
amt: amount
ASAP or asap: as soon as possible
ASHD: arteriosclerosis heart disease
bid: twice a day
bm or BM: bowel movement
BP: blood pressure
BR: bedrest or bathroom
BRP: bathroom privileges
bsc: bedside commode
c/o: complains of

c̄: with
C: centigrade
Ca: cancer
ca: calcium
CABG: coronary artery bypass graft
CAD: coronary artery disease
CAT: computerized axial tomography
cath: catheterization
CBC, cbc: complete blood count
cc: cubic centimeter
CCU: cardiac care unit, coronary care unit
CHF: congestive heart failure
CO: coronary occlusion
COLD: chronic obstructive lung disease
cont.: continue
COPD: chronic obstructive pulmonary disease
CPR: cardiopulmonary resuscitation
CPT: current procedure terminology for outpatient treatments
CSR: central supply/service room
CT: computerized tomography
CV, cv: cardiovascular
CVA: cerebral vascular accident
cxr: chest X ray
d/c, dc: discontinue
D.E.A.: Drug Enforcement Agency
diff: differential
D.O.: Doctor of Osteopathy
DOA: dead on arrival
DRG: diagnostic related groups
DSA: digital subtraction angiography
dx: diagnosis
ECG: echocardiograph
EEG: electroencephalograph
EKG: electrocardiograph
ENT: ear, nose, and throat
ER: emergency room
F: Fahrenheit
FBS: fasting blood sugar
FDA: Federal Drug Agency
FF: force fluids
Fx, fx: fracture
GI: gastrointestinal

gm: gram
gr: grain
gtt: drop
GU: genitourinary
Gyn: gynecology
h or hr.: hour
H_2O: water
HCVD: hypertensive cardiovascular disease
HDL: healthy type of cholesterol
Hg or Hgb: hemoglobin
HIV: human immunodeficiency virus
HS or hs: hour of sleep
ht: height
I&O: intake and output
ICD-9-CM: system to classify diagnoses
ICU: intensive care unit
IPPB: intermittent positive pressure breathing
IV: intravenous
IVP: intravenous pyelogram
JCAHO: Joint Commission on Accreditation of Hospitals Org.
KUB: kidney, ureter, and bladder X ray
L: liter or left
L&D: labor and delivery
lb: pound
LDL: unhealthy type of cholesterol
LL: left lung
LLL: left lower lobe (lung)
LLQ: left lower quadrant
LMP: last menstrual period
LUL: left upper lobe (lung)
LUQ: left upper quadrant
med: medication, medical
meds: medications
MI: myocardial infarction
min: minute
ml: milliliter
MRA: magnetic resonance angiography
MRI: magnetic resonance imager
NA: not applicable
neg: negative
NPO: nothing by mouth (nil per os)
NTG: nitroglycerine

OB: obstetrics
oob: out of bed
OPD: outpatient department
OR: operating room
OT: occupational therapy
oz: ounce
p̄: after
P&R: pulse and respiration
PAC: premature atrial contraction
PAT: preadmission testing
pc: after meals
PCA: patient controlled analgesia; self-administered pain R_x
Peds: pediatrics
PET: positron emission tomography
PFT: pulmonary function test
P.M.: evening; after 12 noon
PO, po: by mouth (per os)
post: after
postop: after surgery
pre: before
preop: before surgery
PRN/prn: when necessary
Psyc: refers to mental health
PT: physical therapy
PTCA: percutaneous coronary angioplasty
PVC: premature ventricular contraction
q: every
q4h: every four hours
QA: quality assurance
qd: every day
qh: every hour
qid: four times a day
qod: every other day
qs: quantity sufficient
R/O: rule out
R: rectal or right
RBC, rbc: red blood cells
RDA: recommended daily allowance
rehab: refers to returning to health
RL: right lung
RLL: right lower lobe
RLQ: right lower quadrant

RML: right middle lobe (lung)
ROM: range of motion
RR: recovery room
rt: right
RUL: right upper lobe (lung)
RUQ: right upper quadrant
R_x: perscription
s̄: without
SOB: shortness of breath
spec: specimen
SPECT: single photon emission computed tomography
stat: immediately
subq: subcutaneous
supp: suppository
Sx: symptoms
TB: tuberculosis
Tbsp: tablespoon
TD Filing: system of organizing medical records
TIA: transischemic attack
tid: three times a day
TLC: tender loving care
TPN: total parenteral nutrition
TPR: temperature, pulse, respiration
tsp: teaspoon
tx: treatment
UHDDS: listing of definitions of diseases and surgeries
UR: utilization review
URI: upper respiratory infection
US: unit secretary
VF: ventricular fibrillation
vo: verbal order
VS: vital signs
VTS: volunteer transport
WBC, wbc: white blood cells, white blood count
wc, w/c: wheelchair
wt: weight

E Ranges of Annual Income by Department

▶ BIOMETRICS DEPARTMENT

JOB TITLE	GROSS INCOME (in dollars)
Cardiologist	130,000–200,000
Echocardiographic Technician	17,000–25,000
Electrocardiographic Technician	19,000–25,000
Electroencephalographic Technologist	19,000–32,000
Cardiac Technician	19,000–25,000
Cardiovascular Technologist	25,000–33,000
Vascular Technologist	30,000–38,000
Neurologist	65,000–135,000

▶ COMMUNICATION DISORDERS DEPARTMENT

JOB TITLE	GROSS INCOME (in dollars)
Otolaryngologist	100,000–170,000
Audiologist	32,000–45,000
Speech-Language Pathologist	30,000–43,000

▶ DENTAL OFFICE

JOB TITLE	GROSS INCOME (in dollars)
Dentist	100,000–140,000
Orthodontist	110,000–150,000
Oral Surgeon	125,000–180,000
Dental Hygienist	25,000–38,000
Dental Assistant	10,000–18,000
Dental Laboratory Technician	10,000–18,000

▶ DIETARY DEPARTMENT

JOB TITLE	GROSS INCOME (in dollars)
Dietitian	25,000–40,000
Dietetic Technician	24,000–33,000
Dietary Clerk	11,000–23,000
Dietary Host/Hostess	12,000–24,000
Dietary Worker/Aid	10,000–19,000

▶ EMERGENCY CARE DEPARTMENT

JOB TITLE	GROSS INCOME (in dollars)
Physician	110,000–180,000
Registered Nurse	30,000–43,000
Licensed Practical Nurse	25,000–33,000
Paramedic	30,000–36,000
Physician Assistant	30,000–40,000
Unit Secretary	15,000–25,000

▶ MEDICAL LABORATORY DEPARTMENTS

JOB TITLE	GROSS INCOME (in dollars)
Certified Pathologist	155,000–170,000
Medical Technologist	28,000–40,000
Blood Bank Technologist	22,000–27,000
Chemistry Technologist	22,000–27,000
Hematology Technologist	22,000–27,000
Immunology Technologist	22,000–27,000
Medical Laboratory Technician	22,000–40,000
Cytotechnologist	28,000–36,000
Histologic Technician	21,000–34,000
Phlebotomist	15,000–25,000

▶ MEDICAL OFFICE

JOB TITLE	GROSS INCOME (in dollars)
Physician (depends on specialty):	
Pediatrician	75,000–120,000
Internist	80,000–120,000
General Surgeon	110,000–200,000
Physician Assistant	30,000–45,000
Nurse Practitioner	35,000–42,000
Dialysis Technician	26,000–36,000
Medical Assistant	12,000–16,000

▶ MEDICAL RECORDS DEPARTMENT

JOB TITLE	GROSS INCOME (in dollars)
Medical Records Director	42,000–63,000
Medical Records Technician	15,000–30,000
Medical Transcriptionist	18,000–27,000
Utilization Review Coordinator	25,000–48,000

▶ MENTAL HEALTH DEPARTMENT

JOB TITLE	GROSS INCOME (in dollars)
Psychiatrist	90,000–150,000
Psychologist	29,000–60,000
Social Worker	25,000–45,000
Occupational Therapist	29,000–43,000
Clinical Nurse Specialist	34,000–45,000
Registered Nurse	30,000–43,000
Licensed Practical Nurse	25,000–32,000
Mental Health Technician	13,000–20,000
Psychiatric Aide	11,000–14,000
Art Therapist	28,000–35,000
Child Life Specialist	28,000–38,000
Chemical Abuse Counselor	26,000–36,000

▶ NURSING DEPARTMENT

JOB TITLE	GROSS INCOME (in dollars)
Director of Nurses	40,000–80,000
Clinical Nurse Manager/Head Nurse	35,000–65,000
RN: Staff Nurse	30,000–43,000
Clinical Nurse Specialist	34,000–45,000
Nurse Practitioner	32,000–45,000
Licensed Practical Nurse	25,000–32,000
Nursing Assistant	11,000–14,000
Nurse Anesthetist	58,000–75,000
Discharge Planning Nurse	32,000–45,000
Social Worker	25,000–45,000
Child Life Specialist	28,000–38,000
Enterostomal Therapy Nurse	35,000–45,000
Midwife	43,000–54,000
Health Unit Coordinator (Sectretary)	18,000–28,000

▶ OCCUPATIONAL THERAPY DEPARTMENT

JOB TITLE	GROSS INCOME (in dollars)
Occupational Therapist	29,000–44,000
Occupational Therapy Assistant	20,000–28,000

▶ PHARMACY DEPARTMENT

JOB TITLE	GROSS INCOME (in dollars)
Pharmacist	40,000–65,000
Pharmacy Technician	15,000–25,000
Pharmacy Assistant	10,000–18,000

▶ PHYSICAL THERAPY DEPARTMENT

JOB TITLE	GROSS INCOME (in dollars)
Physiatrist	120,000–190,000
Physical Therapist	30,000–45,000
Physical Therapy Assistant	22,000–29,000

▶ RADIOLOGY DEPARTMENT

JOB TITLE	GROSS INCOME (in dollars)
Radiologist	90,000–190,000
Cardiac Cath Lab RN	33,000–45,000
CAT Scan Technologist	28,000–37,000
Darkroom Technician	14,000–19,000
Department Director	45,000–65,000
Film Librarian	16,000–20,000
MRI Technologist	29,000–40,000
Nuclear Medicine Technologist	27,000–38,000
Radiation Therapy Technologist	29,000–40,000
Radiologic Technologist	24,000–35,000
Receptionist	11,000–17,000
Sonographer	24,000–34,000
Transcriptionist	18,000–27,000
X ray Assistant/Transporter	11,000–15,000

▶ RESPIRATORY THERAPY DEPARTMENT

JOB TITLE	GROSS INCOME (in dollars)
Pulmonologist	90,000–170,000
Respiratory Therapist	25,000–38,000
Respiratory Therapy Technician	17,000–30,000
Perfusionist	60,000–130,000

▶ SUPPORT DEPARTMENTS

JOB TITLE	GROSS INCOME (in dollars)
Patient Registration Representative	15,000–27,000
Patient Account Representative	23,000–30,000
Credit and Collection Representative	16,000–28,000
Central Service Technician	14,000–25,000
Purchasing Agent	20,000–35,000

▶ SURGERY DEPARTMENT

JOB TITLE	GROSS INCOME (in dollars)
Anesthesiologist	100,000–190,000
Nurse Anesthetist	58,000–75,000
Anesthesiologist's Assistant	58,000–75,000
Surgeon (depends on specialty)	80,000–above 200,000
Surgeon's Assistant	35,000–55,000
Scrub Techs	22,000–30,000
Scrub Nurse (LPN)	24,000–34,000
Circulator (RN)	29,000–45,000
Perfusionist	60,000–130,000
Surgical Transporter	11,000–15,000
Health Unit Coordinator (Secretary)	17,000–25,000
Recovery Room Nurse	29,000–45,000

Glossary

abduction: moving limb away from the body
abscess: sac filled with pus from infection
absorption: taking in nutritional elements thru membranes
abstracting: reviewing charts for data to write reports
accurate: without error
active: exercise that the patient does himself/herself
acute: severe, sharp
adaptable: able to change
addictive: substance or behavior that becomes habit
adduction: moving limb toward the body
ADL: activities of daily living
ad lib: as much as desired
admission: to come into the hospital as a patient
admitting physician: term for doctor responsible for patient care
aerator: machine used to remove gas
aerosol treatment: breathing tiny particles of liquid in air
agility: ability to move quickly and easily
agitated: disturbed; moving with rapid irregular motion
agraphia: inability to write
AIDS: Acquired Immune Deficiency Syndrome; disease caused by HIV that leaves victims without defense against malignant diseases and certain organisms
alimentary canal: gastrointestinal tract

allergist: physician specializing in adverse reactions

allergy: adverse reaction

alphabetical order: arrangement according to letters

alveoli: sacs in lungs where exchange of gases occurs

ambulate/amb: move about, walk

amplification: sound magnification

amputation: removal of a limb

analgesic: medication that relieves pain

aneurysm: weakening in blood vessel wall causing abnormal dilatation

angiography: pictures blood vessels

angioplasty: repair of a blood vessel

anoxia: lack of oxygen to the brain

antibiotic: medication that fights infection by killing bacteria

antigen: substance foreign to the body causing antibodies to form

antiseptic: liquid that kills bacteria

anus: sphyncter at end of gastrointestinal tract

anxiety: feeling of apprehension or uneasiness from an unknown cause, especially related to the future

aphasia: without language; inability to communicate through speech or writing; may not be able to intepret sounds

apnea: lack of breathing

appendicitis: inflammation of appendix, the hollow tube on cecum

apraxia: inability to position, sequence, and move speech muscles

arterial blood gases: test for levels of oxygen and carbon dioxide in arterial blood

arteriogram: X ray of arteries after injection of radiopaque dye

arteriosclerosis: hardening of the arteries; a thickening of arterial walls causing a narrowing of the lumen

arthritis: joint inflammation causing pain and swelling and changes in structure

articulate: pronounce

articulation: clear enunciation

artificial larynx: prosthesis that replaces the voice box to assist with communication

asap: as soon as possible

ascending: beginning of large intestine

assess: to observe all the information about something

asthma: sudden, periodic attack of constriction of the bronchi causing dyspnea and wheezing

atrial fibrillation: quivering of the upper heart chambers

attentive: observant

attitude: behavior that reflects mental view

audiogram: a graphic representation of ability to hear

audiology: a field of evaluating and treating hearing impairment

audiometric testing: evaluating hearing levels

auditory comprehension: ability to interpret the spoken word

ausculation: listening to body sounds

autism: unable to communicate with the real world, reality

autoclave: machine that sterilizes by steam under pressure

automatic stocking: routine delivery of supplies to present par levels

bacteria: microorganisms

benign: self-contained tumor; does not spread

bile: liquid that helps digest fat

billing procedures: informing patients of amount due for care

biometrics: department that measures functions necessary to life

biopsy: piece of tissue surgically removed for study

bitewings: name of X rays of back teeth

bladder: hollow organ that holds fluid

blood: fluid that circulates in vessels; made up of cells, elements, and plasma

blood bank: lab section that supplies autologous or compatible transfusions

blood gases: test for level of oxygen and carbon dioxide in the arterial blood

blood pressure: amount of force exerted against vessel walls

blood transfusion: infusion of cells and plasma into circulation

BP: blood pressure

BR: bedrest or bathroom

brace: device that holds a joint in place

brackets: apparatus on or around tooth; used in straightening process

breath sounds: noise made when passing air in and out of respiratory tree

bronchi: tube that connects trachea with lungs

bronchial: refers to bronchi

bronchitis: inflammation of the tube between trachea and lungs

bronchopulmonary treatment: inhaling medicated aerosol

bronchoscopy: procedure to look into the bronchi

BRP: bathroom privileges

buccal: refers to mouth

calculus: stone; occur in kidney and gallbladder

calorie: a unit of heat

cane: stick used to carry some of patient's weight when walking

carbohydrate: a compound composed of carbon, hydrogen, and oxygen; in sugars and starches

carcinoma: cancer; a malignant tumor

cardiac: pertains to the heart

cardiac arrest: sudden cessation of heart beat

cardiac cath: abbreviation for cardiac catheterization

cardiac catheterization: passing of a tiny tube into the heart to measure cardiac function and detect abnormalities

cardiologist: physician specializing in heart disease

cardiopulmonary resuscitation: CPR; to artificially ventilate the lungs and rhythmically compress the heart

caries: tooth decay and gradual disintigration

cast: plaster mold of part; dental casts from impressions; solid mold immobilizes limb after fracture

CAT scan: uses X rays to picture structures as slices of tissue

cavity: hole in tooth from decay

cecum: blind end of ascending colon

central service: department that sterilizes equipment

cerebral palsy: shaking caused by brain damage

cerebral vascular accident: stroke; interruption of circulation or bleeding in the brain

cerebrospinal: fluid around brain and spinal cord

cervical cells: specimen from lower part of uterus; for Pap test

charge stickers: labels applied to equipment to indicate cost

charges: cost of supplies, services or procedures

chart: medical record

chart analysis: reviewing medical record for completeness

chemistry: lab section that identifies and measures elements in blood serum

chemotherapy: treating disease with chemical agents that are toxic to certain cells

cholangitis: inflammation of bile ducts

cholecytitis: inflammation of gallbladder

cholecystectomy: removal of gallbladder

cholelethiasis: gallstones

chronological order: organization according to date

chyme: mixture of food with gastric juices

clean: free from dirt

cleft palate: a congenital opening in the roof of mouth forming a passage between the mouth and nasal cavities

closed head injury: trauma to head/cranium

cobalt-60: radioactive isotope used in treatment of malignancies

coccyx: tail bone

cochlea: cone-shaped tube; auditory part of inner ear

cochlear implant: replacement of cone-shaped tube in middle ear

coding: identifying diagnostic groups

cognition: mental process used to acquire knowledge

cognitive: ability to think

colectomy: removal of colon

colitis: inflammation of large intestine, colon

collection: department/process of retrieving payment

colon: large intestine

colostomy: opening into colon

common bile duct: tube that carries bile and pancreatic fluid

communication: transmitting messages through speech and hearing

compulsion: a force

computerized axial tomography: (CAT scan), a noninvasive technique using X ray and a computer to visualize transverse planes of body tissue

confidentiality: to respect the patient's privacy about illness

confusion: not being aware of person, place, or things

congestive heart failure: weak heart becomes ineffective as a pump resulting in poor circulation

contaminated: introduction of bacteria or harmful substance

contracture: muscle that has tightened and immobilized a joint

controlled substance: drugs that can become addictive/abused including depressants and stimulants; distribution is monitored

conversion: admission of patient receiving outpatient treatment

coronary angioplasty: repair of blood vessels in heart muscle

coronary thrombosis: blood clot blocking artery in the heart muscle

cough: a forceful exhale

courteous: polite

critical thinking: thought processes that facilitate analyzing and problem solving

Crohn: disease of chronic inflammation of small intestine

cross match: tests if patient's blood will mix with transfusion

crown: covering over whole tooth and made of gold or porcelain

culture: procedure to grow bacteria

cyanosis: blue skin color from not enough oxygen in system

cyst: abnormal sac of clear fluid

cystitis: inflammation of the urinary bladder

cystogram: X ray of the urinary bladder

cytology: (lab section) study of the formation, structure, and function of cells

data: information
D.E.A.: Drug Enforcement Agency
deafness: inability to hear
decay: degeneration of spot on tooth
defibrillation: electric shock to the heart to restore rhythm
dentures: artificial teeth set in plastic mold
dependable: reliable
depression: mental state of melancholy; loss of interest in people and activities
dermatologist: physician specializing in skin disorders
descending: section of large intestine on left side of abdomen
diagnosis: name of illness
dialysate: fluid used in artificial kidney machine
dialysis: procedure to cleanse blood by diffusing waste elements and excess fluid through a semipermeable membrane; used when kidney function is impaired
diapers: applied to those who cannot control the flow of urine
diastolic: amount of pressure in blood vessels when heart is at rest; name of cardiac cycle when heart relaxes between beats
dictation: taping information for typing
digestion: process of breaking down food into usable form
direct: type of admission when patient comes from home or office
dirty: grossly soiled
disability: state/condition of physical or mental impairment from illness or injury
discharge: to release from the hospital; drainage
discs: pads between spinal bones
donor: person who gives an organ
Doppler: instrument to detect blood flow/pulse by sound
DRG: diagnostic related groups
drug levels: test to determine amount of chemicals in blood
drug rehabilitation: recovering from chemical use
duodenum: section of small intestine connected to stomach; beginning of small intestine
dynamometer: instrument to measure hand strength
dysarthria: inability to control muscles that relate to speech
dysphagia: impaired ability to swallow; difficulty in swallowing
dysphonia: impairment of voice production; difficulty with voice
dyspnea: difficult or labored breathing
echocardiograph: picture of heart by sound waves; visualizes cardiac structures by the noninvasive ultrasound procedure

E.C.T. electroconvulsvie therapy; an electric shock to the brain sometimes used to treat acute depression

-ectomy: suffix meaning removal of an organ, part, or limb

edema: swelling

EEG: abbreviation for electroencephalograph

EKG: abbreviation for electrocardiograph, electrocardiogram

electrocardiograph: a record showing tracings of the electrical activity of the heart

electroencephalograph: graph of electrical impulses produced by brain activity

electronic ear: device that amplifies sound

embolism: moving blood clot

emergency room: place to treat sudden serious illnesses

-emia: word ending meaning blood

emphysema: a chronic degenerative disease characterized by loss of elasticity in lung tissue and enlarged alveoli

enamel: hard covering of tooth

endotracheal tube: a plastic airway through the mouth into the windpipe to maintain airflow

enteritis: inflammation of the small intestine

enthusiastic: shows intense interest

epistaxis: nose bleed

equilibrium: balance

esophageal speech: process of burping air to communicate with sound after the voice box has been removed

esophagitis: inflammation of esophagus, gullet

esophagus: tube that brings food to stomach from pharynx

eustachian tube: auditory tube from middle ear to pharynx

evacuation: to move to the outside

exchange carts: mobil shelves delivered with complete stock for department needs

exhale: to breathe out

express care: place where minor sudden illnesses are treated

expressive language: ability to convey information

extraction: removal of tooth

extremities: arms and legs

family practitioner: physician specializing in patients of all ages

fantasy: imagination or illusion

fat: organic compound of triglyceride in fatty acid; lipid; adipose tissue

FDA: Food and Drug Administration

fear: anxiety of real or possible danger

femur: thigh bone

fibrillation: irregular heartbeat

fibula: bone in back of calf

filling: restoration; process of inserting material into a prepared tooth

finance: department that manages money for the institution

flaccid: limp muscle

flight: helicopter crew

floss: waxed or unwaxed thread used to remove plaque and calculus from dental surfaces

fluoroscopy: temporarily pictures organs

Foley: catheter in urinary bladder

fracture: a broken bone

gas sterilizer: machine that kills bacteria on plastic equipment

gastrectomy: removal of stomach

gastric: refers to stomach

gastric juice: digestive liquid secreted by the stomach

gastritis: inflammation of the stomach

gastroenterologist: physician specializing in stomach and intestines

GI: gastrointestinal

gingivitis: inflammation of gums; signs include redness, swelling and bleeding

glomerulonephritis: inflammation of the kidney; a form of nephritis

glomerulus: meshwork of blood vessels in the kidney

glossectomy: removal of tongue

glucose: a simple sugar

gums: tissue covering bone at base of teeth

gynecologist: physician specializing in female organs

gynecology: branch of medicine dealing with female organs and diseases

hallucination: a false perception of sights/sounds

handicap: any mental or physical hindrance that interferes with normal activities

hand washing: most effective way to prevent infections in hospital

health care team: several professional medical personnel working closely together to meet patients' needs

hearing: act of perceiving sound

hearing aid: instrument to amplify sound

hearing loss: decreased sound perception; degree of acuity can be detected

heart failure: diagnosis of inadequate myocardial pumping action

helpful: willing to work

hematocrit: lab test measuring proportion of blood cells to serum

hematology: (lab section) study of the number and type of blood cells

hematuria: blood in the urine

hemi-: prefix for half

hemiplegia: paralyzed on one side of body

hemo-: prefix meaning blood

hemoglobin: red substance that carries oxygen within blood

hemorrhage: abnormal and excessive bleeding

hepatitis: inflammation of the liver

histology: (lab section) study of tissue structure

HIV: human immunodeficiency virus; causes AIDS

Holter monitor: portable EKG machine

house: regular diet

humerus: bone in upper arm

humor: sense of appreciation for what is funny

hyper-: prefix meaning high, above, excessive

hyperalimentation: concentrated nutrients in IV fluids

hypertension: high blood pressure; pressure in blood vessels that is greater than normal

hyperventilation: breathing too rapidly

hypo-: prefix meaning below, under, less

I&O: indicates the need to measure fluid intake and output, in and out

I&O surgery: one day hospital stay for surgical procedure

ileitis: inflammation of the ileum, last section of small intestine

ileostomy: opening into distal section of small intestine

ileum: largest and most distal section of small intestine

immunology: (lab section) study of the body's ability to resist disease

impairment: deficit

impression: outline of whole upper or lower set of teeth

impulse: a force transmitted along nerves

incomplete: medical records that need more information

indicator tape: adhesive paper that changes color in high heat

infection: condition caused by bacteria

ingestion: taking food in by mouth

inhale: to breathe in

initiative: working without being asked

inlay: a solid filling made in a mold then placed into the tooth

inpatient procedures: billing for treatments on admitted patients

instrument sets: implements packaged together

insulin: important in body's use of sugar

insurance claim: application for payment from medical policy

intensive care: department where critically ill patients are cared for

interest: wanting to know

internist: physician specializing in medical treatments

intracranial bleed: oozing of blood into head cavity

intravenous fluids: sterile liquids infused directly into veins to provide liquid, nourishment, electrolytes, and medication

isolation: apart from others

-itis: suffix meaning inflammation of a part, organ or tissue

IV: intravenous

JCAHO: Joint Commission on Accreditation of Hospitals Organization

jejunum: middle section of small intestine

joint replacement: insertion of artificial parts at the juncture where bones meet and articulate

kidney: organ that cleanses blood and makes urine

knowledgeable: informed

KUB: X ray of kidneys, ureters, and urinary bladder

labor and delivery: place where babies are born

laceration: an irregular tear of the flesh

language: organized means of communication; method of transmitting information

language therapy: treatment of sound interpretation

large intestine: stores food waste; reabsorbs liquid

laryngectomy: removal of voice box

larynx: voice box

laser: acronym for light amplification by stimulated emission of radiation; a device that emits intense heat and power as a beam

laser treatment: procedure used in surgery to incise and coagulate

laxative: stimulates the intestinal tract to pass waste

legal: term that describes correspondence sent to lawyers

Lifeline®: system attached to home phones to indicate that help is needed.

lithotripsy: process of breaking up stones in urethra or bladder

L.O.C.: level of consciousness

lumen: the space within a tubelike structure

lungs: spongy organs of respiration containing alveoli

macroscopic: seen by naked eye

magnetic resonance imager: a noninvasive technique to visualize internal organs using powerful magnetic fields

malignant: harmful tumor that can cause death if untreated

mammogram: breast X ray

manic depression: cycle of hyperactivity following melancholia

mastectomy: removal of breast

mast trousers: inflatable pants used to raise blood pressure

mediastinum: space between lungs

Medicaid: a U.S. government program that provides reimbursement for health care given to the poor

medical: treatment of illness with medications, rest, and diet

medical asepsis: clean technique

medical referral: recommended physician

medical staff: doctors approved to work at a hospital/facility

Medicare: Federal reimbursement for hospital and medical care for persons of retirement age

mental health: ability to cope emotionally with stresses of life

mental illness: disorder of the mind

mentor: person who teaches and advises

metabolic: pertains to metabolism, how the body uses food for energy

metabolism: process or releasing energy when food is used by body

metered-dose inhaler: pocket aerosol treatment that mists medication to be inhaled

microbiology: (lab section) the study of bacteria and the substances that effectively control/kill them

microfiche: small film

microscopic: seen only with magnification

mineral: inorganic element found in food

mobility: ability to move

modulation: control of voice intensity

molar: large tooth in back of mouth

mood: emotional state influencing one's perception of the world

motor: nerve sensations to muscles causing motion

mouth: buccal cavity

MRI: abbreviation for magnetic resonance imager

multiple sclerosis: a CNS disease, loss of coordination

musculoskeletal: term for the system of muscles and bones

myocardial infarction: heart attack; necrosis of a section of heart muscle due to a blocked coronary artery

nameplate: patient identification card

narcotic: medication that induces stupor and sleep; relieves pain

nares: openings in nose

necrosis: death of areas of tissue or bone

nephron: basic unit of the kidney

nervous: system that relates to nerves

nervous breakdown: an incapacitating, severe attack of an emotional or mental disorder

neurologist: physician specializing in brain, spinal cord, and nerves

neurology: care of brain, nerves, and spinal cord, and related diseases

neurosis: mental disorder with unpleasant symptoms

nosebleed: epistaxis

NPO: not to eat or drink anything; nil per os

nuclear medicine: specialty that tests with radioactive substances

nursery: newborn care

nursing process: methods used to assess and care for patients

observation: process of viewing

obstetrics: unit that specializes in pregnancy and delivery

obstetrician: physician who delivers babies

obstetrics: process of pregnancy and birthing

obstruction: blockage, obstacle

occlusion: blockage of blood vessel

-oma: word ending meaning tumor

oncologist: physician specializing in cancer

oncology: caring for cancer victims

operating room (OR): place where surgery is performed

oral: refers to mouth

oral musculature: muscles around mouth

-orrhapy: suffix meaning repair of

orthopedics: treating bone problems

osmosis: process of molecules moving through a membrane

-ostomy: suffix meaning opening into

-otomy: suffix meaning opening into

otoscope: instrument to view/examine ear

outpatient: to be treated and released, not admitted; clinic

outpatient procedure: billing for nonhospitalized patients

palate: roof of mouth

palpation: pressing body parts to detect abnormalities

pancreas: makes insulin and digestive juice

pancreatitis: inflammation of the pancreas

panoramic radiograph: continuous X ray of jaw and teeth

par level: number of items requested as standard stock

paracentesis: procedure to remove fluid from abdominal cavity

parallel bars: wooden handrails for stability when walking

paralysis: inability to move muscles voluntarily

paranoia: imagined persecution
paraphasia: using an incorrect but related word
parotid: salivary glands under ear
partial plate: a few false teeth attached to a molded form/denture
passive: exercises/body movements carried through by therapists without patient assistance
patella: kneecap
pathology: study of the nature and cause of a disease
-pathy: suffix meaning loss of normal structure and function
patient accounting: department that tracks money owed to hospital
pediatrician: specialty of physician who cares for children
pediatrics: care of children
peptic ulcers: open sores/lesions in stomach or duodenum
perception: awareness
percussion: process of tapping body parts
peri-: prefix meaning around
periodontitis: inflammation/degeneration of the covering of teeth below the gum line
peristalis: wavelike contractions that move food along
peritonitis: inflammation of the lining of the abdominal cavity
personality: represents the mental aspects of a person
pharyngitis: inflammation of the pharynx; sore throat
pharynx: throat
phlebitis: inflammation of veins
phobias: fear of something or fear of a situation
phonation: production of voice by vibrations of vocal cords
physical deficit: disabled body part
plan: individual treatment program
plaque: film on a tooth that harbors bacteria
plastic surgeon: physician who repairs and reconstructs
-plasty: suffix meaning repair of
pleural sac: tissue that surrounds lungs
pneumonia: an inflammatory disease of the lungs, caused by infection or irritation
pneumonitis: inflammation of lungs; pneumonia
PO: by mouth; per os
polite: courteous
polyps: mushroom-shaped abnormal growths
post-: prefix meaning after
postoperative: after surgery
pre-: prefix meaning before
precertification: approval of insurance company before treatment

preoperative: before surgery

prescription: written doctor's order for medication

pride: justifiable self-respect

prn: when necessary

prompt: on time

prosthesis: artificial part

protein: nutrient necessary to build new cells, heal wounds, and allow muscles to contract

psychiatry: deals with the mind, mental illness

psychosis: mental illness resulting in personality disintegration, loss of contact with reality

PT: physical therapy or patient

PTCA: abbreviation for percutaneous coronary angioplasty

pulmonary artery: carries unoxygenated blood from heart to lungs

pulmonary function test: measures ability of lungs to exchange gases

pulmonary vein: carries oxygenated blood from lungs to heart

pumps: machines that control fluid flow

pus: cloudy fluid from infection

pyuria: pus in urine

quadraplegia: paralyzed from the neck down

radiation: potentially harmful ray used for diagnostic or therapeutic purposes

radiation therapy: X-ray treatments of tumors

radiologist: physician specializing in imaging and X-ray treatments

radius: the outer, shorter bone in forearm leading to thumb

rales: abnormal sound produced by air passing through bronchi that contain liquid

range of motion: exercise that determines and maintains joint movement

receptive language: ability to hear and understand

recovery room: where patients wake up and stabilize after surgery

rectum: last section of large intestine

registration: process of signing in before treatment or admission

regulations: rules

rehabilitation: process of a disabled person returning to maximum function

reimbursement: payment for health care

renal artery: vessel that brings blood to the kidney

renal calculus: kidney stone

requisition: order form

respiratory arrest: breathing has stopped

responsible: accountable for actions

restoration: repair of tooth

restraints: appliances used to limit patients' movement

retro-: prefix meaning behind

retroperitoneal: behind the abdominal cavity

ROM: range of motion

root canal: removal of nerve from tooth

RR: recovery room

saliva: digestive juice in mouth

same-day surgery: patients have an operation and return home in one day

scheduled: term for planned admission

-scope: suffix meaning instrument to look into the body

-scopy: suffix meaning procedure of looking into the body

scrub: term for washing hands, fingernails, and lower arms before performing or assisting with surgery

seizures: brief attacks of shaking movements and/or altered consciousness; convulsions

sensation: feeling or awareness of stimulus

sensory: nerve stimuli to brain

sensory receptors: nerves that carry impulses from sense organs to brain and spinal cord

serology: study of serum and reactions between antigens and antibodies; basis of immune system

serum: clear liquid that carries blood cells; liquid portion of blood

sigmoid: S-shaped segment of large intestine, above rectum

sling: arm support

small intestine: tube-like organ between stomach and large intestine; absorbs food

sodium: element that influences retention of fluid in cells

soft: nonirritating type of diet

sound waves: vibrations that produce noise

spastic: periodic contractions of muscles

special diets: food ordered by physicians as part of therapy

speech: sounds that represent words

speech pathology: study of abnormal voice production process

speech therapy: process of training in verbal communication

splint: device worn to support part

sports injuries: athletic injuries

sputum: liquid made in trachea; spit

stapes: tiny bones in the middle ear

stat: immediately

Steri-Strips™: narrow sterile adhesive tapes

sterile: free from living microorganisms

stethoscope: instrument used to hear internal body sounds

stomach: organ that stores and digests food

stomatitis: inflammation of the mouth

stress test: EKG done during increasing exercise; determines cardio-vascular fitness

stroke: cerebrovascular accident; interruption of circulation to a section of the brain, may cause paralysis and loss of consciousness

stuttering: repetition of syllables when attempting to talk

sub-: prefix meaning under

sublingual: under the tongue

submandible: under the lower jaw

submaxillary: under the jaw

surgeon: physician who repairs by operating on body structure

surgical: care of patients before and after operations

surgical asepsis: sterile technique

suture: sterile thread used to stitch a wound closed; stitching parts together

swallowing: process of moving musculature of mouth and throat; enabling the passage of something from the mouth to the stomach

swelling: edema

systolic: pressure in blood vessels when heart contracts; name of cardiac cycle when heart contracts

tartar: hard crust of calcium salts, saliva, and debris on teeth

TB: abbreviation for the airborne disease of tuberculosis

T, C, D B: turn, cough, and deep breathe; treatment to expand lungs especially after surgery

TD filing: system of filing medical records

teamwork: activity of a number of persons acting in close association

terminal: final, end

thallium: diagnostic radioactive substance used after stress test

third party: term for a company that pays for health care

thoracentesis: procedure to remove fluid from chest cavity

thoracic: chest surgery; physician who operates in the chest

thoracic cavity: space inside of chest

thrombophlebitis: inflammation of veins with blood clots

thrombosis: formation of a blood clot; stationary clot in vessel

tibia: shin bone

tissue: group of cells

TPN: total parenteral nutrition

TPR: temperature, pulse, and respirations

trachea: windpipe; connects larynx and bronchi

tracheostomy; tracheotomy: artificial surgical opening into trachea, windpipe

tranquilizer: medication taken to relieve mental tension, anxiety

transcription: typing from physicians' tape recording

transfer: to move from one place to another from one nursing unit to another

transplant: surgical procedure to replace an organ

transverse: section of large intestine under diaphragm

trauma: serious injury from impact

traumatic brain injury: damage to brain by sudden impact to skull

tremors: trembling or shaking

triage: system to identify degree of illness and treatment needed

T-tube: rubber catheter placed in common bile duct; drains bile

tympanic membrane: eardrum

type: test to determine kind of blood

ulna: the larger bone in the lower arm leading to the little finger

ultrasound: uses inaudible sound waves to outline the shape of body organs

unit-dose method: drug packaging system; medications are packaged in individual doses

ureter: tube that connects kidney to bladder

urethra: tube-shaped canal that connects bladder to outside

urinalysis: test that identifies elements in urine

urine: liquid made in kidney

urologist: physician specializing in kidney and bladder disorders

urology: urinary tract problems

vascular: blood vessels

ventricular fibrillation: quivering of lower heart chambers

vertebra: spinal bone

virology: (lab section) study of disease-causing viruses and development of vaccines against them

virus: organism that is smaller than bacteria

vital capacity: maximum amount of air expelled after a full inspiration

vital signs: temperature, pulse, respirations, and blood pressure

vitamin: organic substance essential for growth and metabolism

vocalization: complex process of talking, singing, laughing

voice prosthesis: artificial device that produces or amplifies sound

voice therapy: treatment of speech problems

volume: amount; intensity

VS: vital signs; TPR and BP

walker: U-shaped tubular support used when walking

wax: thick substance resembling beeswax

wisdom teeth: last large teeth to come into back of mouth

withdrawal: withholding medication/alcohol with resulting physical/ mental symptoms

work habits: attitude/behavior pattern in occupation

X ray: radioactive rays used to photograph or treat the inside of the body

►INDEX

NOTE: Page numbers in **bold** type refer to non-text material.